"Drawing its inspiration from tribal traditions and modern psycho-therapy, this book contains treasures and rewards that are available in few other self-help manuals."

STANLEY KRIPPNER, PH.D.
Co-author of *The Mythic Path* and *Extraordinary Dreams and How to Use Them*

"Beyond facilitating healing, this book points to the real reason behind the human journey—continual expansion, maturing consciousness, and permeability to a multi-dimensional life that transcends the limits of personal history."

DIANE POOLE HELLER, PH.D.
Co-author of *Somatic Experiencing® Training Manual* and
Crash Course: Healing from Auto Accident Trauma

"As a long time practicing Integrative Medicine physician, I am very excited by the new dimensions of possibility offered in *Ritual as Resource*. Alongside innovative transformational opportunities for individuals, communities, and organizations, this book boldly envisions an inspired ascendant pathway to an integrative healthcare system we can all feel good about."

FRANK LIPMAN, M.D.
Author of *Total Renewal: 7 Key Steps to Resilience, Vitality & Long Term Health*

"*Ritual as Resource* shows us a greater understanding and ability to use rituals as a meaningful bridge to health, vitality, and fulfillment in our everyday life. A warm and welcoming guide on how to create desired outcomes through the art and science of ritual."

LINDA G. RUSSEK, PH.D.
Co-author of *The Living Energy Universe*
Director, Heart Science Foundation

"Michael Picucci shares his journey of discovery into the use of ritual for personal and community transformation. His voice is open, engaging, and freely self-disclosing, giving a natural and flexible sense of the many ways that ritual can work in our lives. *Ritual as Resource* offers a powerful, cutting-edge support for anyone engaged in personal as well as community and professional transformation."

DENISE BRETON
Author of *The Mystic Heart of Justice*, Executive Director, Living Justice Press

"Michael Picucci shows us how to create powerful personal rituals that become actual vehicles of transformation, providing enormous healing resources for ourselves and our planet."

ROSHI BERNIE GLASSMAN
Author of *Bearing Witness*, Co-founder, The Peacemaker Community

"*Ritual as Resource* opens up new vistas for all of us who seek inspiration for implementing our potential; to heal from life's traumas and to be rewarded with the benefits of fully engaging with our desires and senses in the world around us."

BARBARA E. WARREN, PSY.D.
Director, Organizational Development,
Planning & Research, The New York L.G.B.T. Community Center

"Bravo…. In a world so void of significant ritual, Michael Picucci offers an insightful book which not only provides a foundation for the importance and value of ritual but also shares with readers an intimate how-to list of rituals for incorporation into daily life."

DAVID FRECHTER
Founder, Spirit Journeys

"Finally, a book that respects modern medicine, embraces Energy Psychology, and is fun to read! This should be required reading for all of us."

ROBERTA TEMES, PH.D.
Author and Clinical Assistant Professor,
Downstate Medical School, Brooklyn, N.Y.

Ritual as Resource

Energy for Vibrant Living

Also by Michael Picucci

The Journey Toward Complete Recovery:
Reclaiming Your Emotional, Spiritual & Sexual Wholeness

Complete Recovery:
An Expanded Model of Community Healing

Ritual as Resource
Energy for Vibrant Living

Michael Picucci

North Atlantic Books
Berkeley, California

Published by
North Atlantic Books
P.O. Box 12327
Berkeley, California 94712
www.northatlanticbooks.com

Cover and book design by Susan Quasha
Printed in the United States of America
Distributed to the book trade by
Publishers Group West

Ritual as Resource: Energy for Vibrant Living is sponsored by the Society for the Study of Native Arts and Sciences, a nonprofit educational corporation whose goals are to develop an educational and crosscultural perspective linking various scientific, social, and artistic fields; to nurture a holistic view of arts, sciences, humanities, and healing; and to publish and distribute literature on the relationship of mind, body, and nature.

Library of Congress Cataloging-in-Publication Data

Picucci, Michael.
  Ritual as resource : energy for vibrant living / by Michael Picucci ;
foreword by Peter A. Levine.
      p. cm.
  Summary: "Demonstrates that ritual can be a potent therapeutic tool for healing difficult emotional/energetic blocks and traumas as well as for finding solutions to stressful everyday problems"—Provided by publisher.
  ISBN 1-55643-566-5 (pbk.)
  1. Psychotherapy. 2. Ritual—Therapeutic use. I. Title.
  RC480.5P52 2005
  616.89'14—dc22
                    2005023510

HEALTH RESPONSIBILITY
We all deserve to get all the help we need in becoming and staying healthy. The rituals in this book (or on the separate CD) are not a form of, or substitute for psychotherapy, or other medical attention. If you are experiencing chronic and/or life-limiting symptoms, you may need to enlist competent professional help. If you choose to do these rituals on your own, and if you should experience reactions that feel too intense to manage on your own, seek professional help. You may find contacts through these websites: www.theinstitute.org and www.traumahealing. com, among many others, or ask a knowledgeable friend for a referral.

1 2 3 4 5 6 7 DATA 09 08 07 06 05

Dedicated to three radiant souls
who have inspired me with their courage.

In memory of the light of
Howard Lesman

the wisdom and
compassion of
Dayashakti
(Sandra Scherer)

and in honor of
David J. Pearson
whose innate intelligence provided
the directive to write this book.

Contents

VIBRANT EROS

Acknowledgments

This book owes its existence to the support of twelve uniquely bright and resourceful individuals who joined with me in a virtual (book writing ritual) circle constantly giving feedback and sustenance to my experience, observations, and writing. They are all mentioned at the end of Chapter One.

I also want to give special thanks to Evan T. Pritchard, who immersed himself in this endeavor, helping me further transform my ideas, experiences, and learning into words of greater meaning. Jane Hart's early edits gave the text foundation. Chuck Stein, who reviewed the full manuscript from outside the circle, gets a *sacred bow*. He offered an array of new and brilliant perspectives for restructuring and fine-tuning that upped the book's amperage. Robbie Tucker assisted in making the text flow as it approached editorial completion with a last exacting edit. And, also big kudos to Susan Quasha for a spirited cover and book design, rendered with poise and good-heartedness.

I will be forever grateful to Richard Grossinger and Lindy Hough of North Atlantic Books for their belief in my work and willingness to offer North Atlantic's imprimatur. I also want to thank Emily Boyd, who gracefully guided *Ritual as Resource* through the publishing process.

I am touched by the synchronicities in recent years that brought the languaging of this writing from my soul to my consciousness, mostly through the contributions of Peter A. Levine (and the Somatic Experiencing® processes he originated). I also thank Peter for appreciating my creations careening off of his own and writing this book's Foreword. The two people who mysteriously led me to

Peter are Dean Sweeney and Steffie Yost, both healing pioneers I respect, cherish, and admire.

All of the expressions above would not be possible without the ongoing support and grounding of some very special organizations and people. The Institute for Authentic Process Healing (IAPH) is my personal and professional *home community*. Here I found respect, support, and empowerment. I thank the Board of Directors, the Advisory Council, the Practitioner's Circle, and all community members who have come, gone, or stayed in the past twenty years. At IAPH is where others sustained and participated in my research, giving it a home and making it real. I also want to extend heartfelt gratitude to the Gay Spirit Culture Project, especially to Patrick McNamara and the core group, for creating the event that sparked the epiphany and catapulted me to write this book. I am also dynamically linked to a medley (too many to mention) of great people, communities and organizations, whom I cross-pollinate with for our own and the larger good. I honor all of you.

I have been blessed with a "best friend" that has been with me for over twenty-five years; his name is John McCormack. Without John's wisdom, friendship, guidance, and faith in me, I don't know where I would be today. The other important individuals who have truly sustained me personally and professional are Mario Cavazos, Nicholas Cimorelli, Jim and Sue Cusack, Sônia Gomes, Jane Hart, Tom Herington, Ian Holloway, Tom Kane, Brian Lynch, Mary McDonald, David Pearson, David Shaw, Billy Taylor, Alice Terson, Gary Topper, Ana Venezia, Jerry Ward, and my long-time ally, Barbara Warren. Thanks also to William (Red) Croker for keeping my body sound and spirit high through this writing.

In memoriam, I want to acknowledge the following people who gave me love, support, foundation and wisdom: Ken Axel, Richard Christian, Dayashakti (Sandra Scherer), David Goodstein, Sensei Sandra Jishu Holmes, Richard Lacarda, Howard Lesman, Michael McMahon, Sheila Picucci, Gil Rubin-O'Keefe, and Peter Simmons.

To all my clients and workshop participants through the years—you know who you are—I sincerely thank you for your trust and confidence in me, and for your support in helping me develop this work as part of our shared journey.

I also want to acknowledge all the great contributors (many of whom are mentioned in this book, as well as those who are not) in the fields of energetic and body-mind-nature healing, who have come before me and have so generously informed this vision of *Ritual as Resource.*

The completion of this text, like the ones that preceded it, demonstrates the steadfast love and grounding provided by my partner-in-life, Elias J. Guerrero, Jr., who sustains and comforts me through extraordinary adventures and challenges. Bravo, Elias, I love you dearly.

Lastly, to the Great Spirit (or higher power) that guides me, protects me, and ultimately graces all of my challenges, I express my humble gratitude.

Foreword

We hold the mistaken notion that we have somehow "outgrown" our need for ritual. In fact, in our post-modern-technical society, it is just the reverse. "High-tech" demands the balance of "high-touch." The great spiritual traditions are about re-connecting to wholeness through rituals and celebrations; they are vehicles for that journey. Though we as a secular society are deluged with information (much of it stimulating and useful), at the same time, we suffer from a paucity of wisdom and have the desire for more personal warmth, connection and engagement.

It is interesting that a branch of science—psychology—has led at least a few hardy pioneers full circle back to the realm that once belonged to religion, ritual, in order to answer the need for more personal connectivity with each other and the universe. I believe this to be an important step forward.

Michael Picucci, in *Ritual as Resource*, reveals ritual as a portal into the rich inner landscape of the true self, and how vital a resource it is in our modern lives. However, unlike in recent centuries, in which rituals have been set by hierarchal societies, we moderns need to participate directly in the creation of our own transformational experiences through ritual. The tranquil feelings of aliveness and ecstatic self-transcendence that make us fully human can also be accessed through ritual. This way they become enduring features of our existence. This book helps fill the gap between ourselves and the divine intelligence in the universe, and in the context of our time.

Picucci at first shows the reader how to develop basic rituals involving the body, and its awareness of "felt sense," and the breath. This foundation is essential. Without access to the living, sensing, knowing body, spiritual experiences—no matter how exultant and transcendent—do not become part of who we are. Then, by breaking down ritual into its dynamic parts, including the special role played by the reptilian brain, Michael helps us to understand the very real and tangible power of prayer, in its various forms. He then weaves the idea of prayer as communication into the many rituals that follow. In addition, he provides schemas (open-ended models) that help us visualize our rituals and bring them into form. This includes intention, resource, and the Curious Observer.

Ritual as Resource presents a course of action in which everyday activities like breathing, community-building, health and personal hygiene, house- and car-hunting, going to work, playing, praying, and just growing up, might be imbued with greater spiritual meaning through the power of ritual.

Perhaps Michael's most original and powerful contribution is in establishing rituals that help us transform trauma. While all of us have been traumatized at some time in our lives, we need not become victims of those events. Through the resources gathered in the previous exercises, we can begin to harness and transform the primordial biological energies evoked in trauma. In doing this, we begin to become the potent master of our own destinies.

And then there are the inevitable challenges that meet us on our journeys through life. Loss, bereavement, separation, divorce, serious illness and injury all have the power to halt our forward movement. Again, with the strength and resilience developed through ritual, even these devastating occurrences can be woven into the rich tapestry of our lives, bringing us more depth, passion and power.

Dr. Picucci also leads the reader through relationship and erotic rituals to help restore connectivity on many levels and awaken the sensuous body. Finally, to complete his task, he introduces the art of dynamic linking, a ritual in itself, which helps individuals cohere with each other, while taking the healing community movement another important step forward.

This is a book to be read, meditated upon, and used as a resource for a life fully lived.

PETER A. LEVINE, PH.D.

Author of *Waking the Tiger: Healing Trauma* (North Atlantic Books, 1997) and *Healing Trauma: A Pioneering Program for Restoring the Wisdom of Your Body* (Sounds True Book/CD 2005)

Introduction

> In order for the mind to see light instead of darkness,
> the soul must be turned away from this world, until
> its eye can learn to contemplate the true reality and
> the supreme good. Hence there may well be an art
> whose aim would be to affect this very thing.
>
> SOCRATES

Could human beings, faced with a rapidly changing world full of trauma and distractions, ever develop an art for filling the mind and spirit with light instead of darkness? Could we learn an art that speaks to our desire for inner peace and to our need to bring happier circumstances into our outer world as well? Indeed, such an art is within our grasp and its name is *ritual!*

"Ritual," a challenging word to define, since at its heart it is about experiencing something. Ritual usually refers to rite, an action sanctifying a certain process. For our purposes, let us expand the meaning of the word "ritual" to include not only physical actions, but energetic, non-physical dimensions as well, such as intention, visualization, and realization. Socrates sought to illuminate our spirit, and if we are to see and experience that light, we need assistance from soulful sources—for healing both our inner and outer existences. Through a contemporary understanding of ritual, we can discover that assistance, allowing the healing arts and the art of living to gracefully merge.

Ritual, partnered with scientific understanding of *energy fields*, gives birth to a new context in which to live a fuller and richer life. That context opens the way for techniques so powerful that I would be dead by now, had I not learned them. In fact, the approach outlined in this book is inspired by encounters with death, both by others and myself. These approaches developed not only out of a need to survive, but to live energetically and fully expressed. A colleague, Diane Poole Heller, states, "Resource is any positive memory, person, place, or action that creates a soothing feeling in our body." Many therapists now use these resources to help clients de-activate the nervous system, bringing forth a response of relaxation to their state of being. Ritual has been a key to unlocking incredible resources, healing, and more joy in living as well.

This book will expand on this idea, using "resource" both in its noun and verb forms. As a noun, it will be used to refer to anything that serves as a source of transformational energy and enrichment, as well as relaxation, especially in the context of ritual. As a verb, "to resource" and its variants, it will be used to express the act of accessing and utilizing these hidden treasures.

Because a new language is developing to describe some of these abstract concepts, the glossary at the end of the book may be useful for any words or phrases unfamiliar to you.

Ritual is not the only form of *energetic healing*. A new clinical field, Energy Psychology (EP) is a moving force traveling through constructs of mental health, physical health, and transformational processes. Building upon both newly emerging and conventional therapeutic methods, EP utilizes techniques from a variety of forms of *energy medicine*, body-mind therapies, along with ancient traditions like acupressure, acupuncture, yoga, qi gong, and ritual, the central focus of this book.

As a practitioner (and so-called *wounded-healer*), I started out with a focus on addiction recovery, a field that later propelled me into the healing of trauma as well as the relational and sexual challenges of our time. So I'm particularly pleased to see that energy medicines are becoming the new centerpieces of healing at some of our most respected and cutting-edge addiction and trauma treatment facilities. Those most familiar to me include Crossroads at Antigua, West Indies, The Life Healing Center in Sante Fe, New Mexico, and The Meadows and Sierra Tucson in Arizona. I understand there are many such emerging facilities around the globe. The techniques being integrated are acupuncture, EMDR (see glossary), Somatic Experiencing®, yoga, Thought Field Therapy, and many others. They are showing up everywhere. In time, they will provide us with a larger understanding of (and greater compassion for) those of us who have, or have had, serious addiction, mental health, or emotional challenges. In fact, they will also give us a greater understanding of life itself. We are entering a time in which the exploration of energy medicine and the field of psychology are becoming one and the same. Perhaps the word "psychology" itself is being gradually transformed by our new understandings of human energy.

Ritual as resource, EP, and all of the healing arts, working with ancient techniques, are helping us create tools of the future: light, belief, self-love, and imagination. We will demonstrate their effectiveness in this book. These resources are not about wishful thinking or the denial of reality. In fact, we will face the traumas of pain and hardship eyeball to eyeball, and we will respond to these challenges effectively in ways that are fundamentally transformational. Once we bring these unseen traumas to light and break down the binary internal logjams that lock us out of our lives, we can begin to make healthier choices. These choices can foster happier circumstances, as we more fully contemplate the reality that Socrates called "the supreme good." I invite you to use these ideas as a foundation for vibrant living.

A Personal Perspective

I've chosen to write this book because I know to the marrow of my bones that we need to learn how to use ritual to develop the resources we need to be able to live full vibrant lives in the twenty-first century. The decision to write this book in a direct, revealing, and disarming tone was not an easy one. It goes against the grain of conventional science writing and the publishing world in general. However, it is essential that I *speak* to you rather than write at you, in order to engage us both in the *authentic process* of healing communication, which is at the core of my work. Ritual is a dynamic, self-disclosing, and totally direct way of communicating with the universe. I have decided to let this book speak to the reader in a similar manner; enthusiastic, conversational, and highly autobiographical. Novelist Tom Spanbauer has referred to this style as "Dangerous Writing." Chris Haigy, in *White Crane Journal* states, "it means putting a piece of yourself in a work, going to the 'sore spot,' and discussing taboo topics.… It means writing for yourself, a concept that in the literary world was thought to make you go broke. It means 'exposing yourself to the tiger,' not physically, but mentally."

In this book both you I will be exposing ourselves to the tiger that sometimes rages within us, and can just as often purr. This tiger escapes the rational mind, like a part of us that can be mastered but never tamed. To liberate this tiger we must first face our own vulnerability. Ritual can access energy from the animal world that, when handled respectfully, is not to be feared. There are deep, healing forces that can make us stronger if we learn how to access them. The resilience I've gained from ritual allows me to stand toe to toe with anyone (or anything) with confidence, and perhaps with only a mild sense of fear. In order to describe to you the long, twisting road of trauma, exploration, and recovery that led me to the doorstep of *energetic medicine*, dangerous writing is inevitable. To convey the importance of ritual as resource, it is necessary to share the path I've traveled, tigers and all.

I was given up for dead twice in my life. The media, the odds, statistics, the opinions of those around me, and the way I felt in my body, all marked me as a dying man. However, I lived to tell this story.

How I survived is complex and involved both *allopathy* (specific scientific, pharmacological and surgical actions directed at specific parts of my body) and *holopathy* (healing practices that viewed me as a field of energy, as a whole being connected to community and humanity). I am grateful to the allopaths who worked on my body. Positive experiences with allopathic medicine have inspired me to make creating the bridge between holopathy and allopathy a part of my life's work. This book, in fact, is an act of ritual holopathy, a healing practice made possible by allopathy. The two in concert demonstrate the power of ritual and its ability to heal whatever part of us seems to have lost its innate integrity.

In April, 2004, I experienced the second most powerful epiphany of my life, illuminating for me an art I had never given much thought to, the very one that Socrates seems to be calling for in this chapter's epigraph. A flash of insight came to me at a "Summit on Spirituality and Global Transformation" at The Garrison Institute in New York. The Oxford English Dictionary defines epiphany as, "Having an aesthetic experience that includes the manifestation or appearance of some divine or superhuman presence." The Garrison Institute was the perfect location for such an occurrence. It is a former Capuchin monastery overlooking the Hudson River in the lower Hudson Valley, situated on the beautiful ninety-five-acre Glenclyffe property. The Institute's programs work towards two goals: a deep, insightful exploration of a given issue, and the articulation of specific steps to enhance society and enrich the human spirit in regards to that issue.

Sponsored by the Gay Spirit Culture Project, the indescribable beauty and sacredness of this gathering place was fertile ground for what happened to me. I remember being in the huge, magnificent temple with 130 other like-minded people on Friday night (the second of the four days of the retreat) as a robust ritual appeared to spontaneously erupt. The *elders* of the group were asked to identify themselves, and, to my surprise, I was one of them. We were honored by all, and at one point, more specifically, by the younger men in attendance. The self-identified youth were then honored for their courage to attend and share. There was a *focalizer* directing the energy and processes in the temple, and at one point he invited the elders to do a special transmission of love, permission, and unconditional support to the youth. We elders were instructed to surround the youth (who were standing in the center of the room after a very energetic movement ritual) and to lay our hands on their shoulders and backs encouraging them to follow their bliss, make room for mistakes, (and the lessons within them), and know that we trust their judgment, and that our spirit is always with them. It was one of the sweetest and most touching moments of my life. Emerging from that ritual the title of this book was born as the experience exploded through my body and mind. The significance of Ritual became supremely obvious at that moment. The second two words in the title, *As Resource,* will take on even greater meaning as we delve deeper in this alchemy.

After that night, I had an overwhelming sense that I understood something that had not crystallized before about what I was doing. No deity came out of the clouds to speak to me, although the insight was nevertheless truly divine, as it came from within.

The new and wonderful turn that my own journey to complete recovery was about to take was illuminated to me at the Summit, where I experienced ritual as an omnipotent resource in our time.

A previous epiphany that I had in 1985 (coincidentally, at another spiritual gathering) led to the creation of my last book, *The Journey Toward Complete Recovery: Reclaiming your Emotional, Spiritual & Sexual Wholeness*. This Summit of 2004 also addressed some of the same issues as the earlier gathering, but this time they were steeped in a sense of ritual, becoming fertile ground for a cascading of further discovery. Thereafter, from day-to-day, hour-to-hour, and moment-to-moment, flashes of insight and integration kept coming to me about ritual as a tool for healing and vibrant living. All my past learning, teaching, and experiences were taking on a new interwoven vibrancy, not apparent to me before. I knew in the core of my being that my perspectives, practices, and teachings would be forever changed. Stunned by possibility, my mind was flooded by the connections that led to the ingredients of this book. While the experience itself was mind jarring, it was accompanied by a sense of calm and resiliency that made me feel very whole and complete.

In the center of this I began to sense the world differently. I could now understand the suffering and trauma that generations of people before me had experienced. Without attaching a judgment, I viewed it as evolution. I could follow the chain of inter-generational pain on and on, back in time, lifetimes fading into lifetimes. It was astounding. All of this came to me in a flash as my years of work in trauma healing became integrated into *Ritual as Resource*.

Rituals address: (1) the urge to comprehend our existence in meaningful ways; (2) the search for a pathway as we move from one stage of our lives to the next; (3) the need to establish secure and fulfilling relationships in the community; and (4) the longing to know our part in the vast wonder and mystery of the cosmos.

Joseph Campbell, one of the most influential cultural anthropologists of the twentieth century, offered two central messages, just prior to his passing, that still resonate in my soul. Both are at the core of what I mean by the title of this book.

Campbell's first message was partially a negative one: The various forms of ritual and ritual-like behavior developed by the early American Colonialists (such as regular church attendance, volunteering for war, big game hunting, fist-fighting over love, marriage, the work ethic, etc.) no longer work in the same way for us in the twenty-first century. Their rituals gave them a sense of meaning, purpose, stability, and a sense that they were part of something larger themselves; that their lives were on the right track. These rituals and myths grounded our forbearers, but *our* world has changed. The mythologies connected to them are sterile, so the rituals that gave context to their lives and times can't ground us. Campbell said that the world has changed so fast in the past sixty years that we have outgrown our own mythologies, therefore we were without sufficient grounding, and we're adrift! Not only had we lost our anchors but there has been no opportunity for new grounding mythologies and rituals to develop, take root, and replace the old.

Joseph Campbell predicted that new mythologies emerging in the 21st century would involve consciousness. "Knowing one's self," and the wealth of new rituals that goes with that, unleashing new sets of energies, is what this book is about. The knowing of the self will bring us the peace and equanimity that the mythologies of the past once provided our forbearers. The new mythologies will be an eternally returning story, one we come back to over and over. This story will illuminate how we learn who we are in a swiftly changing spiritual, material, and scientifically manipulated world. Ritual in an expanded sense will be a doorway to this journey of knowing.

The second message I internalized from Campbell is a bedrock of contemporary ethos: "Follow your bliss!" You will discover that ritual is a place of incubation—far away from newspapers, fears, money concerns, and all other attachments to everyday life. Ritual can be what Campbell would call your "bliss station." From that "station," we can explore new inner landscapes, discovering a wealth of resources to help us realize what is most true and potent about who we are, and what is most meaningful.

Expanding the Circle

What if it were possible for us to use ritual as a resource to fulfill Campbell's end-of-life vision? What if we could fashion a new resource from the old, to gently propel us into a truly energetic way of being?

Out of an awareness of my own limitations, I decided not to write this book alone. Accordingly, I have written it with an editor, Evan T. Pritchard, a renowned mythopoetic writer, musician, and ritualist, together with a circle of twelve diverse and distinguished individuals. While Evan has helped give words, and sometimes poetry, to the concepts I feel and know in my bones, the circle has helped to make the writing as broadly accessible as possible.

This text is published by North Atlantic Books, a highly regarded nonprofit publisher aligned with the Society for the Study of Native Arts and Sciences. The goals of this nonprofit, educational corporation are to develop an educational and cross-cultural perspective linking various scientific, social, and artistic fields to nurture a holistic view of the relationship of mind, body, and nature. We are proud to have the endorsement of this society. In presenting this endeavor, we also honor the 12-Step Movement, the many *authenticity circles* that came before it, and the waves of transformational work that are now cresting on many shores.

We have done everything possible to make this sharing of wisdom and discovery accessible to the widest possible audience. That means we are reaching out to all who suffer the adriftness of modern day life, with its attendant illnesses, addictions, malaise, and despair. We mean cab drivers, doctors, short-order cooks, lawyers, students, CEOs, housewives, and Indian chiefs. We mean women, men, and all of the beautiful gender and color variances that exist. Because this book is not only my own attempt at focusing important discoveries but also that of our circle, I will sometimes use "I" and sometimes "we," as seems appropriate. "I" will always preface my personal experience; "we" will represent a consensus of the entire circle that will sometimes include you, the reader, as well.

My own recovery process influences my writing in the "I." In 12-Step meetings (and other healing circles) I quickly learned I am more likely to remain mindful of others and more likely to be understood by speaking only from "direct personal experience." As a psycho-therapist, "I" communication was further validated by Carl Rogers, the father of Humanistic Psychology. He believed that healing could only take place in the process of "authentic communication of personal experience." Hence the term *Authentic Process Healing* that has framed my research, practice, and life.

It is in this context that I humbly offer *Ritual as Resource* in the most inclusive and responsible manner possible.

Tuning In

1

◇◇◇◇◇◇

Felt Sense and Energetic Living

A felt sense is … an internal aura that encompasses everything you feel and know about a given subject at a given time—encompasses it and communicates it to you all at once, rather than detail by detail.

EUGENE GENDLIN

What you hold in your hands is about how to achieve a powerfully intuitive way of life through exploring the felt-senses of the body, by unlocking hidden transformational energies through ritual. For readers unfamiliar with the term "felt sense," I will quote more extensively from Eugene Gendlin, the man who coined the term in his book, *Focusing.* Gendlin writes: "A *felt* sense is not a mental experience but a physical one. *Physical.* A bodily awareness of a situation or person or event. An internal aura that encompasses everything you feel and know about a given subject at a given time—encompasses it and communicates it to you all at once, rather than detail by detail."

As one who further developed Gendlin's discoveries, Peter A. Levine states in his *Waking the Tiger* (the world's best-selling book for individuals and practitioners on healing trauma), "The felt sense unifies a great deal of scattered data and gives it meaning." Once I experienced felt senses in *my* body, there was no turning back. I began to understand myself through a new inner language that helped me articulate my experience. I began to develop my somatic intelligence, that unique wisdom which belongs to the body, and this brought me deeper into the heart of ritual and what I now know as *innate intelligence.* This innate intelligence is a gift from nature that is often delivered to me through the art of ritual.

When I first began utilizing ritual, I achieved great results, but I did not truly understand this work at a deeper level. Even so, I knew it was more than just having a lucky healing experience. Over time, I have been introduced to its unlimited potential. In addition to healing through our innate intelligence, it can be used to access our inner resources to make them more palpable and accessible for us. We can also use ritual to experience spiritual *openings*. This may, or may not, look like anything we are familiar with from various world religions, and that is okay. Ritual can juice up and empower every step of our life journey, wherever it leads. We only need to accept that this possibility exists.

This reminds me of the enchanting book, *The Field: The Quest for the Secret Force in the Universe,* by Lynne McTaggart, an investigative journalist. In the prologue, *The Coming Revolution*, she writes, "We are poised on the brink of a revolution—a revolution as daring and profound as Einstein's discovery of relativity. At the very frontier of science new ideas are emerging that challenge everything we believe about how our world works and how we define ourselves. Discoveries are being made that prove … that human beings are far more extraordinary than an assemblage of flesh and bones. At its most fundamental, this new science answers questions that have perplexed scientists for hundreds of years. At its most profound, this is a science of the miraculous."

In line with this "science of the miraculous," we are going to explore the "feeling of healing," which is the relationship between our innate intelligence and our well-being. Innate intelligence refers to that energy and/or wisdom that is sometimes referred to as our essence, chi, or simply the mysterious life force that guides us from the inside out whenever we tap into it. It is also the energy that invisibly connects us to the earth and to everything and everyone in the universe. Even if you have worked with energy dynamics as a healing modality before, this book intends to take you one step further by exploring energetic healing within the context of ritual. We will explore this tool for *tuning, focusing, amplifying*, and *directing* energy for healing, as the four distinct intentions that make up a complete ritual.

I have a *Book Ritual* that is coupled with other daily prayers. During the time set aside for these rituals, I begin to *attune* to my higher self and bring my attention away from the outside world. This is *Tuning*. Then I direct my attention inward and toward my awareness of my being and my body, in the very moment. This is *Tuning*. I then *focus* on my intentions for this book, how I want to learn and discover in the process of writing it, how I want serendipity and synchronicity to grace the process, and how I want the book to bring the highest good for myself and others. This is *Focusing*. Next I invite in the heart-opening love and supportive energy of special people, including deceased loved ones (Sheila, Daya, Gil, Howard; you'll hear about them later) and the innate intelligence of the universe itself to hear my intentions and help them manifest. This is *Amplifying*. I may also take a deep breath or two. Lastly, I imagine myself writing and working with the ritual circle, the designers, and the publisher. I direct this *amplified* energy with all of this wonderful imagery toward our mutual goal, to place a powerful new book into the hands of those who need it, offering a tool which can be used to accelerate their own healing process. This is *Directing* Life Energy. By using these steps we develop an intuitive approach to ritual, at times appearing to border on magic.

A dictionary definition will steer us through the many connotations time has placed on the word, "Magic": Having, or apparently having, supernatural powers, producing surprising or remarkable results, effecting or permitting change, or bringing success." Magic can also mean something "enchanting and delightful," as for instance, how I was magnetically pulled, energetically and literally, to attend that Summit. That *was* an experience of magic. It is appropriate that we use the word "magic" here, because medicine finds its historical roots in magic—healing magic. In fact, the word "shaman" in the original Altaic language of Siberia implies "healer," one who heals naturally and supernaturally through ritual and magic. It is interesting that in just over a hundred years, the art and science of psychological healing has evolved from the psychodynamic analysis of instincts to embrace shamanistic and other rituals known worldwide for thousands of years. This is not too surprising when you consider that ritual and the magic it evokes are great ways to get well and stay well, because ritual gives us access to our innate intelligence, our very life force, where both prevention and restoration begin towards optimum health.

My own path to awareness of the felt senses of my body is the same journey to self-discovery that awakened me to energetic living. I first learned of it while healing my addictions and was drawn further along the path facing multiple health challenges and my own traumatic history. Your path can start wherever your feet are planted right now. By the time you put this book down, you will know how to bring a new light of intuitive certainty to your next step in life.

We want to share with you how ritual, gracefully merging with scientific technologies, can help you live a more artful way of life. For example, if you choose the assistance of medical science to heal your body or mind, do not neglect your energy; rather, combine medical science and energetic healing to achieve a more profound, satisfying, multi-dimensional healing experience. As previously mentioned, I would be dead by now if I had not learned to combine energetic healing with modern medicine. These experiences inspired me to develop and implement energetic healing in my life.

Engaging Opposite Energies

In discussing ritual and its connection to modern technology, we will also discuss the role that opposing energy forces play in our lives. It is crucial that we turn the contradictions we experience into our teachers for creating a more enriched life. According to Peter Levine, the dance of opposites is the key to generating energy fields, and I believe it is the key to spiritual transformation as well. Spiritual transformation is a change in a person, an institution, or a tradition that brings about an engendering of greater wholeness.

An example of this dance of opposites is the healing I experienced with my father. Learning that I had the capacity not only to comfortably hold opposite energies in my system, but to transform them, I got the knack of being able to move back and forth between the two energies. On the one hand, my father was a traumatizing, painful force in my life, with many limitations—both evolutionary and cultural. On the other, he was my *dad*, who sacrificed greatly for me. I love him, and now, I get a big kick out of him. This was a huge personal shift, and my use of ritual helped engage these opposite energies. By giving myself room to invite both of these energies into my body, allowing them to dance together—touching one energy to the edge of the other—I opened the door for my own spiritual transformation to occur.

One of the most profound (and timely) examples of opposite energies existing together is our current field of medicine itself. Richard Grossinger writes in his book, *Planet Medicine:*

> *Since earliest times, our species has evolved two distinct traditions for the practice of medicine. One, the art of healing, is exactly that: an art, practiced through sympathy and intuition, cultivating its own training and techniques and requirements of skill and education. The other is academic and rationalist, giving rise to technology, scientific medicine (allopathic). It*

includes ancient and primitive skills of surgery and pharmacy, as well as the sophisticated forms into which they have evolved....
Mostly [the two traditions] are in active opposition.

Richard Grossinger demonstrates how two opposite energies can co-exist at the same time in the same context. He also illustrates three paths to healing (even though he only mentions two); you can take the way of the holopath or the way of the allopath, or both. The first is basically energetic healing, while the second is analytical and anatomical. Both are valuable traditions that can save your life. Perhaps by opening up a dialogue here on this subject, we can come a long way to diffusing the painful challenges inherent in medicine's opposite pulls. Even more important, we can experience these same opposite principles at work in every fragmented corner of our lives, and by understanding how to combine them, achieve greater mastery of life.

Ritual as Resource will focus on the first, the more intuitive type of medicine and intelligence, and invoke skills that embrace and transform the scientific and technological. We can understand this more clearly now because of what we've learned from the deep investigations by people like Lynne McTaggart, who writes, "What they have discovered is nothing less than astonishing. At our most elemental, we are not a chemical reaction, but an energetic charge. Human beings and all living things are a coalescence of energy in a field of energy connected to every other thing in the world. This pulsating energy field is the central engine of our being and our consciousness, the alpha and omega of our existence." She adds, "The field *is* the force, rather than germs or genes, that finally determines whether we are healthy or ill...."

The theme of working with *opposite energies* will course throughout this book, as it is central to all we know about working with our innate intelligence to bring us the felt sense of wholeness and awareness that we seek.

My *"Mary Ritual"* is a quick simple example of playing with opposite energies in a useful way. I do a fair amount of public speaking, some of which can be challenging and bring up fear, anxiety and constriction in my body. Mary is a friend I've known and loved for twenty years. More pertinent is that I *know* and deeply feel that Mary loves me unconditionally: In her eyes, I can absolutely do nothing wrong. It's like having the perfect protective mother. Here's the way I use Mary's energy as a resource in this ritual: Five minutes before the speaking engagement or presentation, I invoke Mary's love, her smile and laughter. By invoke, I mean I recall a memory of us together, and then I *feel* and *sense* that memory. I envision her right in the center of the group I'm about to address. I focus my attention on Mary's image and humor, and my body constrictions relax. From that moment on I am presenting to the whole group with the same kind of loose expansive energy I have with my dear friend. As the two energies meld, I'm not *just* with the group I was nervous about. A third experience exists that makes me feel whole, complete, and comfortable with my task. This works best as we realize that we can hold opposite energies in our being, and at the same time learn to work with them for a positive outcome.

A New View of Ritual

When someone thinks about ritual, they might think back to images of ancient times or perhaps rituals from their own past, such as their childhood religion. Some might think of everyday rituals, such as having a cup of coffee with the morning paper at breakfast, or going to work. In this book we will be exploring a new expansive experience of ritual, one that we may have never consciously considered before.

An example of a mundane task that some might call a ritual is the daily shower. As I've learned more about engaging my innate intelligence and resources, I have a more expansive view and experience of everyday tasks such as my daily shower. It has become my *"Shower Ritual."* As I step under the spraying water, I attune myself to spirit and give thanks to the universe, or God, for this resource of water to wash my body and cleanse my soul. While washing my hair and body, I focus on my desire to have all problems and toxicities from past moments washed away as well. Through prayer, I direct this purification towards a greater purpose, that I may meet every moment hereafter with a clear heart and soul, bringing a *presence* and resource to whatever and whomever I meaningfully engage with on this day. I amplify it as I dry myself off with the feeling that I am starting over a new life. By all appearances, it looks like the same old shower. Yet, I can assure you it feels very different, and my day (and, I feel, my world) is all the better! The difference between my new shower experience and the old way of just taking a shower is the intention and Curious Observer I bring with me. These are two important elements of ritual which will be fully explained later. For now, consider the Curious Observer to be a little sprite on your shoulder who simply witnesses, without judgment or agenda! What is important to know for now is that with all rituals there are (along with the aforementioned) important, powerful elements, like *sense of place*, keeping the ritual actions distinct from the mundane, inviting resources, and invoking styles of speech (even if the words remain interior and not given voice to). Honoring rituals with a name always amplifies the energy, while a sense of *gratitude* for what's good in our lives, whatever our present challenges may be, helps sanctify our experience. This expanded view of ritual includes what we know about ancient ritual from writers like Joseph Campbell, and other innovative cultural anthropologists like Malidoma Patrice Some, as well as from observations made in our own supportive community over the past twenty years.

Paradox Transports Us

An important part of this book involves connecting our knowledge of ancient ritual practice with the needs of today, where ritual still has a place in our super-technological world. Ancient wisdom about energy and ritual emerged from a world in which time passed more slowly and people were more consciously connected to the energy of the earth and the cosmos. We need to re-learn and re-connect with timeless concepts of energy that are beyond human measure and combine them with the more current technological concepts of energy applicable in a world where speed, clarity, and exact results are prized and expected. The ancient world and the modern world are both real for us, and they can complement and transform each other as all opposite energies can. Integrating this wisdom with modern developments can help us create a new way of being and living. In many indigenous cultures there are no "bad" energies, only those that need to be respectfully transformed. An integrated way of living can help us embody a wholeness that utilizes every dimension of our being. This wholeness includes what we experience as opposite energies or contradictions. What I am suggesting is a paradox: "A statement which on the face of it seems self-contradictory, absurd, or at variance with common sense, though on investigation or when explained, it may prove to be well founded." A paradox is like a Zen koan. "It embraces the unknown and makes an ally of doubt," reports John Tarrant in a recent issue of *Shift* (published by the Institute of Noetic Sciences—IONS.org).

Rituals help us step outside the routine nature of life and experience something special and non-ordinary. There are many seemingly paradoxical references in this book. Ritual engages and embraces paradox, allowing us to inhabit a larger space and engage a larger logic that can transport us to our next level of wholeness. Through ritual we can wake up to the next level of what being alive is all about.

If you apply the ideas in this book and experiment with them with an open mind, you will begin to cultivate a new feeling of specialness about yourself and your daily life.

The Ritual of Reading

Consider reading this book as a personal ritual for yourself. Simply invite a sense of blessedness into your experience, such as reverence, love, or gratitude for the good that has come your way. This positive resource exists in our inner and outer worlds. Without a sense that a resource of pleasant energies are at your disposal, it may be challenging to engage this practice. If you experiment with the ideas in this book, they will take on personal meaning rather than remain only words. You must *act* on the words. Experiment with the ideas that these words represent in your life. This new, light-hearted *playground*, where ritual is a resource must be self-tested and experienced. You can start whenever you choose. In truth, you can't know ritual from reading a book, yet you can make it come alive and take root by including these exercises in your own ritual creation. Let a resource keep you company while reading this book. Practice the rituals and notice what happens.

The Book Ritual Circle

As previously mentioned, I wrote this book as part of a larger, long-term ritual circle comprised of thirteen people (including myself). The ritual circle that supported the writing of this book began to form by our making a common spiritual commitment over the July 4th weekend, 2004. The induction to our book ritual circle was simple. We shared a short prayer, inviting in spirit or nature. We each affirmed, *"Being a member of this book ritual circle is in my own best interests, for the good of all participating and for the larger good."* Once we did that, the ritual began. It was that simple. Everyone agreed to read the raw material that I'd been collecting for some time, once I put it in chapter form, and then to respond from their own inner voices in a positive creative spirit. Since they were all people I admired and trusted, I agreed to go back, as my own intuition guided me, and integrate their contributions.

I was empowered by the circle and by myself to be the ritual focalizer, as well as the author. In fact, we are all contributors. The group is intentionally diverse, including young people, elders, women, gay, and heterosexual men, Native Americans, Caucasians, and Latinos. The circle consists of an editor, seven readers, a cover designer and line editor. Of course, many of the roles of the individuals became blurred, as in ritual work nothing remains linear. In alphabetical order the circle consisted of these special people: Victoria Britt, Nicholas Cimorelli, David Conneely, Jane M. Hart, Steven Lansky, David Pearson, Evan T. Pritchard, Susan Quasha, George Russell, David Shaw, Robbie Tucker, and Ana Venezia.

As I complete this chapter, I notice that the current issue of *Utne* magazine (featuring the latest ideas and trends emerging in our culture) has an article: "Do-It-Yourself Rituals: Who needs old traditions when you can make up new ones?" The timing of this publication is synchronistic, and, as you will read again, *synchronicity* both grounds and takes wings from ritual. "Synchronicity," a word coined by Carl Jung, means "meaningful coincidence," a wink from the universe that tells me I'm on the right track. The *Utne* article talks about "ritual-crafting." That's a good term for what this book is about. With a little practice and a light heart, you may quickly find yourself being a ritual-crafter. If so, be prepared to notice any synchronicities along the way!

A special note: There are many rituals throughout this book. It can be difficult to read a ritual and practice it at the same time. You might consider recording the ritual, speaking very slowly and thoughtfully into the recording device (which then becomes a resource for this ritual). Listening to yourself could be an additional way of amplifying the energy as well. You can also order a CD with all the rituals in this book clearly spoken from my website (www.michaelpicucci.net) or using the order form in the back of the book.

2

The Me Nobody Knows

I am going to tell you the story of my life …
and if it were only the story of my life,
I think I would not tell it.

BLACK ELK

The Me Nobody Knows (Well, Almost)

In my community, *focalizer* has come to mean a person who empowers himself and who is empowered by the community to bring focus to the matters at hand. A focalizer brings the community's energy to the highest level for the good of all. And I have earned this title by demonstrating my willingness in group gatherings to respectfully bring intellectual, emotional, and energetic focus to what concerns us.

I'm also a man who has been given a front row seat to the challenges, suffering, and beauty of this life. Appearances suggest that my life has been tragic, yet I have lived an extraordinarily rich and full life. I was abandoned by my mother, terrorized by my dad, neglected and constantly ridiculed by older brothers, and repeatedly uprooted from multiple homes in my youth. I suffered learning disabilities, addiction in my early teen years, and the death of a spouse at age twenty (and another one at age forty-two). I've had a long struggle with my sexual identity, further addiction in my thirties, genetically inherited cardio-vascular disease, a diagnosis of HIV/AIDS (along with a massive loss of loved ones to the disease), two cancers, a heart attack and triple by-pass surgery. And as I write this, I am vital, healthy, and happily living (one day at a time). This fullness has me experiencing contradictory complexities with a sense of aliveness and resilience that continues to surprise and delight me, all nourished by the assistance of ritual.

Brushes with Mortality

In 1983, I was treated for one of the most aggressive of all cancers, Burkitt's Lymphoma, an extremely rare form of the disease. Teams of hospital residents came into my room while the chief lymphoma oncologist pointed to my lump and said, "That's Burkitt's." A strange, ominous look appeared on all faces in the room, and hospital attendants subsequently left my meals outside the door from fear that I was contagious. Well into chemotherapy, with my immune system suppressed, I developed a second cancer. As each near-deadly complication set in escalating an already grim prognosis, I quietly began preparing for death.

On reviewing my life, I had been a relatively good person making some significant contributions to the people in my world. While I felt okay about how things had been, there was still a glaring, heavy regret. I knew I had not come even close to living my potential. My innate intelligence (the voice deep inside me) told me there was so much more I was capable of doing. Listening to that voice, I discovered how fear and ignorance blocked my clarity and energetic potential, and this deeply saddened me. Knowing I had missed out on so much, I felt a deep loss and sorrow.

Fortunately (and, surprisingly) I did not die, and my survival was transformational. Although I didn't realize it at the time, the rituals I was practicing to deal with my illness helped me side-step death and alter my life. Even then I instinctively trusted ritual, though I didn't call it by that name.

Early on in my chemo treatment, I was referred to an energy healer named Barbara Ann Brennan, years before she wrote her two bestselling books, *Hands of Light* and *Light Emerging*. Barbara had several sessions with me to prepare for the chemo and the surgeries, and once she visited me at Sloan Kettering Cancer Center during a particularly difficult time in my treatment. I felt blessed to have such a resource. While she was in my quarantine room working with energy fields, placing crystals on my torso, my oncologist walked in the door quietly, stood in frozen silence, shook his head and exited. Mind you, this was all very weird to me back then, but I was willing to try anything. And I had already told him I was including the alternative and complementary treatments of energy, prayer, and nutrition in my healing program. He scoffed and said, "Let's just see if we can keep you alive through the chemo." In January, 1986, this same oncologist published my case in *The American Journal of Medicine,* referring to my "complete remission." Years later when I read the article, I was upset that he never mentioned anything about my incorporation of alternative healing methods and how they may have impacted the outcome.

I experienced another challenge in 1996 when I suffered a heart attack in the hills of Huatulco, Mexico. It was harrowing to get back to the U.S., and my arrival at the Emergency Room sent the whole place into high alert. While hospital personnel were all around me preparing for surgery, I felt strangely composed. As I lay under the bright lights surrounded by all that commotion, I found myself once again reviewing my life. Thirteen years had passed since my first run-in with mortality, and it was different this time. The inner voice now told me that if I died it was all okay. I had been living to my full potential since my last illness-related awakening. I felt prepared. I could die with only two sorrows in my heart; one for my life partner, Elias, and his sadness at losing me, and the other for an unresolved issue with a friend. I wanted to live more of my life and see more of my potential fully expressed, as I had come to really enjoy the process. Clearly, I was extremely fortunate again as triple-bypass surgery saved me.

Out of my first near death experience, my innate intelligence brought to me an important ritual for maintaining emotional completeness with people in my life: Communicate openly with dear ones to resolve any emotional or energetic estrangement. I learned further to not wait in expressing my love and caring for others.

Another big lesson at that time related to surrender. During my near-death experiences I was unconsciously guided to create a ritual that reminded me to invite in loving, caring energy, and at the same time, letting go of a need to control the outcome of the efforts I put forth in my world. Now I am comfortable with the knowledge that I am not in control, and in truth, I don't want to be in control. This realization has been a gift of relief. Whenever I catch myself desiring to control a person or situation, it doesn't take long for my innate intelligence to take note. With that guidance, along with an inner smile, I am able to surrender to the process of letting go again.

I've lived most of my adult life as a man who loves men, affectionately and sexually. I also love women; it's just not the same. It's important for you to know that for a variety of reasons, the most significant being that energetic living and healing thrives on a diversity of human types. My being gay (referred to by my Native American friends as *two-spirited*) is important to my rituals because rituals are where I have a chance to verbalize who I am and what I care about, without judgment or agenda.

Ritual thrives on bold self-expression. It gives one the opportunity to bring pain, struggle, joy, and the glory of affectionate and erotic energy into healing and ongoing transformation. There is so much confusion, ignorance, and suffering in the domain of sexuality. Ritual helps us let it be and learn from it. I share my preferences to say to others like me, "You are not alone."

There is so much sexual diversity, as the world is full of an amazing variety of humans. We have much to learn from each other; courage, tolerance, compassion, flexibility, and mostly, love. The light of spiritual acceptance can help us live with any confusion that may be present, and we can do that most effectively through ritual.

Three Men Named Peter

Part of the inspiration for this book comes from three men all named Peter. The first one is my dad. He was angry, confused, vengeful, and bitter when my mom left us when I was only four. As the youngest of three boys, the emotional nurturance I needed was painfully absent. In my therapy for early addiction recovery, I began to remember how traumatizing it was to live with such an angry person on a daily basis. As I discovered my feelings in therapy and recovery, I realized how strained and uncomfortable I was as an adult in his presence, even speaking with him on the phone. For decades I wrestled with resolving this emotional conflict. Years of psychotherapy (analysis, cognitive, and experiential processes) brought some relief to the suffering. My dad, Peter, has had a deep impact on my life.

The second one, Peter A. Levine, brought his thirty years of research in the healing of trauma to help me dissolve and transform *all* the pain related to my dad. From this Peter, I learned that the results of my childhood traumas were encoded *somatically*, living in my body in the form of frozen energy. My dad activated the hyper-energies trapped in my body. You may know this feeling inside your body, as if your foot is on the accelerator and the brake at the same time. All this energy and no place to go. That can cause a venomous rage or an inward contraction of silent depression or anxiety. Through Levine's Somatic Experiencing® (SE) rituals I learned how to let my body, my natural organism, heal itself by renegotiating these energies under

supportive, ritualized conditions. I realized that the trauma was neither in the event, nor in the person who caused it to happen. *It was
in me, and I could do something about it.* This was a very empowering
awakening. In relating to my dad I went from wanting to avoid any
relationship with him, to caring about him deeply, as I do now.

Experiencing SE and other energetic healing practices got me in
touch with a core energy in myself, that innate intelligence, and a
sense of wholeness. In SE, through the felt senses of the body, I fused
expansive (resource) energy with contractive (trauma) energy. This
fusion of opposite energies produces a new possibility that helps me
feel whole. It is to intimately blend, merge, and unite into one whole,
as if by melting together. With this fusing of two opposite energies,
there almost always comes a third possibility (or experience) that I
hadn't considered before. In each case, this new way of experiencing
old conflicts makes me feel more whole, present, empowered, and
resilient. I first experience the felt sense as a surreal otherworldly
image, but then it integrates with my intellect, becoming part of my
everyday being.

The third is Peter Russell, author of a little masterpiece called
From Science to God. His book speaks of the mystery of consciousness
and the meaning of light. Similar to Peter Levine, Russell informed
knowledge hidden within me, rendering it in present day language
and giving me an understanding of its purpose. In his book, Russell eliminates the conflict between science and spirituality. He illustrates how holopathic (or naturalistic) and allopathic (or scientific)
medicine are indeed one. His observation, supported by hard science,
turns our reality inside out by making the distinction that *all* things
derive from consciousness and not matter. According to William
James, considered to be the father of pragmatism, this is true. He
says, "The truth is whatever proves itself to be good in the way of
belief, and good, too, for definite assignable reasons." It is a fact that
people are 99.999 percent, space, being made up of atoms, molecules,
and subatomic particles that are mostly empty.

Everything observable in our world, including our bodies, is moving in unimaginable vastness. Most of these specks are zooming too fast to spot—or even to determine a position for them! The only thing that makes things seem like *things*—objective matter—is the electromagnetic energy field that holds the teensy weensy fragments in relationship to each other across mind boggling expanses of emptiness. In other words, it's not that there is energy moving through bodies and matter, but rather, our bodies are all a matter of energy. (One vital energy is *love*.) In 1907, in *The Varieties of Religious Experience*, James also wrote, "Design, free will, and spirit instead of matter, have for their sole meaning a better promise as to this world's outcome."

Many find it helpful to have visual representation to support their understanding of the body as energy. Alex Grey (alexgrey.com) was kind enough to allow a reproduction of his beautiful painting, *The Psychic Energy System*, shown on the following page in black and white. The illustration gives us an idea of what this energy system might look like. The artist combines traditional Asian images with his own imagination to depict the energy dynamics that give rise to human form and being. The chakras, from the Indian system of energetic healing, are the glowing orbs you can see along the central axis of the body. Each chakra is whirling at a particular frequency of energy. The lattice of "energy-skeins" superimposed on the whole skeleton represents the meridian system of traditional Chinese medicine. These systems give us a concept of how life energy flows though us at all times, the flow, blockage, *contraction* and *expansion* of which determine our health, mood, and consciousness at every moment. In western medicine, these systems have been described in terms of the electromagnetic nervous system function, and more recently in terms of the electromagnetic field generated by the human body. Our journey in this book will focus more directly on the newer western interpretation, because it is more accessible and directly relates to illuminations shared by Peter Levine and Peter Russell.

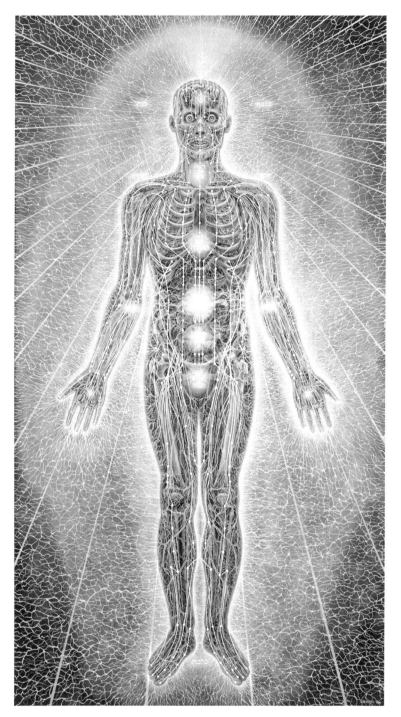

"Psychic Energy System," painting by Alex Grey;
from *Sacred Mirrors: The Visionary Art of Alex Grey*

These two authors, among others, present us with an expansive *holographic* image of an emerging reality where ritual becomes a tool for detecting and interacting with natural, cosmic, and sub-atomic forces. It is exactly this *turning inside out* of our reality that makes room for the new playground of healing that ritual offers. Ritual can provide all the resource energy necessary to transform contractions in our ways of being, making us more clear and more whole. I am grateful to these three Peters for challenging me to turn on the light within.

A Curious Observer's Playground

I like to think of ritual as a form of "playing," and the general practice of ritual as a playground. This playground may seem unfamiliar or even scary, yet it doesn't have to be. You venture onto it in your own time and at your own pace. You are invited to conduct experiments with your own Curious Observer, that invisible part of us that perceives our experiences (thinking, feeling, bodily felt senses, and imaginings) without judgment or agenda. The Curious Observer perceives and knows all we see, do, feel, and think. Ken Wilber, in his novel *Boomeritis* calls it "the witness." I prefer using the word "curious" because in our culture, and in my experience, it helps remove judgment or agenda … it just notices. When I think of "playground," I also think of Wilber. He writes, "Leave seriousness at the door … for this is hallowed ground, and bow to the Lightness and Humor that begin to replace solemnity."

The Curious Observer remains detached and can report what's going on inside of us, whether our felt senses are pleasant, unpleasant, numb, tingling, or just neutral. Also, through our felt senses the imagery in our world is often awakened, be it contractive (tight or pulling in) or expansive (calm, present, whole, perhaps with a tingling or wave sensation). These are the types of distinctions we want to make as we curiously observe. An interesting and healing aspect of the felt senses is that when we become aware, these sensations almost always transform into something else. As Peter Levine wrote in *Waking the Tiger*, "Any change of this sort is usually moving in the direction of a free-flow of energy and vitality." Whatever else comes forth feels like an illumination of many forms, cutting through the often intrusive cognitive processes.

To connect with your Curious Observer, borrow a paradoxical creed from energy medicine: *Slow is Fast*. Taking in a breath of spirit ("spiritus" means breath in Latin), your body will generally relax, allowing observations to emerge that are more clear and informed in more nuanced ways. "Slow is fast" seems contrary to our social conditioning, but it makes sense if we are, as Peter Russell suggests, *turning our realities inside out*.

Nancy Napier, a colleague and author of *Sacred Practices for Conscious Living*, introduced me to a simple exercise that helps people get in touch with their Curious Observer and their felt senses:

> *Imagine that a really annoying person is about a foot and a half in front of you, and they just keep bothering you. Now allow yourself to imagine that you are pushing them away. Curiously observe what that felt like. Do it again, but differently for the second time. As you go to push away that same imaginary person, do it in very slow motion, as if moving molecule by molecule. When you are finished, observe what you notice differently this time.*

The slow movement activates the autonomic nervous system that often brings a different and calmer resolution to the exercise. Your Curious Observer will understand and perhaps stay in tune to continue the exploration.

An Opening in the Universe

Seeing ritual as a healthy way of living and healing, I get sensory images and experiences, as if energy is coming through the floorboards of my study, through the sidewalks, the paved streets, even the chair I sit on. I sense energy coming from the earth and deeper still from the universe and the galaxies. Here we are dealing with what Peter Russell calls "the unknowable reality." He says, "With the development of quantum theory, physicists have found that even sub-atomic particles are far from solid…. They cannot be pinned down and measured precisely…. They are like fuzzy clouds of potential existence, with no definite location. Whatever matter is, it has little, if any, substance."

Opening to an unknowable reality invites us to be ever new in our ways of seeing, feeling, doing, and thinking. The frontier of knowing, without knowing, is a paradoxical place where we dance between the total uncertainty of life, and the intuitive sense of what feels right in our hearts. When we enter that frontier, led by nothing but the felt senses, we are broadening the bandwidth of our experience (like switching from dial-up internet to high-speed cable). The flow of energy and information is efficiently and radically quickened with our capacities become greater. Through this opening of energy, we inexplicably find a comfortable level of connectivity with ourselves, with others, and with nature.

It can be difficult to open up to the unknown through ritual, especially in very busy times when it can feel utterly impossible, not to mention frightening. However, by experimenting with the belief that slow *is* fast, we will be better able to trust our own experience. Readiness is important, so you never want to proceed too fast. It can cause us to become overwhelmed, and if there is an enemy against energetic living and healing, it is being overwhelmed. *Too much too fast!* Energy systems build organically. There is no rush; evolution is long. Simply check in with the felt senses of your body and let them tell you whether you are ready.

To quote an old spiritual axiom, *"The diamonds are in your own back yard."* (Mind you, noticing and mining them can be another matter.)

Expansion

3

Clearing the Way to Effective Ritual

I believe the very purpose of life is to seek happiness.
That is clear. So I think the very motion of our life is
towards happiness.

THE DALAI LAMA

Trustworthy Tools

To build inner knowing in ritual as a passageway to the unknown, you need trustworthy tools. These tools include ideas, practitioners, and groups, and there are certain things to look for when choosing them. A practitioner or group should exude respect and safety, and you should feel a comfortable resonance with your chosen path of exploration. You should experience a sense of being grounded, as if your body is truly connected to the earth from the soles of your feet upward. Groundedness can come from a felt sense in your own body that who you are with and what you are doing can be trusted. In creating your own rituals, you need only to trust that you yourself and whatever unseen energy you invite in are part of your creation. All of the above are safeguards, as no one really knows what's around the corner. And that's a good thing, keeping us on our toes.

The Five Wisdoms

The *Five Wisdoms* are principles we have defined over twenty years of experience and research in a number of groups and communities, especially our own, The Institute for Authentic Process Healing (www.theinstitute.org). They are: 1) *Being real;* that, is coming from authenticity and personal experience. 2) Knowing that living and healing can become more vibrant by joining with others in the spirit of community. 3) Knowing the value of sharing an intention with others and/or spirit. 4) Knowing the value of sharing a belief that the intention can be realized. 5) Grounding ourselves through our resources.

These are all essential for the ritual healing process to work, as long as they include (in order) *respect for self, then others, and respect for other existing realities.*

Rewriting the Past ... and the Future

The four-day Summit mentioned earlier was an opportunity to cross-pollinate ideas with 130 spiritually engaged men from around the world, movers and shakers who shared their intention of supporting transformation on the planet. It was a mind-blowing experience—sharing energy and ideas with brilliant, diverse, and accomplished men of all ages. During this Summit (that was steeped in ritual), I gained the insight that the Five Wisdoms we had been using for community healing also worked for creating individual rituals. (I'd been unconsciously using them in my own personal rituals for years.) Individualizing the Five Wisdoms offered the potential for experiencing ritual as a way of living and healing, and those ideas could be passed on to others.

Linda Russek and Gary Schwartz suggest in their book, *The Living Energy Universe,* "Too often we make the mistake of defining ourselves by our histories, by our past systemic memories…. Fortunately, we are not the mere history of our stories. We have the energy and information to create new stories."

As we become more fluent in drawing energy from our inner and outer resources, we can experience possibilities beyond our wildest dreams.

Healing Trauma

A life trauma is an event that was overwhelming when it occurred, often resulting in the creation of psychological barriers and the experience of deep shame. It is worth noting, however, that trauma is not just an event: trauma deregulates our nervous systems. According to Peter A. Levine's most recent book, *Trauma Healing: A Pioneering Program for Restoring the Wisdom of Your Body*, "… trauma is about loss of connection—to ourselves, to our bodies, to our families, to others, and the world around us … it can happen slowly, over time, and we adapt to these subtle changes sometimes without even noticing it. Human beings are born with an innate capacity to triumph over trauma. I believe not only that trauma is curable, but that the healing process can be a catalyst for profound awakening—a portal opening to emotional and genuine spiritual transformation."

Trauma healing is not about telling the story again, over and over. Life changing trauma healing is often undertaken in modern clinical rituals like Somatic Experiencing® (SE), EMDR (Eye Movement Desensitization and Reprocessing), Thought Field Therapy (TFT), The Wave Work® and other body-mind-spirit integrations. These approaches access focal points to our own innate intelligence, previously blocked and weakened from trauma. "Trauma resolved is a gift from the gods," says Peter Levine. Releasing those blockages through the healing of trauma will help strengthen our intuitive innate intelligence, and ritual can be the tool.

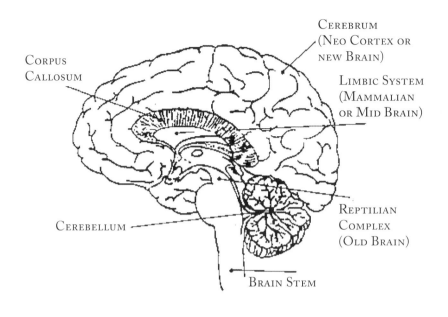

The Human Brain

Trauma Healing and the Triune Brain*

Paul MacLean, the former director of the Laboratory of the Brain and Behavior at the United States National Institute of Mental Health, developed a model of the brain based on its evolutionary development. It is referred to as the "triune brain theory" because MacLean suggests that the human brain is actually three brains in one. Each of the layers or "brains" were established successively in response to evolutionary need. The three layers are the reptilian system, or *R-complex*, the *limbic system*, and the *neocortex*. Each layer is geared toward separate functions of the brain, but all three layers interact substantially.

*The following text, through page 44, is an extract from: Renate Nummela Caine and Geoffrey Caine. *Making Connections: Teaching and the Human Brain,* Incentive Publications, 1990.

THE REPTILIAN COMPLEX *(THE OLD BRAIN)*

The R-complex consists of the brain stem and the cerebellum. Its purpose is closely related to actual physical survival and maintenance of the body. The cerebellum orchestrates movement. Digestion, reproduction, circulation, breathing, and the execution of the "fight or flight" response in stress are all housed in the brain stem. Because the reptilian brain is primarily concerned with physical survival, the behaviors it governs have much in common with the survival behaviors of animals.... The overriding characteristics of R-complex behaviors are that they are automatic, have a ritualistic quality, and are highly resistant to change.

THE LIMBIC SYSTEM

The limbic system, the second brain to evolve, houses the primary centers of emotion. It includes the amygdala, which is important in the association of events with emotion, and the hippocampus, which is active in converting information into long term memory and in memory recall. Repeated use of specialized nerve networks in the hippocampus enhances memory storage, so this structure is involved in learning from both commonplace experiences and deliberate study. However, it is not necessary to retain every bit of information one learns. Some neuroscientists believe that the hippocampus helps select which memories are stored, perhaps by attaching an "emotion marker" to some events so that they are likely to be recalled. The amygdala comes into play in situations that arouse feelings such as fear, pity, anger, or outrage. Damage to the amygdala can abolish an emotion-charged memory. Because the limbic system links emotions with behavior, it serves to inhibit the R-complex and its preference for ritualistic, habitual ways of responding.

The limbic system is also involved in primal activities related to food and sex, particularly having to do with our sense of smell and bonding needs, and activities related to expression and mediation of emotions and feelings, including emotions linked to attachment. These protective, loving feelings become increasingly complex as the limbic system and the neocortex link up.

The Neocortex *(The New Brain)*

Also called the cerebral cortex, the neocortex constitutes five-sixths of the human brain. It is the outer portion of our brain, and is approximately the size of a newspaper page crumpled together. The neocortex makes language, including speech and writing possible. It renders logical and formal operational thinking possible and allows us to see ahead and plan for the future. The neocortex also contains two specialized regions, one dedicated to voluntary movement and one to processing sensory information.

We have mentioned that all three layers of the brain interact. The layers are connected by an extensive two-way network of nerves. On-going communication between the neocortex and the limbic system links thinking and emotions; each influences the other and both direct all voluntary action. This interplay of memory and emotion, thought and action is the foundation of a person's individuality.

The full extent of this interconnectedness is unclear. However, it is entirely incorrect to assume that in any situation one of our three "brains" is working and the others are not. What we can do, tentatively, is assume that at times one particular focus may be dominant while the rest of the brain acts in support and that education can influence which focus dominates.

You'll never find an animal in the wild with Post Traumatic Stress Disorder. In the trauma healing model by Peter Levine, he demonstrates how the programming of animals is more in tune with their autonomic nervous systems. Their Old Brains guide them to release the activated charge of an overwhelming event immediately through a natural release mechanism in their bodies. In the case of us humans, contending with our New Brains, rather than the powerful chemical energy resulting from a trauma being released, it often gets encoded and stuck in our bodies. From there where it's stored it can cause depression, wreak emotional havoc, and cause illness and other health problems. Left unattended, there is no telling how long it can lie in waiting before it ignites.

The Old Brain is the part that is most connected to the soul, and I've observed that when resourced properly, with calmness and clarity, spirit can speak to us through it. While the New Brain recognizes and filters the images that come, the Old Brain seems only able to recognize six basic categories, informing these questions: 1) Is this person (or thing) someone to attack? 2) … to submit to? 3) … to run away from? 4) … to mate with? 5) … to be nurtured by? 6) … to nurture? But the New Brain has already started to ready the body to make its move: to relax, if it's friendly; prepare to fight, if it's a foe; or flee, if it's too dangerous to fight. Unlike the animals, for us it takes some doing for the New Brain to calm the emotions, reverse the preparations, drain the adrenalin, etc.

This is where ritual and the many new methods of accessing the Old Brain come in to support the restoration of equilibrium to the autonomic nervous system, bringing a sense of balance.

We can be relieved of not only the terrible repercussions and symptoms of stored trauma in the body, but also of the so-called "schemas" that are stored in the upper regions of the brain. A schema is a hypothetical mental structure for representing generic concepts stored in memory. It's a sort of framework or plan or script, like an information processing program, that creates our expectations. These schemas are written about by Charles H. Elliot and Maureen Kirby Lassen in their book, *Why Can't I Get What I Want?* Charles H. Elliot and Maureen Kirby Lassen help us understand how from infancy our brains try to make sense of our world by organizing information on different topics into clusters.

Once formed, these schemas not only organize our experiences, but they also cause us to interpret and react to events in consistent, predictable ways—like templates or lenses through which we view the world. By incorporating the rituals of these new healing arts, either the ones you read here or ones that you make up yourself, perhaps it can be possible that **you *can* get what you want!**

What the Old Brain knows you can't learn in a book, so we need to access it through ritual. Some of the Old Brain's wisdom is timeless, nearly primordial.

In the ritually awakened Old Brain there are no rigid barriers between the wisdom of our animal powers and those that are distinctly human. The Old Brain has no sense of linear time. Yesterday, today, and tomorrow do not exist. The past and the present are the same. So the instinctual response may bear little relationship to the current situation. For example, spouses frequently overreact to seemingly trivial provocation, leaving the person who blew up unable to explain why he did so. The spouse may have been operating from schemas long ago programmed by incomplete trauma resolution in the body. Through ritual, we can complete those responses by accessing the Old Brain and allowing the New Brain to integrate experiences and expectations grounded in an updated reality.

These rituals should be experienced without self-conscious shame or anxiety, as they are coming from a very instinctual place. But they must be entered into responsibly and ethically.

The root of meaningful ritual that lies deep in our innate intelligence and felt senses, once discovered can become a never-ending voice of positive encouragement and reinforcement in our lives. It not only can give us access to vibrant living; it can heal trauma, heighten intuition, and enhance fulfilling sensuality and sexuality, as well.

Ritual may not always *look* like ritual. Mundane tasks like taking out the dog or preparing for work in the morning are not usually seen as the kind of spiritual ritual that can reinvent your life. And yet these actions can be tools of transformation. It's a matter of intention and belief. A client of mine, John, walks his dog in Central Park every morning. For him this walk is sacred. And by all John's accounts, his dog, Rochester, experiences it that way too. They go to the same big rock every morning where John sits, meditates and prays, while Rochester dutifully takes care of his own outdoor business. For John, this is not just walking the dog! It is a ritual, rich with desire for prayer and reverence (intention), and the love of Rochester, the park, himself, and whoever is in his prayers (resource).

It only requires inviting in the invisible resource of the Five Wisdoms in whatever creative, fun way that works for you. It's important that you are always empowered to guide your own processes, always tuning into your own felt sense of what is right for you and respectful of others, and what isn't.

But a paradox exists here. On the one hand you are being told that ritual is *all* about energy and consciousness we can meaningfully engage with. On the other, I've said that scientifically speaking, matter—even our bodies and what we perceive and use as a basis for action with our senses—is only energy. Solidity is an illusion.

Still, you'll notice that the fundamental words and energy grounding the Five Wisdoms are: *Respect for self, then others; Respect for other existing realities.* "Others" and "other existing realities" can look a lot like matter, while we must never forget that these elements of people or organizations are also manifestations of spirit, universal energy, and evolution. By respecting these other manifestations of energy we can bring our own resource energy to them, often engendering meaningful transformations.

Innate Intelligence and Trauma Healing

In my experience over many years as a psychotherapist and healer, I've seen a multitude of twisted bodies suffering, trying to figure out what's wrong–only to find out it was really a symptom of a deeper energetic paralysis, usually stemming from the trauma of broken connections (remembered or forgotten) and the schemas created by them. Each of these people found, as did I in the beginning, that it is hard to look at the constrictions in the felt senses of their bodies. It reminds me of Ken Wilber's similar awareness in his book, *No Boundary,* of which he writes:

"Contrary to most professional opinion, this gnawing dissatisfaction with life is not a sign of 'mental illness,' nor an indication of poor social adjustment, nor a character disorder. For concealed within this basic unhappiness with life and existence is the embryo of a growing intelligence, a special intelligence, usually buried under the immense weight of social shames. A person who is beginning to sense the suffering of life is, at the same time, beginning to awaken to deeper, truer realities. For suffering smashes to pieces the complacency of our normal fictions about reality...."

This "special intelligence" Wilber speaks of can be achieved through energetic healing and ritual. It is a version of what I refer to as our innate intelligence. Once a person sees through new eyes and has this awareness, they shift their focus from the pathology of their interior challenges to begin to discover possibility, resilience, wisdom, and resource. Trauma is a fact of life—some have had worse traumas than others. Our varied responses to it certainly play a huge role in the creation of personality and humanity. Whether it seeds a life-affirming growth experience, or an unconscious, crippling blockage, it's a part of life. If we are scathed from earlier years, it's because healing was interrupted or impossible. Yet trauma is a normal human process, and ritual is uniquely suited to serve as a powerful resource for healing it.

Energy Blocks and Fear

Few, if any, survive the ordeal of childhood entirely unscathed. Some emerge with scars, eye injuries, burns, and fractures. Others carry those scars and burns deep within where we cannot see them. Which is worse? As expressed below by Stanislav Grof, a modern founding father of energetic medicine, we all have inner wounds to some degree. They form bioenergetic blockages that eventually manifest as symptoms. ("Bioenergetic" refers to the body's energy and biology. If the energy is affected, so is the biology, the physical and the chemical, etc.)

> *Every one person is carrying a variety of more or less latent emotional bioenergetic blockages that interfere with full physiological and psychological functioning.... The manifestation of emotional and psychosomatic symptoms is the beginning of a healing process through which the organism is trying to free itself from traumatic imprints and simplify its functioning.*
>
> STANISLAV GROF, M.D. AND CHRISTINA GROF
> *The Stormy Search for Self*

We encounter bioenergetic blockages when we notice something unseen, yet felt in our bodies, that holds us back from following our bliss or fully expressing ourselves. Sometimes the blockages even blind us from noticing that we are not moving in the direction in which our soul longs to travel. Once we become aware of this blockage, we often discover that it feels like fear: The fear of what others will think; that one does not know enough, or is not good enough; that one will not succeed; that one can get hurt or might be rejected, to name a few.

Fear can usually be traced to an energetic block, having a biological/biochemical basis as well. Depending on the circumstances, a person can heal through energetic treatment, medical (biochemical) treatment, or a combination of both. The energetic and biological approaches are both valid and sometimes connected. This is why I sometimes suggest that people support their healing process working through blockages and traumas with the aid of medication. For some individuals the combination of energy healing and chemistry adjustment can make the process more graceful. This was certainly true for me at a couple of crucial junctures in my life. Although this book focuses on energetic healing, it is important to note that healing can also benefit from Western medicine's allopathic biological/chemical methods.

Whatever our approach to healing might include, we need to respect where our blockages (our fears) originate. Fear is sometimes rooted in outer realities, but that is seldom the only cause. With most people I find that about twenty percent of their fear is actually appropriate for the situation, while eighty percent evolves out of personal or cultural history. Once the symptoms of energetic blockages become evident, they may be traced back to their source, the original fearful experiences or generational patterns of fear. Or, they may not be. It is not necessary to remember every trauma you or your ancestors experienced. In these rituals we are dealing with what your body is presenting *now! The story is less important than the sensations.* Either way, through energetic healing (or what trauma-healing work refers to as the "renegotiation of the nervous system"), our blockages can be dissolved so that symptoms will often disappear by themselves.

There are many schools of energetic healing developed since the 1960s, mostly with group research at places like The Esalen Institute in California. The field is burgeoning with new techniques, originators, and teachers appearing often. However, energy medicine has always been with us, dating back to the Stone Age, if not before. There is evidence that our predecessors, the Neanderthals, were deeply involved with ritual as a core energetic healing modality.

Ritual as Self-Expanding

Before we go too far into the book's ritual suggestions, we will discuss the basic principles of ritual, what makes it such an effective tool, what blocks and diminishes its power, and what to do about these blocks. Even tentative attempts at the process are useful for restoring our inner strength, helping us remove blockages to a full experience of living. The key is to start by applying ritual to the problems that are in our face right now. The technique with which you develop will help you face new challenges as old problems disappear. Ritual is self-expanding; it opens us to energy with which to do more ritual that opens us up to even more energy. It's a delightful, mind-boggling, ever-expanding journey that can lead to new vitality and self confidence.

I have used ritual to heal my deepest wounds. After working through the blockages I described related to my relationship with my dad (mom also), a whole new energy opened up. It was full of love, self-appreciation, and an intriguing mix of humility and self-confidence. After experiencing that healing, I embraced this new energy for whatever was next on my plate to help me sweep away challenges.

The Four Intentions of Ritual

Regardless of whether a person performs ritual in a group or as an individual, there are four main intentions to ritual: *Tuning, Focusing, Amplifying*, and *Directing* Life Energy. Each step entails intentions for manifesting and working with energy. Intention shows up in hundreds of different forms, and in every avenue of life: the artistic, spiritual, sexual, athletic, and scientific, to name a few. Over time we develop not only the intention, but also the skill to bring energy in tune and into focus, amplifying and directing it at will, bringing it into harmony with our innate intelligence, a higher power, or the universal force. The following steps illuminate intentions for both groups and individuals. They address how "universal life energy" or "the spirit of the universe" is relevant to all, regardless of one's spiritual or religious background. They themselves are collective or private expressions of intention.

1. *Tuning (Group):* "We have gathered together with the shared intention of tuning into and linking up with the universal energy of life and of healing. We agree to drop our masks and personas and stand here together in authentic process to be real with each other and speak from our hearts with words that ring true."

(Individual): "I stand (sit) here with the expressed intention of tuning into and linking up with the universal energy of healing. I vow to drop my masks and personas to stand in authentic communication with myself and the universe, to be my real self and to speak words of prayer that ring true."

2. *Focusing (Group):* "We agree to remain focused on the universal life energy without distraction from scattered or unhelpful energies that do not heal us. We agree to focus on love rather than selfish anger, and on helpfulness rather than foolish pride. We agree to keep our hearts simple, focusing on one thing at a time or nothing at all."

(Individual): "I vow to stay focused on the universal life energy without the distraction of unhelpful energies that do not heal. I vow to focus on love, not selfish anger, on helpfulness, not foolish pride. I vow to keep my heart simple, focusing on one thing at a time or nothing at all."

3. *Amplifying (Group):* "Through the ritual we are about to do, we agree to amplify the subtle flow of spirit into a great wave of energy with the power to transform our lives and this world. May the spirit of the universe show us through signs and indications that our work is good, as well as how we can improve our practice."

(Individual): "Through the ritual I am about to do, I amplify the subtle flow of spirit into a great wave of energy, with the power to transform my life and this world. May the spirit of the universe show me through signs and indications that my work is good, and how I can improve my practice."

4. *Directing (Group):* "We agree that our goal here is to heal and experience living to its fullest and deepest potential. We all share this goal and give ourselves wholeheartedly to it. We direct this energy to an agreed outcome, which is for the good of all. Let no one be harmed by this intention."

(Individual): "I vow that my goal is to heal and experience living to its fullest and deepest potential. I give myself wholeheartedly to it. I direct this energy to a stated outcome, which is for the good of all. Let no one be harmed by this intention."

When an Altaic Shaman from Lake Baikal in Siberia begins a ritual fast from food and water, he is tuning his body to higher frequencies. A stuffed belly is thought by shamans to distort the perception of some of the higher vibrations. When that shaman becomes totally still through the ritual of meditation and focuses his inner eye on light, sound, or a particular vision, he reaches a concentration of purpose, losing all sense of time. This is when the shaman steps into liminal space: the place between the worlds, the place between habits, the only place where true transformation can take place. Sometimes this is accomplished through striking or ringing a bell, or through singing a song, chanting, or drumming. He then performs ritual actions to amplify that energy. Drawing a picture in the soil, for example, to correspond with the energy coming through, amplifies the inner vision. Finally, that energy is directed. Offerings made in gratitude to spirit serve to direct the energy of life back to its source. Or he directs it to the Bear for protection, to the sun for warmth, or to the caribou for a good hunt. To summarize, the Shaman performs a ritual in the following steps: He fine-tunes energy by fasting; He focuses energy through meditation; He amplifies it through ritual. While most people today do not feel inclined to adopt the rituals of the Altaic shamans, ritual still has a place in our modern lives. We are not bear hunters, but we can still use ritual to empower ourselves to navigate through the challenges of life.

I learned from Evan Pritchard that these same four concepts are applied in music by anyone who has ever played an instrument. First you tune the instrument, and then you focus the emotions you want to express through the way you play the instrument, shaping what's called the timbre, or the quality of the sound. (There are many ways to get different sounds out of any instrument.) Then you modulate the volume by amplifying, then directing the music towards your chosen audience in your performance.

Orchestral and chamber musicians often use ritual to help them focus before a performance. And after the curtain opens, when the conductor taps their baton facing the players, a few seconds of silent breathing is observed before the music starts. Even rock bands have been known to form a circle holding hands in a ritual prayer before going on stage.

Why such elaborate ritual? Because for most people, giving a performance worthy of Beethoven or Brahms (or The Rolling Stones) is hard, requiring the musicians' being in tune with each other, being focused, and being able to transcend all distractions to reach the heart of the listener. Removing energy blocks in a healing-community setting requires that we focus on what we're doing, acting in concert with each other, and allowing the energy to flow and sing with great resonance like an orchestra.

If you are not a musician and can only play the radio, these same four terms: tuning, focusing, amplifying, and directing, also apply. A radio must first tune into the energy of the broadcast frequency. This is done through the tuning knob, which locates the signal on the dial. With focus, it locks into that signal to then be amplified, traveling through speakers that can be directed to any room in your house.

The Nature of Universal Energy

A group of people may enter into a healing circle, retreat, or other gathering in a wide variety of states of consciousness. These can range from angry and negative, to overly optimistic and vulnerable, from scattered and flighty to obsessively tunnel-visioned. The goal of the group focalizer, like the orchestra conductor, is to tune the group's energies into the best and most helpful areas of consciousness by stating a shared intention. The role of the focalizer is also to help the group focus on the goal so that it does not get sidetracked. And then to amplify the energy through group dynamics, directing it towards the good of all.

Let's take a look at how these four aspects of energy: tuning, focusing, amplification, and direction, can be applied to ritual, whether group or individual. The first thing that must be clearly understood is that there are many types of energy running rampant in the universe. Not all are good for you at any given moment. Focusing on unpleasant energies and thought fields is not helpful, and unadvisable. Anyone who is serious about healing energy blocks needs to work mainly with their innate intelligence, or their primary universal energy source (also known as love, or expansiveness). Primary universal energy can be felt, seen, heard or imagined, and experiencing it is unique to each individual. Some feel the universal energy as a pleasurable experience in the body, a sense of connectivity or harmony, or even just adequacy. Sônia Gomes, a Brazilian practitioner of Shamanistic roots and a Somatic Experiencing® senior faculty member, taught me that adequacy is good (and a healing resource). The dictionary defines adequacy as: "The state or quality of being adequate or sufficient for any purpose; equal or amounting to what is required; fully sufficient, suitable, or fitting sufficiency." This understanding has helped many of my clients in their resourcing.

Some see universal energy as light, often white, sometimes blue. The various healing aspects of light may be spoken of as green, violet, blue, orange, or yellow in color. Others sometimes see tan or brown, which they relate to as an earth connection. Some healers say a red light can be revitalizing to the soul or the base chakra. There are those who do not see light, but hear sounds (like a pleasant buzzing) or simply feel the presence of a universal energy. Not being a very visual person, I mostly feel it in my body as a sense of tightness, tingling, expansion, well-being and wholeness. I sense that I am in my own skin and that I like being there. I feel mysteriously connected to all there is, and sometimes I get the felt sense of being formless, an unexpected delight.

What is most important for any ritual is that the intention is good. We want to basically tune into what feels right to us, wherever we find it; in our being, in our vast memory banks, or in our surroundings.

Individual Expression and Community Exchange

When we enter into personal ritual, we often come to that private room, sacred space, or natural setting, with confusion. Our ears may be ringing with all the crazy things people said earlier in the day, our nerves could be jangling, and all the things we may have neglected are still trying to get our attention. That's when we need ritual the most. Just as a group can begin with a chaotic mix of scattered energy, so too can one person. Even in solitary ritual, we must take time to tune, focus, amplify, and direct the best energy we can link up with.

In contemporary healing communities, the use of ritual has been developed over time as a necessary means of transition from individual expression to community exchange. Ritual has been tremendously effective in group settings, like the retreats we frequently convene. Our success has led to the awareness that we can take healing tools of ritual home, and continue our own healing privately.

Community is important to support the healing of the individual. People have come to retreats where, in the magic of community, whatever needed attention would organically surface and healing would occur with the joy of feeling a connection with others. It is also important that each individual be encouraged to create their unique process to use on their own for dealing with their personal life issues. While community is a surprisingly powerful resource, historic tribal rituals were empowering by the strength of connection between the participants, without individuals being individually empowered. In our current community work, ideas about ritual include recognition of shared intention, but we also like to give individuals a lot of space and freedom to be unique in following their own path.

Energy as Resource

Life is no brief candle to me. It is a splendid torch
which I have got hold of for the moment and I want
to make it burn as brightly as possible before handing
it on to future generations.

GEORGE BERNARD SHAW

From Power to Wisdom

The gifts of the Summit on "Spirituality and Global Transformation" expanded beyond my life, also transforming others I had
met there, and my perceptions. For several years, community members and practitioners were discussing The Five Powers for dissolving
barriers to wholeness, but not everyone understood their meaning. It
became evident that there was also wisdom for daily living in applying each of these powers. David Nimmons, author of *Soul Beneath the
Skin,* and a Summit attendee, suggested we switch the word "powers" to "wisdoms," since each derived from experiential knowledge.
"The Five Powers," that had guided the community for years, evolved
into "the Five Wisdoms." The prior formulation of five powers of

community-based healing had grown out of almost twenty years of experience, developed by a particular circle of devoted souls working together in community. These powers were an adaptation of what we had learned really worked in 12-Step and other communities. Through our experience we recognized that what we were doing all along was ritual. As we made the jump from *healing* to *living*, we found that the same five powers that dissolved our barriers to wholeness in recovery were now five *wisdoms* for daily living that helped us as individuals and helped the community from backsliding into unconscious behavior and poor communication.

As mentioned earlier, the Five Wisdoms of group ritual are grounded in the basic principle of respect for self, then others. Without this no group effort can be truly effective, as the attention of the participants will wander and the energy will scatter. As we begin to consciously apply energy as a resource, we don't want that energy to be scattered, we want it focused. When living and operating within the Five Wisdoms, we are consciously agreeing to go into a luminous ritual space, a spirit-led activity. This means those present must be spontaneous, in the moment, humble before spirit, and completely honest before each other. This can be in a one-on-one meeting, therapy session, or a community gathering. Ritual involves using physical realities to invoke the unseen reality of shared energy. Therefore, even agreeing to enter into a ritual, by definition, is a ritual.

Here are those the Five Wisdoms as they have evolved:

Authentic Process: *Coming from authenticity and personal experience; being real.* Speaking from the heart within a circle of others, or even to one's self, is necessary, yet rarely present in conventional society, so that people all over the world are stepping out of their conventional contexts, following their inner wisdom and creating their own circles for authentic process. You can get a glimpse of this global process on the web at: www.wisdomcircle.org or www.culturalcreatives. org. "Being real" is the keynote of authentic process. When we present a false front, we are not interacting energetically with others in the group; we are "holding energy back," the opposite of using energy as a resource. "Being real" is the minimum requirement for using ritual as resource. That's the first law of energetic healing.

Community Based Healing: *Knowing that living and healing can become manifest by joining with others, in community and with spirit.* A community is a group of two or more people interacting. As defined by M. Scott Peck in *A Different Drum*, "a community is a group of individuals who have learned how to communicate honestly with each other, whose relationships go deeper than their masks of composure, and who have developed some significant commitment to rejoice together, mourn together, and to delight in each other, making others' conditions their own." There is an unexplainable magic that occurs when people join together with a shared intention to heal and to become more alive. When they let down their masks of composure and non-judgmentally share struggles, joys, and sorrows in a ritualized format, an indescribable healing takes place. We need that reinforcement, especially in an urban setting where we're constantly confronted with challenges to our sense of self-worth. As we learn more about the potency of personal or private ritual, community becomes another dimension of support.

Shared Intentionality: *It is valuable to share an intention with others and/or spirit.* When two or more people consciously bring their attention to healing and self-discovery in a specific, structured way, this is *shared intentionality.* Shared intentionality can also be present in personal rituals performed by one person with an unseen reality (a higher power, the forces of nature, or the spirit of love). This brings us into alignment with each other, creating a conscious bond that reinforces and stabilizes our wavering intentions for positive growth. When I first went into a recovery program, I needed to do *something.* It was that, or go nowhere given my state of affairs. Among all the incredible things that happened at that first meeting, the most powerful was meeting people with whom I shared an intention to recover.

Years later, I see even more clearly the wisdom of seeking that shared intention, and more important, of vocalizing it for a group. (For further discussion, see *The Journey toward Complete Recovery* where the ten specific intentions identified by my research in long-term recovery are described and can be shared in a community healing process.)

Shared Belief: *It is equally valuable to share a belief that an intention can be realized.* Belief creates experience, experience shapes belief. Tending to proving us right, belief is an equal partnership between you, spirit, and the rest of the world. Bond with others who share your beliefs and those beliefs will affect your experience. Belief is sometimes changed from negative to positive by sharing. It's not hard to see the wisdom in that. When I first went into recovery, I didn't actually have the belief that I could do it. I couldn't envision a sober life. It was unimaginable. But through hearing the stories of others, I came to share the belief that I could do it too. The positive benefits in my life have followed from that ever since.

Grounding through Resources: *We are safer, clearer, and more comfortable when we ground ourselves through our resources.* To fully grasp this wisdom, you'll need to have the experience behind the words. This is a process that one perfects with practice, yet we can all do it instantly if we allow ourselves to. Imagine a time when you felt loved or you were extending love to another (love is one of the great invisible resources). In this imaged recollection, circle in your mind the best moments and invite your body to connect with the image. You may begin to notice a subtle felt sense of expansiveness, calm, or warmth in your body. If you don't at first, then you are trying too hard. Imagine stepping outside yourself, what I earlier called the Curious Observer, just noticing what happens as you give your body permission to connect with the circled image. From that Curious Observer place you may hear yourself saying: "Hmmm, what's that?" or "I feel that," or "That's interesting," "That feels calmer," "That hurts," or "I feel numb." The last one is always most interesting to me. If we allow ourselves to stay with the numbness (or any other sensation) long enough, it will change. We just need to continue to curiously observe it without judgment or agenda. The numbness *will* thaw, and other sensations will come to the fore. No sensation stays the same too long. Our innate intelligence is too eager to teach us as we become more able to learn from it. Without expectation, notice the felt sensations that present themselves. Perhaps they are subtle at first, and that is good. Give the experience time and note if anything happens. If you experience sensations of calm or warmth or connectedness, you may have discovered your first resource.

Resource Energy: Turning Our Reality Inside Out

In creating or participating in rituals, we always want to find grounding through what we call resource energy, rather than through our thoughts. We all have thousands of "resource reservoirs" inside of us to connect with and to draw upon. The reality is that we've been conditioned *not to* pay attention to our vast resources. Because of this, we have not realized the potential they offer us. We've been trained to focus on our problems, deficiencies, and on what needs to be done. We have not been acculturated to look at our moments of blessings, or to hang out with the gifts bestowed upon us. Many of us deprecate such moments because either they are not honored by our culture or because they seemingly do not last. It is true that some things are not meant to last forever, but they still are alive in our living memory. By connecting to our resource energy we begin to turn our reality inside out.

My deep understanding and appreciation of the energetic meaning of resource came from Diane Poole Heller, a dynamic therapist who co-wrote the *Somatic Experiencing® Training Manual* with Peter Levine. She was also my teacher in the first two years of the SE training. (Peter taught the third year, Advanced Training.) Diane also wrote extensively on resource in a book she co-wrote with Laurence Heller, *Crash Course: A Self-Healing Guide to Auto Accident Trauma &*

Recovery. Diane discovered SE and the trauma-healing field when nothing else relieved severe and mysterious symptoms she was still experiencing four years after a traumatic auto accident. She eventually found Peter Levine, and not only were her symptoms resolved, she was able to transform her life. Diane has distinguished herself in trauma healing by developing a strong focus on resourcing, resiliency and empowerment.

I often invite people to compose a written inventory of their inner and outer blessings as they begin to use ritual as a resource. It's a way to start thinking in this direction. I ask them to think about what the experience of their healing is going to be like, and how they have all they need inside themselves to begin to heal.

All of your pleasant or meaningful moments are energetically stored in your body memory as cumulative properties, not energyless events from a linear past as many believe. One of the things we've learned from Peter Levine's thirty years of research in trauma healing is that for every vortex of trauma *(contractive)* energy we have in our bodies, we have at least an equal potential for finding our resource *(expansive)* energy. We each can become more skilled at tapping into these resources, gradually learning to let them enliven us, dancing at the edge of *contractive* energies. By naming our resource in ritual, we give it power. As soon as we call in imagery, the felt senses, and other invisible realities, we are invoking spirit. Connecting with spirit itself is a felt sense, powerful though unseen. We want to pay a lot of attention to invisible realities because they become guiding powers and principles. As we learn from the felt senses of the body to tune into these unseen guides, they direct the course of our lives. When we stay with the felt senses in ritual, we are also stepping out of the time-space continuum for as long as we need to or are able to, and this can be very insight-provoking. One of the invisible realities becoming apparent for us is *possibility.* We hold kernels of possibility inside ourselves that we could plant and bring out into the world.

The Tastes and Potentials of Ritual

Ritual seems to be a more inclusive term than spirituality, but it is not. Ritual is a structure that both attracts and is made from spirit. It can guide spirit toward many forms of connectivity, creativity and vibrant aliveness. In anthropology, a ritual or "rite" is generally visible. It is an action. For our purposes, a ritual may also be a thought or word filled with intention and focused on qualitative change. In this sense, ritual is a conduit and a tool to help us create a better life. It is a way of life that leads to yet other ways of living.

There is a sight, feel and sound to ritual. You know it when you feel it, sometimes seeing it with inner eyes. In its unique expressions, ritual both derives from and evokes spirit, ever present and available for everyday life. We want to bring ritual into the ordinary, so it can be discreetly invoked at any time by anyone for their own good and the good of all.

During any ritual, actions speak louder than words as we engage in a kind of solemn dialogue between spirit and ourselves. Unless it's a playful ritual, and many group rituals are, there is a solemnity that is comforting. It's like coming out of the everyday stuff and saying, "Now it's time for the sacred, now it's time for me!" We can then ponder our needs and desires with discernment, as we come into the center of our selves, our very being, and the innate intelligence of life.

Coming into the center of our being takes us beyond ourselves as well. During an invocational ritual, humans call on non-humans, spirits, lost ones, and memories. Without these beings we are on our own. Even when I am physically alone, I never feel alone as long as I can hear the gentle, unexplainable whisper of spirit in my ear, creating soft music for the soul. Ritual gives us this, and more, guiding us through realms of grace, serendipity and synchronicity.

With ritual, self-empowerment is crucial. There are teachers, facilitators and focalizers, but no higher authority than your own consciousness and experience. Teachers can help us reconnect with our innate intelligence, which then becomes the empowering force. Another significant aspect of ritual is that it can be repeated. This means that the actions and structures of rituals may be the same each time. When you light a fire, the lighting of it stays the same. In many of the rituals we talk about here, what remains the same is the intention, not necessarily the physical actions.

Intention opens the ritual, and closes it. Ritual space is opened whenever spirit or resource is invoked. Many traditions believe it is very important to send the invited spirit away with thanks, at the end of the ritual, coming to complete closure. It feels right to give thanks to the forces or people who give and share energy with us. It reminds us that we are not alone, and that we are grateful for that.

Beyond Healing

Living life purely for the joy is very different from chasing our next healing opportunity. Both are resource-based, and yet there is a difference. The former is based on inner resources, while the latter is based on outer resources. Drawing on both of these to heal is an excellent idea, but we all have much to learn. We open much more when we draw on the inner resources of the universe, in its many different seen and unseen forms. These cosmic energies are healing and restorative in nature (and if they are not, you're tapping into some other energy). They are able to do more than heal: they are able to connect you with all that is. They form a reservoir of feeling and experience. They are the creativity and knowledge that we call resource, while some simply call it the "source."

There was a time when I didn't have a language for what I was doing, not knowing where this work was headed. Turning a corner, we found we were looking at a much bigger picture, a place of abundance, of joy, of calm. *Connectivity*, for example—the intuitive ability to find what you need when you need it (even against seemingly impossible odds)—is beyond healing. It is part of the language of living. By truly living, we mean being on the frontier of the unknown, and knowing you're there.

Cutting-edge author Jean Houston refers to "the fulcrum of evolution" where there is an aliveness that is both personal and universal. It can be a scary place because we've been so conditioned to believe that "we should know." However, we can transform the fear of not knowing into a feeling of apprehensive wonder that is creatively stimulating and enlivening. By tapping into our inner and outer resources, we can arrive at a sense that it's okay and good to not know; that being right on the frontier is where we are supposed to be. This experience is beyond healing and recovering, that's why we say it's a whole new playground.

Spider-Man is a potent symbol for many spiritual thinkers. The streams of web-like plasma that shoot out from Spider-Man's hands are metaphors for the connectivity that emanates from our own bodies when in ritual. Ultimately, everyone benefits from the web of *connectivity* that the hero weaves. We too can become silent, humble heroes, using ritual to benefit all sentient beings. What better word is there to express *ritual as resource* and to connect to the heart than the word *"connectivity"*? But there is a whole language that we can discover that expresses that connectivity: *The Language of the Living*.

The Language of Living

This language of living is primarily a silent language of action and perception. There are many key words that are able to lift us above the dualities of sickness and health, and a few more that require explanation. Hanging out with this language, making it a part of our being, helps us get comfortable in the process of turning our reality inside out. Here are a few of those key words and other words that link to them:

CONNECTIVITY: Love, Presence, Joy, Laughter, Eros, Transcendence, Integration.

PRAYER: Discovery, Peace, Calm, Freedom, Dignity, Meaningfulness, Compassion, Lucidity, Intuition, Insight, Curiosity, Cosmic, Epiphany, Expansiveness.

WHOLENESS: Non-duality, Paradox, Harmony, Beauty, Universality, Discernment.

SELF-RESPONSIBILITY: Wisdom, Non-linear-ness, Empowerment, Self-surrender.

CREATIVE ALIVENESS: Creative positivity, Fearlessness, Illumination, *Gratitude*.

ACCEPTANCE: Deep knowing, Fluidity and Flexibility.

In addition to familiarity with these words, thinking in the language of living involves *non-positional thinking*. This means we can shift positions at a moment's notice to catch the next wave of energy. By not being rigidly attached to a position, we can stay flexible and open to many possibilities.

One final key word is "gratitude." If we're not grateful, we're not really living, we haven't found the edge of our own existence, and we haven't looked at our life as if every trauma, every problem, and every difficulty were something moving through us to make us more alive. (Even dying can happen in a way that nourishes life and the living.)

Focusing on Resource

The language of living is focused on resource, and resource is purely positive and energetic. It is helpful and healing to look at our resources rather than just focusing on conditions of scarcity. Man's brain is hard-wired for problem-solving, but it has been trained to focus on what's lacking rather than on what IS. For example, rather than fret over the fact we have no bread, we could focus on what we do have: crackers, oats, and cereal, for instance. As the old adage says, "Make do with what you've got!"

In truth we have thousands of sources of energy to draw on as resource. The following exercise clarifies this: While engaged in an act of healing, we can shift our perspective away from the presenting problem and flash to a thought or memory of a pleasant moment when we felt love or some other quality we are grateful for. When we locate a source of energy, a resource, we dwell not only on the thought of it, but the bodily sensation of it as well. When we remember a pleasant moment, we feel good. Invite this pleasantness to make contact with a felt sense in your body at the present moment. Bringing memories of pleasant things that are permanently lodged in the past into contact with the *felt sense* of the body in the present moment will link the energy of those memories with the energy of the present making contact with our innate intelligence. Becoming aware of internal sensations in the present, as mentioned before, will almost always transform them into something else. As Levine's research has shown, any change of this sort is usually moving in the direction of a free flow of energy and vitality. When the sense of present vitality is linked to pleasant memories permanently stored as a resource, we actually can get a feeling of that which is timelessly true—the eternal now.

When I am working one-on-one with clients and they find a memory buried deep in their past that is imbued with great quantities of resource energy, I ask them to stop the memory in time, to "circle" it, surround it in its own little bubble and hold it in a timeless place. They are then able to come back to that circle for additional energy when they need it.

Getting Outside of Linear Time

When working with energy, we need to go into non-linear time; we need to step out of linear thinking in general. Otherwise, we're caught in a trap. Energy is not linear! Energetic healing happens outside of time and works mostly in the Old Brain, not the cerebral cortex (which is linear).

Energy healing happens outside of linear time. When a healing practitioner is not there to help a client bring attention to a resource, the mind tends to continue the story and come to its own conclusions. It remembers that in the physical world of time and space, the pleasure (the resource) did not last forever. Something happened. Night fell, sunrise came, the school year was over, we went on with life, and sooner or later, the connection to the positive energy came to an end, at least in a physical sense.

One way to help us work our way outside of linear time is to think of memories *accumulating* rather than *occurring* in the past, present, and future. Many people don't think of memories as a selectively cumulative experience. They only think of how that connection to a loved one or that experience of life's abundance was lost along life's way, and so they throw it mournfully on top of a pile of loss. Yet if we rise above time, then all of our favorite surprises, encounters, perfect moments—all those influxes of healing energy, are *happening right now!* (Of course, the tough stuff is happening now too, but we don't have to focus on that until we're ready.) And to our surprise, we find we have a great capacity to hold both; in fact, we are made for it.

When we rise above the chain of events of life, past, present, and maybe even future, they are all like stories. We can open the book to wherever we want to look, and we don't have to turn the page. We can just close the book and go back to the challenge in front of us with new insight and enthusiasm. That's what a stored resource is. Keeping the energy fresh in your life can happen when you realize that there are no losses at all—some things just leave to make room for other things. The key to living fully is to let go of attachments to the things of the past (and present), moving towards more growth and exploration, knowing that each moment is still with us energetically.

We Are Light

I believe we are an energy called *light*, not existing in the time-space continuum, only in the *now*. What we generally think of as light is our interpretation of a source—like consciousness itself—that cannot truly be found. We are each a great manifestation of this energy, each one totally unique. When we are really living, we feel grateful to be in this form. When we tap into awareness of ourselves as light, life becomes an energetic adventure.

Getting to the innate intelligence of life requires that we move beyond duality and polarity to a place of integrity and oneness with the universe, where words often fail us. This is why it is important for you to rely on your own experience in this realm; no one can tell you how to live. When we focus on living, we find a fresh source of energy, and we can use that to heal if we need to. Negative energy gets in the way of living fully, happily, and productively. It is toxic and useless.

When we are on the frontier of evolution, we can't necessarily see what's beyond the next hill, but we can be prepared. I have by watching squirrels. Knowing that winter is coming, they spend the fall scurrying for acorns. The more I trust my Curious Observer and the Old Brain, the more I prepare for what's next.

Four Basic Types of Resources

There are four kinds of resource energy we need to discuss, and you may discover more as you think of them.

First is **inner resource,** our inner spiritual strengths, our intuitions, our core values, etc. Many of these are listed in the "language of living" outlined earlier. Our #1 greatest inner resource is being full of life and knowing how to live. Nothing can take that from us.

The second type is **stored resource.** Memories of healing, encouraging events, special teachers, and incredible people from our past become what we call stored (inner) resource.

The world is full of incredible opportunities, communities and people who would be happy to help us. We can call this third type ***ambient (outer) resource.*** We have to draw these events and people to us in a non-linear way, to invite them into our lives. Developing a "high *connectivity* quotient" really helps us enjoy and be nourished by these ambient resources.

The fourth type of resource is ***future resource.*** If I'm going to Mexico next week, having the photo of the resort in front of me on my desktop is a ritual that serves as resource to inspire me forward, to get everything done before I have to leave. Of course, there are future resources not yet imagined that come through serendipity and synchronicity, coming from ritual.

Think of how Walt Disney created a whole world out of nothing that is now a resource for millions of children of all ages.

Connectivity

A primary key word for living that helps us understand *ambient resource* is what we have been referring to as *connectivity*. One of my biggest thrills is to try to catch a wave and body surf towards the beach. I can't always calculate logically the ideal place to stand, but using my intuition, I can generally connect with that perfect spot where I get carried away. Even young kids, who aren't particularly good at this, find that it works once in a while if they try it. To do this, feel a connection with the wave and practice with the felt sense. There is an old expression, "follow your feet." We can catch a wave of energy in life by developing the knack for being in the right place at the right time. People say, "Follow your nose." "Follow your heart." "Follow the spirit." "Follow your hunches." Joseph Campbell, "Follow your bliss."

We can't think too much about it, we can only intuit. We can tap into the energy of synchronicity that is already around us, and ride it.

The science of quantum physics views sub-atomic particles behaving sometimes as waves. At this microscopic level of understanding, there is no ultimate differentiation between matter and energy.

The Power of Not Knowing

In order to increase our *connectivity*, the most important thing to do is to let go of certainty. The more we are comfortable not knowing, the better positioned we are to catch the next wave. We become as keen as a hawk, perched on the limb of a tree waiting for prey to come along. When the prey appears, there isn't time to think and debate, there's only time to act. One of my greatest healing moments over the last several years was having a clear understanding that I didn't have to know everything! I then was able to surrender joyfully into the unknown. For some time my knowing had been blocked by the pressure of my needing to appear knowledgeable. An enormous revelation was in saying the magic words, "I don't know." That's when my innate intelligence kicked in, like a mystical wisdom illuminating my knowing.

This realization was a lesson from a great yogi friend, Sandra Scherer, who passed away from breast cancer. She chose to use only holopathic treatment; because she believed that allopathic (Western) medicine would have been too intrusive, interfering with nature's plan for her. While I struggled with her wishes out of my fear of losing her, I respected her choices and ultimately, her leaving.

Better known to most by her Sanskrit name Dayashakti, which translates as "awakened spiritual energy of compassion," she lived and taught at the Kripalu Yoga Center for many years, and I loved her. Daya taught a very elegant, refined ritual technique, called The Wave Work® because it was not uncommon to feel an extraordinary connectivity in the form of energy waves moving through the body. Her process enabled me to access inner healing wisdom in a gentle and simple way. By simply lying down, being supported and coached in a particular way, I discovered how to rest in the natural flow of life, riding the waves of energy that arise within me. I learned to be a loving observer of thoughts, emotions and body sensations, from moment to moment. When I stopped resisting or judging my experience, a shift in consciousness occurred and my body felt more whole and connected.

Rituals with Daya afforded me the opportunity to integrate their illuminations with my everyday life. Healing insights beyond the limited concepts of my mind revealed themselves, moving me to a place of peace, trust, and connectedness.

At the time in 1999, I was the Director of The Institute for Staged Recovery, which grew out of my Ph.D. research and my first two books. I was responsible for a group of therapists in training, mentoring them through the process of practice building, and this was too much for me. I didn't like a group of people looking to me for the answers, and because of my position, I felt I should always have them. After working with Daya, I asked to be gradually relieved of the burden. Slowly the organization transformed and I was freed of needing to know.

Compassion for Self

Please don't proceed beyond this point without performing the most important personal ritual of all, compassion for yourself. To abandon compassion for self will not be in your best interest, nor will it fulfill our best intentions for you. Love is giving space, especially to our selves. If you cannot bring even an inkling of self-compassion with these processes, you may not understand what we are trying to share with you. If you cannot invoke even the intention to be compassionate toward yourself at this point, at least be patient with yourself!

Following are rituals that I encourage you to proceed with in the order they are written. However, trust your innate intelligence and feel free to pick whatever calls to you for experimentation. As you proceed with self-compassion, we remind you that we are with you in spirit whenever you want us to be, even though you can't see us. If you already have ritual tools at your disposal, use them. We know that this light-hearted place we want to share with you is one of reverence, and above all we honor that.

Everyday Rituals

5

Enter the World of Ritual

When you are complete in your self, fully integrated within and without, then you enjoy the universe, you do not labor at it.

SRI NISARGADATTA MAHARAJ

It's My Ritual

One of the great things about both personal and community rituals is once you perform them, the experience becomes uniquely *yours.* When I go into ritual space and the sense of expansion comes, it has a very personal and private flavor much to my delight.

In this chapter we will get into the heart of ritual in its most simple and fundamental nature. Here are basic sacred practices that help vitalize and fulfill our lives, transforming ordinary events into extraordinary tools for change. These are the very personal rituals that have become instinctual elements in my daily life. They've become my spiritual air and water for living.

Grounding Energy and Spirit

In all rituals it is important to ground our energy and spirit. Daya-shakti left some heart-opening teachings with me that help develop one's connectivity during rituals. She also taught me I could ground and contain my energetic experiences to function in the everyday material world while also living with my heart open. I learned that a sense of balance, alternately expanding and contracting energy, is an important foundation of ritual. She said, "As in macrocosm, so in microcosm," meaning that all of the wisdom in the universe is within each of us. In ritual we make contact with universal wisdom, our innate intelligence. When we tune into this wisdom it guides us to the next step in our evolution. She often said, "No harm will come to anyone when we learn these things, develop a strong abil-ity to ground and concentrate our energy, and learn to integrate. In memory of Daya, I pay a great deal of attention to my feet on the ground, sensing gravity to safely be as connective and expansive as I am able, giving myself the gift of ritual as often as possible.

A Visual Resource

**FOUR
INTENTIONS**

1. Attunement
2. Focusing
3. Amplifying
4. Directing Energy

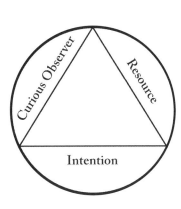

**FIVE
WISDOMS**

1. Being Real with Self
2. Connecting with Resource, Spirit and/or Community
3. Having Intention
4. Having Belief
5. Using Resources to Ground Self

As a visual aid in creating your rituals, we use the symbol of the circle and the triangle, a hallmark of many healing and spiritual disciplines, including Alcoholics Anonymous. Representing unity, it is the unbroken circle of spirit, the cycle of Life-Death-Rebirth, and the seasons. It also represents the feminine power, wholeness, eternity, and the Sacred Space in which we dwell, Mother Earth. The triangle is the strongest of all geometric forms: it cannot collapse unless one of its joints gives way. The triangle points upward, symbolizing masculine power, the active principle. Together they represent the Unity of Mind, Body, and Spirit. Hence the symbol illustrates the balance between structure and freedom—an instance of the unity of opposites—as we might find it in a harmonious partnership or marriage between two dissimilar individuals.

The words on the three sides of the triangle: intention, resource and the Curious Observer, indicate factors any of us can activate in a ritual. This symbol reminds us that the universe of resources and our own innate intelligence (embodied in the Curious Observer) are always present. The circle/triangle configuration is an incubator in which the ongoing miracle of creation can take place.

The Curious Observer is the only part of us that is wise and grounded enough to hold that context of creation. Because resource is universal and unlimited, and because the Curious Observer is much wiser than our own linear and binary thinking brain, the outcome of ritual may actually be far greater than the intention.

As you explore each ritual and begin to enter the process, you can use this graphic to remind yourself of the essential points from the earlier chapters. You may want to put this graphic on a little piece of paper, invoke it with special resource energy, and keep it with you for occasional reference on your experimental journey.

A BREATH RITUAL

Find a quiet place without distraction. Make yourself
comfortable. Close your eyes. This will help you notice the
felt senses of your body and your breath. If you are more
comfortable with your eyes open, then experiment that way,
or just squint a little. Bring awareness to your body. This is
finding attunement with yourself. Gradually draw in a slow
breath. This is *focusing.* On the second, third, or fourth
conscious breath, imagine one special moment in your
life. Take whatever comes immediately and organically
from the Old Brain as your Curious Observer watches.
Allow yourself to be surprised, it may occur. Invite your
breath and entire body to connect with that image (just
the best focus point of it). Notice your body sensations
as you heighten your awareness of conscious breath at
this special moment. You are now *amplifying* the energy.
Taking your time, watching your breathing, noticing the
felt senses of your body (even the subtle ones), just keep
making room for whatever happens. No judgment, no
agenda. (Many people experience a Zen-like simplicity
during breath ritual, a clearness and cleanness of being,
or perhaps a pleasant emptiness). Now, when ready, invite
in a realistic intention for something you would like for
yourself, one that you believe could possibly manifest. Now
as you breathe, imagine the feeling of already having what
you desire, however that comes to you. As you give yourself
some time and space with this, you are perfectly *directing*
the energy of the ritual. When you feel you are finished,
if your experience was pleasant or informative, give quiet
thanks for your breath. Now, as you softly open your
eyes, let your Curious Observer keep noticing in its clear,
detached way as you re-engage with the life before you.

This is the end of this part of the ritual. Remember, you can always repeat it, change it, or do similar rituals in community, and that will amplify the energy as well.

Caution: If you are not able to do the above ritual, chances are you are running up against a constriction, probably one resisting relaxation or the unknown. You can work with this too. This is where compassion for self comes in. We each have different and diverse blocks. Give yourself permission to have yours. Hold the block or barrier in the light of your self-love and acceptance and you will soon find yourself doing this exercise, or a similar one, naturally and organically. Your body and the Old Brain want you to have this delicious experience.

It's good to register the fact that interrelatedness makes whatever personal breath ritual we perform have an impact on culture, politics, and ecology. This happens in subtle (and not-so-subtle) inexplicable ways. Thus we want to come to all rituals with what Wayne Dyer calls "authenticity and a calm heart."

Opening to Life through Breath

Sometimes our whole world seems upside down. Things that ought to be just common sense, like being respectful to ourselves and others and growing organically, are stymied by what we call constrictions. A great thing about breath ritual is that when I look at the absurdity of all that seems to encompass the entire planet, I have a simple truth to come home to for comfort—my breath. It's always there for me, and the more attention I give it, the more I come into my own calm nonattachment in relation to the craziness caused by everyday personal and cultural constrictions. Breathing is always expansive. By allowing air into our lungs we are opening to life and to the resources that exist around us.

I first learned the power of breath ritual in a meditation class about twenty-five years ago, simply by bringing awareness to one's breath. The teacher spoke about diaphragmatic breathing (fully into the stomach and diaphragm) but my breath was still shallow. As I periodically observed my new breath awareness over the following weeks, I began breathing naturally into my diaphragm, which was quite pleasing. But the real benefits came gradually, as my insights deepened.

Spectrum of Breath

In 1995, I attended a meditation and Holotropic Breathwork retreat, facilitated by Jack Kornfield and Stanislav Grof. During each of the five days we would do Insight (Vipassana) Meditation, with gentle breathwork half the day. The other half we did the more vigorous Holotropic Breathwork (HB), where you lie on a full body cushion assisted by a partner (a "sitter"). My partner for the week, David Pearson, a more experienced breathworker, was in training to be a facilitator. When you do HB, you don't just breathe. While lying blindfolded you almost hyperventilate, breathing very fast and deep as you listen to loud provocative music in the background. Your sitter makes sure your space is protected on the floor. At first this breathing seems like hard work, but after fifteen minutes it becomes quite natural. Breathing deep and fast has its own rhythm, often mysteriously in time with the music. It's a bit like a runner's zone, where the effort disappears.

HB was my most vivid experience of transpersonal healing. It transported me beyond space and time where transpersonal events could occur. Deeply into the breath ritual with David's protection, I lost all sense of physical boundaries, experiencing myself as pure energy. This taught me the awesome power of breathwork, vividly reminding me of the transpersonal aspects of ritual.

There are numerous types of breath ritual that are already well-established in addition to a few just mentioned. Breathing practices are found within Hinduism and Buddhism, for instance. In Buddhism, doing breath ritual, you are freeing your mind of everything. You are also awakening a subtle sense of connectivity with the universe. The Latin term "respirare" means to breathe, to blow in a contrary direction, and to recover from fear. When we are consciously breathing, we are connecting to the opposite to fear.

When I start an individual session with a client, they often notice how I unconsciously take a big deep breath before I start. I know it awakens my Curious Observer, bringing light to what is present that will most benefit my client.

We can breathe with the intent of being present in our uniqueness. Yet we are all invisibly connected, each bringing something important to the table of life. Honoring this is one of my daily rituals and a great resource. Every conscious breath is an awareness of this precious resource. Breath is energy, and the key to energy medicine. Ritual is an embodiment of energetic healing. It's in our body, it's physical, and it's something we can do in almost any circumstance.

Personal Prayer Ritual

The most important aspect of personal prayer ritual is that it's *yours*. No one else in the world ever has to know about it unless you choose to share; it's your private, personal ritual. I frequently do prayer and mediation on a Life Cycle Machine at my health club in Manhattan. That is where I go to as a place of resource. I can go to a deeper place of resource and expansive energy, and pray for things I want to manifest. I can pray for many from that humble but energetically alive place. It is a very personal form of prayer ritual.

The inspiration of my *Life Cycle Ritual* helped me come up with the following prayer:

I am the water. I am the wave. I am always part of the whole, and I am a manifestation of that same whole. Through the unique ways I bring my energy and light into the world, I contribute to and honor the whole. I pray that I remember that my differences, my unique qualities, are my gifts, even my reason for being in this larger process of evolution.

In my own unique wave manifestation, I live in a vertical reality connecting the energy of mother earth to father sky. From the earth's perspective, I live in the sky. From this lofty and humble place of knowing, I invite in the guiding light of all the spirits whom I've loved and been loved by, my ancestors, those dear ones who have passed before me, and the Great Spirit of which I am a part. I ask these spirit guides to light my way, bringing grace, synchronicity, and serendipity to my own life journey and the journeys of all my friends and relations. I pray that our daily challenges are graced with compassion and wisdom.

I pray that I can continue to let go of pushing and trying, becoming more the awake receiver of the inner and outer gifts that come my way; that I may continue to learn to rest, enjoying the sweetness of moments, being ever more present for what comes to me.

I pray for my well-being and the vitality of all my relations. May our suffering be minimized and our dreams realized for our own good and the benefit of the whole.

I am thankful for who I am, where I am, and the lessons of this life. It is with humble gratitude that I say Thank You, Thank You, Great Spirit for the awareness, understanding and love I bring to this very moment. Thank you for showing me who I am. Thank You! Thank You!

Sometimes personal rituals become public. An untold number of people have idiosyncratic rituals that fit into their life perfectly, that no one would want to do. They are just as important as those handed down in prayer books.

Prayer Types, Attitudes and Principles

There are many kinds of prayers and ways to connect with unseen reality. There is prayer for protection, prayer for guidance, prayer for transformation, prayer for strength, or prayer for assistance with grief, forgiveness, and anger. There are prayers for finding the right house, car, job, etc.

Prayer is a process of connecting and communicating with unseen realities. During prayer ritual, we send our own voice out into the invisible sea of resources; we send our song, our poetry, our emotions, needs, wants, desires, hopes, and realizations. Then, most important, we open our inner ears as wide as they will stretch and listen to what comes back.

Prayer and ritual historically have a lot in common, both developing out of a need for connecting to a higher power, something larger than us. There are many types of prayers in shamanic societies, as well as in modern ones. Some people, repulsed by religion because of past experience, see prayer from the outside only as people sitting together, doing as they are told rather than acting from their own convictions. Yet indeed it is a very rich resource, one where an individual can truly express themselves freely and openly.

In exploring just two types of prayers, communicating and communing, we can redefine ritual prayer in energetic terms. Both involve the four intentions: attunement, focusing, amplifying, and directing energy, but with different degrees of emphasis on each. Don't hesitate to incorporate music and dance into your prayer ritual, as we are not restricted to any one tradition here.

In the first, we enter into a single chain of highly focused messages with the Supreme Being, a deity or entity of our choice. Some people focus on the content of their message, sending it to the universe for general delivery, trusting that the right resources will respond. Others focus on the recipient of their message, letting their mind wander freely in conversation with their beloved deity. Still others, perhaps filled with a sense of urgency and purpose, focus one message to a single recipient, again and again, a powerful prayer technique yielding surprising results. Each of these three is a type of communication prayer ritual. We are *attuning* to the recipient, focusing on the recipient, directing our message toward the recipient, and amplifying that message through reverence and repetition.

In the second, we holistically enter communion with the totality of all life, all resources, and all deities, sending and receiving countless conscious and unconscious messages all at once. There does not need to be the expectation of a particular outcome. The experience of communing deeply with all life can be far more satisfying than worldly success.

One of the greatest gifts that ritual brings us is the ability to go into a spiritual zone, helping us attain a deeper level of consciousness. Some prefer to enter into a physical, sacred ritual space before praying, with a temple they can go to, or a room in the house set aside for that purpose. Others walk to a certain place in the woods, as the walk itself may be the sacred space. You can use a stick to draw a circle on the ground to create sacred space, or a small rug or cushion, which is portable and creates a consistent space in any environment. The important thing is to feel safe in your sacred space.

PERSONAL PRAYER RITUAL

For one whole day, make a ritual out of everything you do,
the more commonplace and practical the act the better.
Fill each mundane act with the awareness and intention

that it is of great spiritual importance. As you sweep the floor, verbally repeat an affirmed intention to the effect that you are sweeping away the inequity and confusion of the world. As you wash your hands, visualize the intention that you are washing away your old, negative karma and attachments to the past. (You may want to periodically touch your thumb to your third finger on your favored hand as a tactile, energetic reminder of holism and your day's intention.) As you make breakfast, imagine you are making breakfast for a holy man or woman in the next room, and imbue the meal with love. Then take the plate into the next room and eat it! As you are filing away papers, ritually visualize that you are putting the loose ends of your spiritual life in order as well. As you empty the trash, do a little burial ritual to honor the effort of those who provided those resources for you.

Take a piece of paper and write down a list of totally original prayer rituals nobody has ever performed before. Let some ideas flow out of what you think is unusual or different, and others flow out of what you really need to do. Try them out in privacy, and retain the ones you like best.

With some knowledge and experience of breath and prayer informing our reading, the next chapter widens out to additional areas of life. We will explore rituals for health, self-love, overcoming resistance, seed planting, finding what you want, and work challenges. We will also glimpse the vast powers of transporting ritual into community and vice versa.

Everyday Rituals

> What is even more thrilling is that we, ourselves, are
> capable of rewriting the play or changing our roles by
> applying intention, grasping the opportunities that
> arise from coincidence, and being true to the calling
> of our souls.
>
> DEEPAK CHOPRA

"Applying intention, grasping the opportunities …" If we bring
our knowledge of what we know about ritual so far, and blend
in a bit of wisdom of breath and prayer, we can let good intention,
focus, and our Curious Observer further inform us in this chapter
about the value of *"Everyday Rituals,"* beginning with our health.

Health Rituals

I would like to present a radically different view of health itself,
based on the energetic model of healing. Then maybe we will see the
essential importance of ritual in the pathway towards greater health.

The true, uncontracted self is healthy. It is the real you. The contracted, withdrawn, constricted self is not who you are. My own

pain-bound, constricted self doesn't *feel* like me, and it *isn't* me, but it took me years to realize this. The painful isolation that comes with not knowing about the felt senses of expansion and contraction is a big dimension of poor health. It is a cultural learning deficit. When there is no fresh inflow and outflow of energy, the organism becomes toxic. When the physical self becomes uncontracted or more expansive, it leads to a more healthy state both physically and spiritually. In our modern, busy, pollution-laden world, it is ALWAYS a struggle to restore the physical self to an expansive state that feels whole with aliveness running through it. In fact, it is almost impossible to live in a fully uncontracted state; we have to work at it with focus, like a practice. It takes a kind of self-nurturing discipline, a paradoxical state of vigilant self-indulgence. We especially see this in the struggle for physical health, but also in the spiritual realm. This is why most of us need doctors, therapists, healers of all stripes, medicine men and women, wonder drugs, special herbs, etc. We have been trained from childhood to be neither self-loving nor self-disciplined concerning our own health. In fact, most of our early caretakers lacked any awareness of energetic health. It wasn't knowledge of *their* time. It is now manifesting as wisdom of our time. Only self-love can move us from contraction to expansion. And, out of a growing adult self-love, which ritual engenders, comes the nurturing self-discipline required to re-negotiate energetic, physical and emotional states of contraction and expansion. In order to apply these negotiation skills, we need to be able to "hold" expansion and contraction in our bodies at the same time in a grounded way. For this we need ritual and our Curious Observer.

As children, we often experience healthcare as communicating constricting, tension-causing messages of fear. The practices associated with staying healthy: brushing teeth, regular bowel movements, three squares a day, the right kind of hygiene, etc. were forced on us along with threats of horrible illness or even beatings, spanking, scolding, or deprivation. These functions often became painful in themselves. This does not prepare us to be adults taking care of ourselves. Instead, when we leave the nest, we rebel and go crazy, abusing our bodies, until our health falls apart, and then we go to doctors to admonish us, deprive us, and scare us like our parents did. These constrictions only serve to make us sicker, more isolated, and more guilt-laden.

Reframing Self-Love

Ritual can help us reframe health care as self-love, not self-punishment. It allows us to use these rituals of daily hygiene as expansive and heart opening expressions of spiritual self-love and positive self-indulgence. This makes it much more possible to take responsibility for our own good health. Think of the benefits that modern (allopathic) medicine has to offer when practiced in the context of ritual as resource.

When I floss my teeth, I think of it as a *"Self-Love Ritual,"* and I visualize all the good it is doing to my whole system, making my mouth healthier. At the same time I meditate on the simplicity of the act, using it to clear my mind the way a child might focus on a lady bug crawling on a single blade of grass. I do similar meditations while exercising, walking, swimming, whatever. I also have to make reasonably healthy choices in what I eat in order to be healthy. Again, I make those choices into a *"Self-Love Ritual,"* not what is right or wrong.

Getting to the gym is always a struggle, and I experience conflicting emotions, including dread, and guilt; but once I'm there, it's great. In addition to weight training, I can work out on the "Life Cycle" for thirty minutes and do an expansive meditation at the same time. In fact I can't think about anything too technical while on the cycle, because it's too physically demanding, so I remain in a relaxed, expansive state, ideal for the *"Life Cycle Ritual"* mentioned earlier. It's also great for my predisposition to heart disease, as the cardio-exercise is when I do the above ritual which includes prayers for good health. I often update and reconfigure the *"Life Cycle Ritual"* and the prayers it includes to meet my present needs and those of loved ones and clients. For example, if someone I know well is really suffering, I bring them into the light of the ritual, front and center, right after my own health. This "ordering" comes from the principle in the Five Wisdoms of *respect for self, then others.* In this ritual I also pray for the well-being of "all of us" and our mother earth. But, I first have to take care of me and my health or I'll be short on energy to offer others. Health has been a consistent central ingredient to this ritual since I began it. We can make amazing configurations to suit our ever changing needs and purposes.

During the Thanksgiving holiday of 1996, I was still recovering from my heart attack and by-pass surgery. I used Thanksgiving luncheon to create a *"Get-In-Shape Ritual"* with my partner. I needed his buy-in to make it work for me. In my enthusiastic focus for some years on my work, research, and writing, I had let my health suffer. I was overweight and out of shape. This is not good for someone with heart disease. At that private holiday meal, just the two of us, I gave thanks for being alive and for many other things. I then asked him, in a very earnest way, if he would support the above ritual that I intended to undertake. In the ritual language of this book, I had been inwardly *attuning* myself for this commitment for several weeks prior. I declared to him that after the meal I was turning over a new *dietary leaf* and that I was becoming more serious about my exercise program. It was a very real and practical way of showing my "Higher Powers" that I was grateful for the gift of life and intended to take better care of it. I said to him, "As of today, I am going to be very conscious and prudent with food intake and maintain a regular structured exercise routine to alleviate my heart problem and feel better overall." I asked him to support me in this intention, and the belief that I could do it, and he did. I lost the excess weight over the months ahead and have stayed consistent with the exercise. I am presently in the best physical shape of my adult life. This ritual continues now, almost nine years from its sacred inception of us joining in spirit. I'm still at the gym three times a week and being conscious about my food choices.

Rituals for Overcoming Resistance

Use the power of this ritual to help you get past your resistance to health care (and to get to the gym on time in spite of busy and hectic schedules).

> Look into your bathroom mirror and say: "I intend to get to the gym (or, start riding my bicycle, flossing my teeth, going to therapy sessions—whatever you know you should be doing but are NOT doing) today for the greater benefit of myself, my family/community, my work, and my world. I vow that this noble intention stay in my heart and manifest in a successful outcome, so that I can enjoy a more expansive, healthy, and more fulfilled state of being.

If you still experience a difficulty getting to the gym (or start bicycling, or whatever) on the day you perform this ritual, that night try a *"Seed Planting Ritual:"*

> Look into the mirror and say: "I intend to get to the gym (or start bicycling, or whatever) tomorrow morning (or evening). I invite into this ritual any experience of love-giving or love-receiving I have known, and a felt sense memory of it. I set forth the intention that all obstacles and inner resistance and debate against achieving this goal will disappear without effort, or be gently put aside. I will work out tomorrow, for the benefit of myself, my family/community, my work and my world." At the end

of the ritual, it is good to close with a "send" gesture. Snap your fingers, clap five times, blink three times, or knock on wood, whatever gesture works for you. Repeat this each day in the same way, until you over come the obstacle and the new activity becomes a healthy routine.

Seed Planting Rituals

"Seed Planting Rituals" can be very effective in all areas of resistance. They allow the unconscious energies time to reorganize and align themselves with your intention. While we want to have nurturing discipline in a self-loving way, we also want to honor our energetic system and its present limitations. These particular rituals are very helpful in learning how our energy system works and responds. With *"Seed Planting Rituals"* and some patient observation, we can develop a mastery co-creatively working with our energy resources.

Finding What I Want Ritual

History's oldest rituals are probably hunting rituals. Since hunting is not central to most of our lives today, we can learn from the old and go after and find what we want. The intention of this ritual is to find something of value to oneself or one's community, or to let it find you. Learning to more effortlessly find what you want involves faith in the power of connectivity. Looking at the designs on the walls of the Lascaux Caves in France, we can see how the old hunting rituals may have developed as early as 30,000 years ago. Those pre-historic artists knew how to connect with big game through expressed intention. They would draw a picture of the animal they intended to hunt and then draw a spear through its heart. Through these beautiful paintings they were able to make their intentions visible. It has also been noted by some scientists that the pictures are placed in areas of the caves that are not easily accessible, but are unusually energetically (sonically) resonant. This has been interpreted to mean that prospective hunters must have sung songs and chanted while painting the pictures, or while gazing hopefully at them before a hunt. There is, in any case, clear evidence that the hunting party prepared for its mission through ritual. There is no reason why we can't do the same when "hunting" for a house, a job, a car, a college, a dentist, a doctor, a lost object, lost pet, lost love, or the answer to an important question. Try this modern day version of the *"Finding What I Want Ritual"* below:

> Say you are hunting for a new home (or whatever). Sit down with a box of crayons and a piece of paper, and take three deep breaths. Use the crayons to help you visualize what your new home will look like. Draw yourself into the picture, smiling and happy, with a bright sun or romantic moon floating overhead. You can also draw other objects or symbols close to the house or to yourself, as a way of "hunting" and connecting with them as well. Now either with a statement or a song, state your intention for connecting with that place where you will be happy. Dedicate this intention to the benefit of yourself, family, community, and the world. Then draw a circle around the picture of the house. At this point, place it in a drawer, burn it ritually or tear it up. What matters is that you let it go completely.

If you don't have time to do this entire ritual, going over the intention that it embodies mentally might do just as well. Consider the way I found a car recently (with no time to devote to the process):

I live and work in New York City during the week, where cars are not really necessary. However, I recently was in a situation where I needed to buy a "station car," something to get me to and from the bus station.

The hunt for a perfect vehicle was underway. I didn't want to spend over $1,500. I didn't have time to draw a picture of the vehicle, or sing a song or chant, or even look around much; I created the energetic intention to connect with this car, for my convenience and the greater good. I told some people at the gym that I was looking for a simple station car. Someone said, "My best friend has three cars and wants to sell one." That person called me, I asked to see the least expensive one, and he came by my office in the car, right to my door in fact. I gave him a check to hold it until I could take it to a mechanic. He said he would loan me the car to do so over the weekend and left me the car and keys. The next day (Saturday), the man who mows my lawn (and who lives down the road) visited, and I mentioned that the speedometer and directional signals didn't work for this car that I otherwise liked. He said his mechanic had the same car and loved it, and would probably enjoy working on mine. I brought it over for him to look at and appraise. He said that it would be $300 to fix it up to pass inspection. As it turned out, the man had another car of the same make, model, and year, but it was broken down and had all the parts this one was missing. In several hours this mechanic had fixed the entire car I brought him to check out. Of course I bought the car. The entire process from ritual to real live car took forty-eight hours. This *"Finding What I Want Ritual"* can bring results and happier circumstances into our lives in two minutes, two days, or two years. Who knows what the hidden power of resource can do?

One thing we need to remember about connectivity is that the first pet, house or car we connect with and look at may not be the one in the picture, and the one we need to choose for now may not be the one in the picture either. It might even be better than what we drew from our limited concept of possibility. With any ritual, we need to rely heavily on intuition and tap deeply into our Curious Observer so that we won't panic and make our final choice prematurely. We need to be able to let the small fish get away, but also "know" when we have found the right one.

Rituals for Work Challenges

Everyone who is focused on his or her work is expected to be able to work within the concept of a goal, (quota, etc.) and the buzzword today is "get it done!" Yet that word "goal" has become contaminated by exploitation and greed. When we focus only on the goal, the process suffers and quality suffers as a result. That is why we use the word "intention." A work team may want to use ritual to enhance their camaraderie and focus their intention. (There is presently an increasing demand and need in corporate and health care settings for just such ritualized camaraderie.) This allows the team to yield to the lay of the land rather than marching forward into an unseen brick wall. It also allows benevolent, unseen energies some room to interact in the process and say, "Your intentions are good, but here's how to really prosper and benefit others as well."

ALIGNMENT RITUAL

We may like our work to varying degrees, but one constant is, *this is where we are,* and only from here can we create the ritual to feed us as we move along the way.

I'm reminded of a career I devoted many years to, loved, and then grew to need something else. It was advertising. I was good at it (loved the psychology aspect of helping clients see what they *really* had to offer) and a *Success* magazine cover story once referred to me as "a shining star on Madison Avenue." The shine dulled when I got sober and my values began to shift. Also, by then I had become a partner in the firm and really disliked the different kind of responsibilities that came with my success. It was all about money, "putting out brush fires," and personnel challenges. The creation I used to enjoy with clients was now an occasional dog and pony show—the juice was gone. I began to dread my work. My 12-Step sponsor (who was a partner in a financial services firm) and I created a ritual to help me get through the days. Every morning I would call him at 8:45

from my office (with door closed) and he would read Unity's "Daily Word" to me over the phone. It was very soothing, and in short order it inspired me to create an *"Alignment Ritual"* for all who reported to me. I acknowledged to my staff that I needed their support to better fulfill my responsibilities to them. I asked them to abstain from coming to me with problems as soon as they arise. Instead, I invited them to save them for a scheduled time of the day when we could focus together, and to ask themselves four questions about problems *before* bringing them to me. The questions were: (1) What is the problem? (2) What is the cause of the problem? (3) What are the possible solutions? And, (4) what solution do I like best?

The results of this ritual were amazing to me and my sponsor. It dissolved much of that crazy "I can never catch up" energy. In fact, most problems were resolved without me. When I was called in, the choices were clearly laid out so I could offer my input for resolution. This ritual got me through the next several years as I saved money to go back to school for another career, one that focused on psychology and counseling.

INTENTION RITUAL

In fact, all work is a ritual, whether we choose to call it that or not. If we choose to make it one, we bring a lot more empowerment to the process. We can then bring more elements and resources to the table. A friend of mine from the IAPH community was very unhappy at his workplace. He decided to perform a ritual in which he would express his intention to others that by the end of the year he would either resolve the issues at his work place or find another job entirely. He invited me to be one of the people who would share the intention with him, and the belief that he would do it. I accepted in the spirit of the Five Wisdoms of our community and the awareness that this sharing of intention and belief amplifies the energy of the ritual. There may have been a third option out there that he hadn't thought of, but that didn't matter because intentionality is part of a process that is always open to better ideas as they might come along. In fact a third possibility did come along. The business he worked for was sold in a blink. After a three month ambiguous orientation with the new ownership, my friend became pleased, even excited. It seems, without anyone knowing, the old boss (owner) was in a bad way for personal reasons and his mood contaminated everything. The new owner was full of new ideas and enthusiasm. It made my friend feel like he had a renewed bright future with the company.

In certain work activities there is a barrier or threshold which seems to limit our ability to get satisfaction from it or to reach our maximum potential in performance. For instance, some jobs are satisfying in many ways but have some unpleasant aspect such as emotional stress, repetitive stress, physical discomfort, potential conflict, or temporary failure. When these aspects of a job are present, it is common to procrastinate or have difficulty beginning the workday or "getting in the groove." This can lead to showing up late for work or missing deadlines. Getting through the barrier of this unpleasantness may seem like an uncrossable threshold.

In my experience the barriers mentioned are often symptoms of psychic overwhelm (in energy medicine this means too much *activation*, unhealed trauma buttons are being pushed by one or more things). Being late for work and missing deadlines are the most common work symptoms of this type of contraction. Once we identify that psychic overwhelm is the culprit, and contraction is causing overactivation in the nervous system, we can address it through ritual.

Just "naming" the problem begins to help. It's not our fault; this type of activation gets triggered on the most primitive unconscious survival levels. What we want to do in situations like this is look for resources and grounding as soon as we are able. Try this simple ritual:

Find a quiet, calm place to spend thirty minutes, somewhere you won't be disturbed. If you can't find it right away, remember that slow is fast. Hold the intention that when you do find your quiet place, a new opening in awareness awaits you there. Trust the universal spirit to help you find the right place in the right time. Just knowing that what you are preparing should bring some resource energy to the edges of the contraction should take some of the edge off. Don't bother trying to figure things out, just invite your Curious Observer to notice what it notices.

Once you've found your place, begin to settle (tune) into this place. At the same time, begin to tune into your body in this very moment. See if you can find a location in this place where your body feels as comfortable as possible. Take your time. As you begin to feel even a bit settled here in this place, notice your feet touching the floor or ground, and the surface of whatever you are sitting or lying on. Just take your time becoming aware of energy of gravity that is supporting you in place, right now.

Notice that this place, and this ritual, and gravity from the earth are all being resources to you right now. As you do so, tune in to the felt senses of your body and notice if there are any places that feel pleasant or interesting in some way. If so, just bring gentle awareness to these sensations giving them some time and space. Let your innate intelligence be with your body sensation, as your Curious Observer just notices, without judgment or agenda. If your thinking mind should come in, just invite your Curious Observer to respectfully ask it to relax for a while as we notice what the body wants you to know. Give yourself time. Bring some awareness to your breathing; remember that breathing is always good.

Ask your higher power and Curious Observer to "uncouple" or sort out all the challenges of your present life, so they are not one tangled ball. Notice that this can be done in a second without thinking. Ask the Curious Observer "what one thing needs to come to the surface now for focus and resourcing." Take whatever comes and hold it in the "presence" of your experience. Don't do anything with it, leave that to your innate intelligence and your body's self-organizing nervous system. Just give some time and space as you continue to notice for an organic process to take place.

Now, without abandoning whatever was presented or trying to do anything with it, gently put it aside as we do the anchoring part of this ritual. Bring your focus to the following visualization and the three instructions following them as best you are able, just noticing your full body experience as you do.

Close your eyes. Imagine yourself inside the center of a triangle, with the point above your head, lines going down the outside of both sides of your body, and the base under your body.

Imagine a blue colored light above your head, at the point of the triangle, and notice that the light represents these words that you say to yourself *slowly,* inwardly or out loud, repeating them twice: "I am who I am. I am who I am."

Now, imagine that this blue light begins to travel down the right side of the triangle. And, as it travels it represents different words that you say to yourself *slowly,* inwardly or out loud, repeating them twice: "I anchor myself in the awareness that I am who I am. I anchor myself in the awareness that I am who I am."

Now, as the blue light reaches the base, it turns red. Notice the red light slowly traveling across the base of the triangle, underneath you, and that red light represents these words that you say to yourself *slowly*, inwardly or out loud, repeating them twice: "I do what I need to do, to have what I need to have. I do what I need to do, to have what I need to have."

As the red light intersects with the line that travels up the left side of the triangle that holds you, notice that the light turns green. As this green light travels up it represents these words that you say to yourself *slowly*, inwardly or out loud, repeating them twice: "I have what I need to have to be. I have what I need to have to be."

As the green light gets to the point of the triangle, just notice your overall sense of being in this very moment. Just give that some time and space as we prepare to direct your energy out of the ritual and into the world.

As you prepare to gradually and safely bring your energy out of this formal ritual; focus on the principle of "always respecting yourself and then others." See if you want to hold that as an intention bringing this energy out into the world.

As your focalizer for this ritual, I want to leave you with words of offering: Whatever surfaced for you during this ritual, or whatever your experience, let it be. Trust your innate intelligence to guide any actions that feel appropriate or just trust time. If when we started this ritual your sense of overwhelm (or activation) was a ten on a one-to-ten scale, notice where it is now. Notice that within you is the ability, with resource and grounding, to modulate this. Also, as you return to your work setting, with no judgment or agenda, notice if anything has changed.

You may complete the ritual at any time by offering gratitude in whatever way you see fit to the forces that be.

That is the end of this *"Ritual for Work Challenges"* and while many rituals don't appear logical to the New Brain, they have their own unique results. I trust this one ended in a good way. It can be returned to at any time for additional illuminations and energy balancing. It can also be redesigned by one's innate intelligence or by inviting in someone who knows how to focalize such rituals. This can be a tool for crossing that threshold on a daily basis, once you "know" your centering spot (or that you need to find it) and it can help you get into exploring and playing with possibilities more effectively in your life; it will go further and your attitude towards work will also become more positive.

Just as with the *"Health Rituals"* mentioned earlier, the main goal of *"Rituals for Work Challenges"* is to bring your energetic system into balance, back toward a place of feeling whole and connected. This, of course, affects our emotions and our physical health. Just like flossing your teeth, going to work is something you do for yourself, for your companion, family, community, and your world. It is taking responsibility for your well-being in a way that requires nurturing self-discipline. Ritual will help overcome the constrictive responses to present situations and triggered unresolved traumas in our nervous system (often interconnected).

Speaking of *"Rituals for Work Challenges,"* I have discovered that getting to our work earlier than on time (even a little) is tantamount to an empowered energetic work experience. (This is even true for people who work at home; it just requires creating a ritual of structure so they know what that would look and feel like for them.) There may be many reasons for this "arrive early" phenomenon, but this book is not about reasons, it's about ritual and energetic transformation. Getting an early start gives one a dramatically different context for all else that occurs in a given day, particularly the resilience we bring to the matters at hand. For that get "on top of your workday" experience, you may want to try this ritual:

Look into the mirror the evening before a work day. Take three deep comfortable breaths (resource) and say to yourself: "Tomorrow morning I am going to work and no obstacles will come up to stop me. I will be prepared and earlier than on-time. My day will be happy and productive, bringing abundance into my life. This day's work will benefit me, and the world. I will arrive at work early and everything will go as smoothly as possible."

Some may choose to close this with a ritual by petting a dog or cat, or feeding the birds, or touching a lucky or meaningful object on the shelf. Some create a new morning routine in the same order every day to insure an early departure and few obstacles. Some make a daily ritual of buying a newspaper and reading the comics as a treat to reward them for leaving for work early. Others may reward themselves just by enjoying the sense of well-being all day for being on top of their game.

Entering Communal Sacred Space

For ritual to be present in community, first and foremost, a focalizer is required. The focalizer is empowered by the community and empowers him or her self to bring focus to the matters at hand. She or he should be someone who has an innate ability to bring the community energy to a place that serves the highest good of all. Depending on the type of community you are creating, be it a community for a one-time event, a weekend retreat, a residential commune, or simply a coming together of two people (for instance, the way I work with clients), the focalizer role can be fluid and interchangeable. What's important is that someone clearly and distinctly has their eye on the ball and is *holding* the space and intention for the necessary attunement, focusing, amplifying, and directing of energy. As a matter of reality, whoever in a community is doing this at a particular moment is *focalizing*. Yet, it is good to have a primary focalizer who has accepted responsibility for holding the energy of the larger space.

In the attunement phase, the focalizer assists the community in becoming aligned around its purpose for coming together. Using the Five Wisdoms is one of the easiest and most dependable ways I've discovered for achieving this alignment and for the attunement of community energy. Here's how the Wisdoms apply in this context:

1. We bring an intention of respect for self, others and the power of community healing and manifestation.

2. We agree to be authentic and real, sharing from our experience only and respecting the experience of others.

3. We create a shared intention for coming together.

4. We create a shared belief that our intentions can be realized.

5. We ground ourselves and our experience in resource energy.

Once we have done this, *the ritual has begun*. We have now entered that sacred space where more of the unknown can become manifest. Here, we recognize that our logic systems are limited so far as fulfillment and true living are concerned. We notice that our rational minds do not account for our capacity for rapture, joy, and connectivity. *Numinous* or felt sense moments which ritual often provides connect us with parts of ourselves ordinarily hidden. We may experience blinding insight, firm inner instruction, or a "knowingness" that far surpasses any previous conviction. Using the ancient tradition of alchemy as a metaphor, we transmute sorrow to wisdom and anguish into greater connectivity. When we have such an opening of consciousness, we are forever changed.

Intention varies from one type of community to another. Just as there are powerful communities for getting sober and getting away from drug misuse, there are equally powerful communities presently working to create a "Department of Peace" in the United States Government, to reconnect sexuality and spirituality, to nurture and sustain our planet earth, ecologically and emotionally, and to simply heal in ourselves whatever organically presents itself next for transformation. Notice this: For a community to be anchored in the magical powers of ritual it must be "ascendant," aspiring to a higher cause, not fear-driven or self-absorbed.

The brilliance of community ritual is that we can draw inspiration and energy to fuel our personal rituals from the collective resources. One affects the other when they intersect, but they are two separate aspects of life. It is most potent when the intersection of personal ritual with community ritual empowers the individual and the individual's presence empowers the community. Ultimately it is the person who makes the choice to work in community and in ritual with it. People don't at first go to 12-Step programs because they feel empowered to go. They go because they need to go. They may get a lot out of it as both a practical and energetic (or spiritual) resource. In 12-Step programs there are flexible but specific group rituals, and each person adapts their own "program" with the help of community elders and spiritual and communal principles. Ideally, they grow through these until they find themselves creating their own rituals and allowing their program (or community ritual) to be a resource for self-created personal rituals. The rituals of our own creation perfectly address the multidimensional needs of our own being and well-being. If we are not using our available community ritual to ignite and support personal rituals we may be using only about thirty percent of the energetic potential that community ritual has to offer us. Experiment with crafting your own personal rituals in and around available community rituals. Tap into that other seventy percent of the energy waiting to be utilized. Don't take my word for it; let your own Curious Observer notice this phenomenon in your own experimentation.

These are the basics for community ritual. Beyond this, each of us has the opportunity to cast out into new or existing ritual communities.

(What is in fact a ritual community need not use the word "ritual.")
As we notice in them the responsible attunement, focusing, amplifying and directing of energy, we can safely drop back (or forward or
upward) into our Curious Observer. We can then gradually let down
our masks of composure and non-judgmentally share our struggles,
joys, desires, and sorrows. By doing so we allow them to be trans-
muted into grounded creativity, greater connectivity and inner fire—
a light gently cast on the frontier before and around us.

Community Ritual

Let's not make this too serious. Since there are so many possibilities of what a community may be coming together for, I won't try to
be specific. I will leave that to you or your community focalizer. Here
we foremost want to share fundamental energetic principles for community rituals.

We already know the Five Wisdoms are excellent for individual-
ized attunement and focusing within any community. Energetically
and practically, they work on both the individual and community
levels simultaneously. Use them or your own variation; it's the energy
that matters, not the words.

Next, after attunement and focusing it is important to amplify the
energy. At one of our retreats, and at a more official gathering in
Washington, D.C., Alice Terson, one of our Institute Board members, focalized the corniest and funniest energy amplifiers I have ever
seen. After all the participants were tuned and focused, she wanted
to get energy moving to support the shared intentions and beliefs
with connectivity. Alice asked the whole aligned group to stand in
a circle around the room as she led us in doing the Hokey-Pokey. It
was entirely successful on both occasions. If you care to try it, here are
the words as I remember them:

You put your right foot in,
You put your right foot out;
You put your right foot in,
And you shake it all about.
You do the Hokey-Pokey,
And you turn yourself around.
That's what it's all about!
You put your left foot in,
You put your left foot out;
You put your left foot in,
And you shake it all about.
You do the Hokey-Pokey,
And you turn yourself around.
That's what it's all about!

You put your right hand in,
You put your right hand out;
You put your right hand in,
And you shake it all about.
You do the Hokey-Pokey,
And you turn yourself around.
That's what it's all about!

You put your left hand in,
You put your left hand out;
You put your left hand in,
And you shake it all about.
You do the Hokey-Pokey,
And you turn yourself around.
That's what it's all about!

You put your right side in,
You put your right side out;

You put your right side in,
And you shake it all about.
You do the Hokey-Pokey,
And you turn yourself around.
That's what it's all about!

You put your left side in,
You put your left side out;
You put your left side in,
And you shake it all about.
You do the Hokey-Pokey,
And you turn yourself around.
That's what it's all about!

You put your nose in,
You put your nose out;
You put your nose in,
And you shake it all about.
You do the Hokey-Pokey,
And you turn yourself around.
That's what it's all about!

You put your backside in,
You put your backside out;
You put your backside in,
And you shake it all about.
You do the Hokey-Pokey,
And you turn yourself around.
That's what it's all about!

You put your head in,
You put your head out;
You put your head in,

And you shake it all about.
You do the Hokey-Pokey,
And you turn yourself around.
That's what it's all about!

You put your whole self in,
You put your whole self out;
You put your whole self in,
And you shake it all about.
You do the Hokey-Pokey,
And you turn yourself around.
That's what it's all about!

You must think I'm silly using all this space for a childish song we probably all know. I *am* silly, and I am making an important point. After Alice led us in this energy amplifier, we broke into small groups with specific predetermined focuses. In these groups we used a wisdom circle format. The energy was abuzz. Most of these people did not know one another prior to coming together for the purpose of the event. They had only been focalized through the Five Wisdoms and Alice's amplifier, yet they were sharing experiences and possibilities as if they were excited about reuniting with lost intimate friends.

Sometimes we need to take up some time and space, however awkwardly or skillfully we do it, to honor the energy in the room (waiting to express itself) as we are attuning the whole community and each person to the Old Brain. Once it feels at home, in safety, it will know exactly what needs to be brought forth, on individual and community levels. Whenever I focalize such a happening, I look out from wherever I'm standing in the room and get a certain sense and feeling that there is a collective Old Brain that is also paying us a visit and making a very soulful contribution to all that occurs.

Before the community ritual comes to a formal close, there is one more step: Directing the energy. A separate occasion, or as a part of the closing, it is wise to invite people and the community as a whole to envision and possibly speak how they'd like to direct the energy this ritual has created. What would they like to see manifest differently in their lives, their relationships, and their world. And, what may already be manifest that they want to make a different kind of peace and relationship with. The possibilities are endless.

In a discussion about focalizing community rituals being an initiation experience in itself, one of the manuscript readers asked me to write about a tough one, so here it is: The most challenging experience I had focalizing ritual with a "work group" was at a mental health and addiction conference in Washington, D.C. sponsored by the federal government. The event's purpose was to align the grantee organizations from around the country with major changes in the focus of their funding. Fundamental shifts had to be made in how all of these organizations operated in order to maintain funding. Not only were the grantees in a very irritable, ambiguous mood, but the government officials, who invited me, were in business attire (suits and ties, etc.) and not accustomed to my use of ritual to communicate. I was invited to be the keynote speaker and to do a break out group. When I realized where I was and what the delicacies of concerns were, my cerebral cortex, or New Brain, became full of static that generated fear and contraction. As soon as I realized what was happening to me I stopped myself and did my personal Michael, "Save Yourself" ritual. That simply means I took a few real conscious breaths and invited my Curious Observer to balance my energy and observations. It worked and the quiet voice inside reminded me "I am who I am." I was reminded I was invited here to share "just that" in a way that may bring light to the challenges at hand. My contraction relaxed. It went beautifully. In the keynote address I invited the conference attendees to align their energy and intentions for the event using the Five Wisdoms.

To give the audience an experience (which is important) of the fifth wisdom (Grounding through Resource), I actually did a Resourcing

Ritual with the large group. They were great! In the break-out session I was able to demonstrate (with a volunteer) the renegotiation
of opposite energies in the nervous system as a way of healing trauma
(and why this is of value to the populations they provide services for).
We even created a Wisdom Circle Ritual for sharing reactions to the
demonstration. While I could see that a few people were reserved
around the intimacy that ritual fosters (especially those "at work" for
the sponsoring agency), many participants were genuinely affected
and expressed gratitude.

The richness of Community Ritual always enlightens me and
reminds me of something I am often surprised by. That is the reality
that, just as each of us has an innate intelligence, so does the group or
community as a collective. Watching and hearing this wisdom express
itself is beautiful and humbling. By the time the community or work
group disperses, there is a palpable sense in the air that our shared
intentions have been realized. Usually each of us has a felt sense that
our experience is true and that illumination has occurred.

What we offered in this chapter are very general ritual frameworks
for health, self-love, overcoming resistance, seed planting, finding
what you want, work challenges, and the sacredness of community.
It's important to understand that we present them as starter ideas to
experiment with so readers might be inspired to create and perform
their own personalized rituals. In the next section we'll build on this;
picking up on the trauma discussion in Chapter Three, in surprising
ways, we will explore resolution and liberation.

Trauma Resolution

7

Growing Up with Your Shadow

> Responsibility is acknowledgement and recognition of the choices and actions one has made during his/her lifetime. Acceptance of one's feelings, understanding, perceptions, and experiences as his/her own, without blame, anger, apology, or qualification.
>
> JOYCE A. KOVELMAN

Growing Up!

An easy example of the effect of cultural trauma is the thirty-two years it took me to "come out" of the societal straitjacket that forbade the very existence of my sexual and affectional variance. Or ask any person of color, or any woman, about cultural trauma. It's all over the place. Even white men, whose dwindling power has made them the newest minority, have begun to feel its scourge. Let's intend our healing advances efficiently, continuing to diminish culturally induced suffering for all.

This section (in two chapters) on "Trauma Resolution" will build on the last, where I showed that taking responsibility for my own breath and prayers was a doorway to another dimension of my own maturation process. We will explore what "growing up" really is: It's about taking responsibility for our lives! We recognize that doing so naturally includes the resolution of trauma, both cultural and personal. Cultural trauma is inflicted, intentionally or not, by society. Let's diminish culturally-induced suffering once and for all. We will begin our journey by uncovering the shadowy elements of trauma that we sometimes keep even from ourselves.

By integrating our shadow elements we can stand taller and feel more whole. In Chapter Eight, we will access cleansing energies to heal the traumatic episodes that have shaped us. We will see how such transformative practices can open an even wider experience of Vibrant Living. Let's look at growing up as a way of shining light on our shadow.

Let's start with relationships. A person might have a hidden fear of encroachment that gets in the way of any kind of deeply fulfilling relationship. Or it may be like a fear of envelopment (losing one's identity in the enormity of another's being and neediness). With these fears come physiological responses that can be confounding. How can we bring light to these fears? How can we work with them in a way that works better for us? I'll share my story with you to give you a peek at a hidden fear mentioned above. The people with these opposite shadows often have a magnetic pull for one another. This is nature's way of bringing us back to what in us needs our care, understanding and attention.

My mother abandoned me when I was a young child. She never came back. Nothing can possibly fill the gap created by her absence. In each relationship, I'm looking for my mother, and when I find that lost love, I cling to it. If I slip into unconscious patterns in an intimate relationship, I am one pain in the behind, and my partner hates it (as all of my partners have had hidden fears of encroachment). I know that *my* central core issue is abandonment. In a relationship, I become very needy from the unhealed wounds of childhood. Knowing that, my ritual is to observe it, bring the resource of understanding to it, I can then consciously choose when I'm going to act on it and when not, and when, or if, I'm going to share it. I've discovered that sharing it brings me to the center of intimacy and vulnerability. That's when I discover vulnerability is strength, rather than a weakness. Again, we are *turning it inside out!* When I make such choices, I'm being a responsible grown-up. I'm taking full responsibility for who I am from my history, how it manifests at this time, affecting my partnerships. It's fully my responsibility to navigate my being and all that has impacted it, pleasure, pain and all!

This neediness can be a barrier to intimacy. By "barrier" I mean an internal wall that hiding my neediness can cause. There have been times it stopped me in my tracks, confounding me with whomever I was engaging with. People with encroachment fears also have hidden barriers—different, yet equally distancing. As a more responsible grown up, I've learned I can hide my barriers by playing it safe avoiding intimacy. Or, I can allow my heart to open, learn to navigate and heal my traumatic deprivations. I can do what nature is calling me to do: Let my Old Brain rule and drop deeper into it for guidance. When choosing the latter it's important to be able to share verbally, since my partner needs to know my inner struggle. I am always amazed how uplifting it is to bring this out into the light of understanding. From this clearer sense of myself, I can teach my partner things he can do to avoid triggering these issues, while he can teach me his sensitivities (usually about encroachment or needing space). If he is going to be away for a day, but gives some assurance that he's looking forward to being with me the following evening, it automatically disengages my unconscious activation of abandonment. My feeling that he is going away from me forever, is deeply rooted in the fabric of my being.

When I feel the needy pull from within and meet it with compassion, something instantly loosens up. I realize I have a choice: *Instead of demanding love, I can give it.* Mysteriously, with a little patience and without requesting it, love does come in ways I never would have imagined. The results validate both my adult sense of self-responsibility, and respect for my residual unmet childhood needs. Do these feelings ever completely go away? I'm not sure, but they can become manageable in a playful way that enhances intimacy.

In all of these situations there are ways to acknowledge our shadow selves through ritual, and open the doorway to healing and connectivity.

To put light on some of these issues, it is great to do the *"Grow Up Ritual."* It is a practice for those of us who feel we don't get our needs met in the world, those of us who paralyze ourselves with victim statements: "Life hasn't been fair to me," or "I'm lonely and can't seem to connect with people."

Life's Unfair—Respect Isn't!

I won't deny that the world can be unfair, but that has little to do with respecting ourselves and others in our choice of actions and words. Cursing our fate shows disrespect for existence as it is, and for the unseen realities that guide and connect us all. We need to acknowledge that everything, even things we don't like, happens for a reason. Only through this acceptance can we engage in the never-ending process of reaching maturity.

I myself was a prime case of victim-think. At thirteen, I looked up the word "homosexual" in the dictionary. The first three words of the definition were: "a mental illness." I slammed that dictionary shut and ran from the library trembling with horror. I buried that part of me until after my wife, Sheila, died so young. I didn't yet know the word "gay." I definitely did not like being "a homosexual." My only frame of reference for that was Herbie "the town queer," who hung out at the train station in my suburban village. I certainly didn't want to be him! Homosexuality remained a mental illness until 1974, when the American Psychological Association changed its status to: "*a variant, normal manifestation of life*. It seemed my life was a slot machine of loss, only dispensing jackpots of grief and misfortune. I didn't ask for HIV, cancer or heart disease, but I got them anyway. I didn't like becoming an addict either and having to deal with a difficult recovery process. Why me? Most of all, I hated that I could not sustain a loving relationship and keep sexuality alive at the same time. It always died after three months or so. My "What's wrong with me?" I didn't even know I was in the victim orb, it was unconscious.

Some years ago, I read a lecture that had been given by Eva Pierrakos in the 1960s on "Separating Real from Unreal Needs." Her lectures were published in *Pathwork to Self-Transformation*. She was one of the early seers (in our time) in energy medicine. Her husband, John, cocreated Bioenergetics with Alexander Lowen, and later Core Energetics, with Eva. They made major contributions to my understanding of the human condition, and though both are now deceased, I always carry them with me. In my early writing I found it helpful to reframe some of Eva's ideas on *separating adult needs from childhood needs*. The results and responses were very illuminating.

So how do we separate our past deprivations from our present needs? This separation must take place in a very private part of us. That's why ritual helps. There is a strong pull or push that accompanies all unmet childhood needs. That's how we begin to distinguish them and accept that these needs can never be truly met. This is because they are in the past, yet the traumatized person clings to them as if they were happening now. As adults we can often get many of our basic needs met, but that has little to do with those tugs from our past. We must respect these tugs and gently put them aside (temporarily) so we can engage in adult give-and-take relationships, free of the demands of the needy child within.

In adult relationships we all have free choice. We can ask for anything we want, as long as we are willing to allow others the freedom to say no. As the Al-Anon saying goes, "Freedom is when I can be happy whether or not I get what I want."

The *"Grow-Up Ritual"* we will soon get to is all about free choice and empowerment, having both and giving them away to others. The ritual focus I encourage is on defusing unmet childhood needs. You can always spot them if your Curious Observer is noticing demanding pulls, feelings or images. They can have associated words and images like: "I must have that," or "You have to do it my way," or "If she leaves me, I'll die." Notice the demanding push or pull. In fulfilling adult relationships, there are no demands, only choices.

And what, you may ask, does this growing up have to do with intimate relationships? Only everything! I've counseled couples in which one proclaims how independent he or she is, yet all the while exuding an energy and body language that screams, "Please take care of me! Don't leave me! I can't survive without you!" Obviously this person is giving very mixed signals to their partner. The partner simultaneously lives with a gut feeling that no one could ever meet those needs. Typically the partner of a needy person will have their own unmet childhood needs that communicate, "Don't you dare fence me in! I won't give up my freedom for anyone! I don't want to feel manipulated or duty-bound!" You can imagine what a twisted dance this creates. These are not adult needs; they are charged remnants of unmet childhood ones. Neediness or the fears of encroachment are not to be judged, but we need to identify and take responsibility for them so that they do not unconsciously sabotage our best efforts.

It is important to take compassionate responsibility for our inner needs, while realizing that we cannot wait for good feelings to be delivered to our front door like chocolates. By taking responsibility, you become less dependent on praise and love from others, because you are able to give those to yourself. As we give up secret, childish ways of demanding love, gradually the childhood emptiness is neutralized through self-love.

As we separate our childhood needs, the adult needs begin to tell us what our unique path in life is. We begin to seek our purpose.

Now let's explore more of our adult needs. When I study the authentic expressions of people I have counseled, their adult needs become apparent. Besides the basic physical needs, adults have needs for personal growth, self-expression, meaningful connection, and the realization of their potential. Once I learned to separate and respect childhood deprivations, I was able to free my adult self to bring more passion to my life and work. Writing is a direct manifestation of my own focus in this area.

Our adult needs *never* require others to give us what we want. The adult need for love and companionship can only be fulfilled when we are ready to love and share. This is very different from the childhood need to be loved. If we think we are ready for love, but through some fate of the universe it has not come our way, we are still operating with a cloaked childhood need for a perfect parent. When we accept this as separate from it, love will come to us. Willingness to enter this awareness will begin an energetic process where inner constrictions relax and love flows. That is the great mystery of it all. When we come out of our self-delusion, we can flow life and trust the universe to meet our needs.

I am always amazed when I watch people do their own rituals. The world begins to provide them with exactly what they need. It is as if they draw gratification to themselves. As the process continues, we realize that we can obtain fulfillment, contentment, pleasure, and happiness.

The following ritual begins to open the door to one's life purpose. I am reminded again of the old axiom: "The diamonds are in your own back yard." When we clear our vision by untangling our adult and childhood needs, we are better able to see the diamonds.

GROW-UP RITUAL

State the intention that you will notice the inner energetic, demanding pulls, pushes and tugs in your relations with others in your world, or the world itself with greater clarity. Whenever you notice one, at your first opportunity, quietly go into ritual space. Make yourself comfortable and find your energetic grounding. Curiously notice as you bring awareness to your body so you can access the "felt senses" of whatever your body is experiencing. Notice your breath. Now bring forth in your awareness the situation that caused you to feel the tug of unmet childhood needs being acted out in your present life. Notice the felt sense of it in your body and follow that sense back to your childhood, like following a string of yarn backwards through long twisting hallways. Follow it back to a golden room full of feeling and see what images come to your awareness. Take whatever comes. When you find an earlier, previously repressed incident associated with the feeling, ask yourself an even more important question: "How much of my present demanding is based on past factors, i.e., factors charged with earlier emotion? How much of it is present-day appropriate?"

Using your incredible imagination (that is, without limits) notice the image you have and then imagine that it was different—corrected in some way. Now imagine you had the opposite experience and your need was met. However unlikely in real-time, circle the corrective, fulfilling image and invite your body to connect with it. Notice the felt sensations gradually giving them room (space & time) to be exactly as they are, continuing to notice what happens next. You may begin to gradually experience expansiveness. Allow as much space and time as you are able, and keep noticing. At some point, bring some of the expansive energy to the edge of the original image where you felt the tug that brought you into this ritual. Allow the two energies to touch at their edges, or peripheries, just softly bringing your attention to the demarcation line between them. Don't try to make anything happen; just give space and time, gently noticing as your body transforms and heals in its own mysterious, organic manner.

Take a piece of paper and divide it into two columns. Make a list on the left-hand side of all the outer, solid, real factors in your life about which it is clearly appropriate to experience fear. List dangers that you feel your fear and unhappiness are trying to tell you to do something about. Leave a line of space after each entry. Then, in the right-hand column, make a list of all the fears and sorrows that are not attached to present-day circumstances, or are things you cannot do anything about. You can include fears from childhood, adolescence, even recent fears. You can include anything you like, events, heartbreaks, unmet needs, poor choices, and so forth. Again, leave a line of space after each entry. Underneath each entry on the left, write-in the one best thing that came out of that situation in the long run. For example, "Death of mother—met lost cousin at funeral and became friends." "Car crash—learned I can survive almost anything if I really want to." "Loss of job—felt a sense of freedom from crabby boss and learned new skills." You may even have to stretch it to the point of what might seem like insincerity, but the effort may change the way you perceive and live life. If you find an entry you can't make a happy ending out of, think of something you can do in the future that will bring it to a meaningful conclusion. This type of ritual is one of the most powerful of all. For example, "Was homeless for two years. As part of my Grow Up Ritual, I will volunteer and work in a homeless shelter for two years, part time." "Dog killed by car. Will volunteer to work with PETA, and will adopt a pet from a pound that plans to put him to sleep."

Then take a look at the items on the right hand column, and think about what you can do in the future to eliminate those fears while benefiting others. Each answer should not depend on another person taking care of it for you. Underneath each entry, write in your insights.

As you complete your two lists, bless them in whatever manner feels right to you, and say to yourself, "May these fears be released, may I be guided by a higher power which is stronger than my fears. I am no longer a child, I am no longer a victim, and I no longer wait for other people to decide my fate. I am an adult. I have grown up!"

If you have any bioenergetic blockages while performing the ritual, return to them gently. Bring compassion and new understanding to them, and observe without judgment. Repeat the first part of this ritual every time you feel another demanding tug. It only takes a few minutes. Before you realize it, you will do it automatically, like it's second nature—which it is.

By practicing these techniques regularly, we become familiar with what works for us. Have fun with them; try out any variations that come to mind in a spirit of playfulness.

Me & My Shadow

As we grew up, we received messages that all expressions of need were either "good" or "bad." We decided which of our characteristics were acceptable to society, and which ones needed to be hidden. Unfortunately, some of the characteristics that are considered bad never go away. They create their own domain in the dark corners of our personalities and eventually take on lives of their own. These dark corners constitute what Carl Jung called the "Shadow." Because the shadow-self has enormous hidden energy, it can become a warty monster lurching around the repressed regions of our psyche when it is out of our conscious control. We have our whole lives to gradually unravel the mystery of accessing our shadow-self to keep more of our connectedness to spirit alive. Most people put it off too long. Here's hoping you won't!

We will shortly engage in a Shadow Ritual to help shed light on some potential psychological pitfalls. If at any time the shadow material or forthcoming hardship-healing ritual material overwhelms you, stop and put it aside for awhile. Find your familiar resources: Go back to Breath Ritual and Prayer Ritual. Then revisit these areas with a fresh mind.

Carl Jung referred to the shadow as a "dumping ground" for all the characteristics we disown. He believed that to honor and accept one's own shadow is a profound spiritual discipline. Author and therapist Robert A. Johnson called this acceptance "the most important experience of a lifetime" because it makes us whole again. Some theorists refer to the shadow-self as the lower, destructive self. The pejorative connotations of "lower" create a strong negative value judgment that can keep us from understanding its meaning in this context, and therefore is not useful to the process of self-acceptance.

The attributes of the *shadow-self* are different for each person. For some people these are aggressiveness, violence, and destructive desires. For others, they are secret sexual desires like incest, fetishes, or sadomasochism. Still others use this consciousness to store their cynicism, jealousy, and mean streak. Conversely, vulnerability, tenderness, and loving exploration may be relegated to the shadow-self. There is an early developmental stage when traits that the ego sees as negative are repressed. This enormous energy encoded in our bodies and psyches festers there, begging to be released. Hence, the shadow!

When our feet are in the fire and our soul tested mightily by the bitter winds of misfortune, we want to be able to tap into the hidden power of the shadow-self, not to harm or take advantage of others, but to ensure that we won't harm others. By knowing the terrain of our inner darkness, we won't suddenly find ourselves at the mercy of our own hidden vampires and goblins that cause us to isolate ourselves just when we most need to reach out for help and resource.

The shadow-self encases more of our concealed spirit and innate intelligence than any other aspect within us. But the shadow-self is also full of judgment, fear, hatred, and cruelty. As we bring it into conscious awareness, it unites with our adult self and our resource energy, allowing us to become whole.

Larger than Our Shadows

The endeavor to integrate our shadow-self is well worth the grapple. In maturity we can responsibly handle the integration we couldn't deal with in earlier years. As we embrace the concept and experience of vibrant living we will come to embrace and integrate both the shadow and the light. Once more, it is the dance of these opposite energies that generates new energy fields within us that enormously affect all that we do and are. Once transformed and brought into the light, shadow energies bless us immeasurably. We need to make ourselves larger to contain and accept these unconscious paradoxical aspects of self—primitive, contradictory, devouring, destructive, and weak—along with those that better reflect who we really are. We must make ourselves so large that all our parts can coexist peaceably. We must always remember that we are larger than our limitations.

Awareness and Transformation of Shadow Energy

Whatever one's shadow-self attributes may be, there appears to be a powerful sexual force—or the denial thereof—central to the understanding and discovery of this realm. It is a mythic, primal force that will get copious attention in the *Vibrant Eros* section (Chapters Twelve, Thirteen, and Fourteen) on *Erotic Rituals*. For many of us the shadow aspects of our personality are encased in a cocoon of shame. Shame often manifests itself as a barrier. Only when we are willing to dissolve this barrier through the felt senses of the body will the shadow-self begin to enlighten our liberation process. Seen in the light, without judgments, the shadow turns out to be alive, passionate and luscious. Once freed and accepted, with respectful management it can guide our lives truly and richly, through stormy seas or smooth sailing.

I interpret the relationship between the shadow-self and holism as follows: The mask of composure that we present to the world was created by our ego defenses in childhood to keep us safe and help us get through life. The shadow is the flip side of that mask, an under-belly swarming with all the repressed opposites. Sometimes these shadow elements seem extreme or very charged because of repression's "inherent defiance" and the raging vigor it contains. In the act of repression, there is a natural organic force and defiance that our bodies are begrudgingly obliged to live with. This mask of composure can be flipped over by both internal and external triggers when we least expect it. Though this is an oversimplification, a quick glance at our shadow will illustrate the importance of its integration if we are to achieve real fullness of being.

SHADOW INTEGRATION RITUAL: PART ONE

Find the most comfortable place possible to sit on the floor (on a pillow or low chair). Sit there for a few minutes in a darkened room, with a lit candle to your right, positioned so that your body casts a shadow on a wall to your left. (If there is no wall, simply note the shadow on the floor.) Immediately to your left, place an unlit candle on the floor or low surface between yourself and the wall. As you settle in, remind yourself that "this sitting" is done with the intention of transforming shadow elements in the fabric of your being. As you begin to notice the felt senses of your body, notice where your body parts are touching whatever you are sitting on, and notice what your breathing is like. Simply drop into your Curious Observer, that part of you that can

notice all without judgment or agenda. As you do so,
recall a moment in your life when you felt very alive, in a
positive, constructive way—a meaningful moment. Take
whatever comes without editing. Look towards the lit
candle and gaze gently into the flame. Feel its warmth
of color entering your consciousness, underscoring the
beauty of your recollections. "Circle" the loveliest aspect
of that imagery experience in your mind. Now close your
eyes and invite your body to connect with the image. Let
the candle's light shine through your closed eye lids. As
this connection occurs, remembering that slow can be
fast, curiously observe any body sensations you become
aware of. As you do so, invite yourself to give those
sensations time and space. Give even more time and space
to whatever is happening, noticing if anything changes.
Continue to do this until your body begins to feel very
calm and present. Perhaps you'll detect an energy or
aliveness running through your whole body, or parts of
it. There may even be color or textures to this energy.
Allow yourself to just notice. This is a place of resource
and expansiveness. We want to remind ourselves that this
expansiveness is our ground of being: it is most central
to who we are. We can draw on this energy at will; we
can also gently put this energy aside and still return to it
when we want to.

Now, from this place of resource, I'm going to ask you
to gently shift to something about yourself you'd prefer
others did not know. Just let your Curious Observer
notice what pops up, no need to edit. Turn your head to
the left and touch your shadow on the floor. Trust your
body's intelligence. When you have something in your
mind's eye, just let it settle there for a moment, while you

invite your body to connect with the thought or image. Notice what begins to happen in your body, what changes occur in your breathing and your felt senses. Focus on the unlit candle. Let it symbolize the things about your inner workings that you do not yet understand or don't want to look at. Then look at the shadow on the wall that your body is projecting. Is this how you see yourself when you are feeling angry, jealous, greedy, and fearful? Do other people see this shadow? Whatever insights come to your mind at this time are completely valid, an "inkblot test" if you will. You may feel a constriction or contraction of some kind. If you do, just give it time and space, curiously noticing if anything happens next. Perhaps you suddenly feel butterflies in your stomach followed by tightness in the back of your neck. Trust that the body has mysterious ways of bringing things to our attention, elaborating on them, and then transforming them.

Once you feel that a glimmer of new understanding has entered your being about the importance of looking at and working with your shadow, pick up the unlit candle with your left hand and give it to your right hand. Now gently shift back to that earlier image of when you felt very alive. Notice as you return whether the body sensations are the same as before or if there are any nuanced changes. Notice if you can find that resource, that place of expansiveness you found earlier, or a similar one. If you can, just hang out with it for a bit, allowing it to heal you. Notice if there might be a color, feeling, or light to the energy.

Light the unlit candle with the lit one, then pass it slowly back to the left hand and place it on the floor to the left. Contemplate the difference in the mixture of shadow and light that takes place, dancing there together on the wall. They are no longer separate. Now there is light and shadow to your left, and to your right. Take whatever distinctive, pleasurable qualities that energy held for you and begin, in your own way, to bring that energy over to the edge of the contraction in the shadow image you had. In whatever way feels natural to you, allow the resource energy to touch the contracted energy right at the edges. Give yourself time and allow the process to be organic, no "trying," no pushing, just trusting that you can somehow invite these two opposite energies together, allowing them to touch in any way that seems right, all the while curiously observing. Continue to do this until you get a felt sense in your body that feels new, grounded and empowered. Also be aware of any images or thoughts that may want to be illuminated as firm inner instruction and a base for further transformation.

Use any part of this ritual that works for you: change it, play with it, and add to it. Remember, it's *your* ritual. Each of the experiments presented in this text are meant to be open-ended. If for any reason you got stuck somewhere doing the above Shadow Integration Ritual, return to self-compassion, appreciate your willingness to experiment, and come back to it in a few days. You may have a very different experience next time. The same holds true for Part Two of the ritual below.

SHADOW INTEGRATION RITUAL: PART TWO

Write on a piece of paper no one will ever see, two column headings, "I love it when …" and "I hate it when …" In the first column, write down all the things you enjoy that you feel guilty about or ashamed of. Really, let yourself get outrageous. Let forbidden pleasures and indulgences come to your mind. No one will know what you write, except you; and that's the whole point! In the second column, write down a list of your pet peeves, hatreds and fears, loathing, complaints, blasphemies. Now fold the piece of paper and write on the outside: "I am capable of monitoring my own actions. I harm no one, and am therefore free to think and feel whatever I need to think and feel." Then bless the paper with your self-love and self-compassion, asking that such thoughts and feelings be directed to the highest good and purpose. Then burn it or rip it up and let it go.

Ritual is like any practice, and it must be taken in that light. Over time we become more proficient, but for now even practice produces tangible results.

Trauma Transformation and Vibrant Living

> This energy we work with in the healing of trauma
> will significantly increase our ability to achieve both
> our individual and collective dreams.
>
> PETER A. LEVINE

As we continue to explore Trauma Resolution, I hope you will understand the value of Chapter Seven's "Grow Up" and "Shadow Integration" rituals. Both are entry points to the transformation of all the traumas that shape and limit our daily lives.

Trauma Healing and Vibrant Living Share Roots

Trauma healing is at the heart of all energetic healing because lingering reactions to trauma make everyday challenges more difficult. Trauma makes growing up much more complicated. It can cause ungovernable fear in natural situations that call for reasonable caution. Trauma scrambles our delicate self-regulating energy systems and makes them malfunction. Because trauma complicates the clinical situation, many mechanistic models of healing and "talk therapy" don't always work. Traumas are monkey wrenches in our bodies. Energetic healing is the resource and antidote for trauma's constrictions and physical injuries resulting from our body-mind-nature imbalance.

In Chapter Three, I shared a respectable foundation for trauma healing. It was important early on to plant seeds for what we will further develop here. In traditional psychotherapy, trauma and its effects are part of the hard focus on "what's wrong with us." In *Trauma Transformation Rituals* the focus is on reconnecting with and discovering resources, what's *right* about us, how our complex organic bioenergetic system works, and how it can heal itself.

My life has been formed and informed by trauma, and trauma healing has become my central learning and teaching. Obviously not everyone has the kinds of early traumas I did. But I've found that most of us suffer from more traumas and internal traumatic conflicts than we're aware of. They are built into our culture and are pretty much universal. Our so-called civilized culture *is* traumatizing, as is every culture. We get traumatized in subtle and not-so-subtle ways by the expectations society puts on us with binary morality and linear thinking that both condition and constrict us; for example, being made to feel "less than" because you are have a sexually variant nature, or you're a Muslim, a woman, a person of color, or you have physical or emotional challenges.

Traumas can be dramatic or subtle. Sometimes they are shocking events that happen in a moment in time in battle or a car crash or a cancer diagnosis. Sometimes they are low-grade threats to our sense of safety and acceptance in the world, which slowly and insidiously throw our nervous system out of whack. The lingering effects of both forms can be quite the same. We are traumatized whenever life stomps on our life force, passion, curiosity, or love.

Traumas live repressed in our bodies–in our psyche, in our central nervous system, in our sinews–either re-enacting themselves or restricting our life force through visceral, physiological fear. Their effect on our entire organism is one of the major causes of disease, the most obvious ones being addiction, chronic fatigue syndrome, fibro-myalgia, irritable bowel syndrome, depression, panic disorders, anxi-ety, chronic pain, etc. Repressed trauma energy in the body causes some of these ailments and others it exacerbates. It is a prominent, often overlooked, cofactor in most diseases. This constrictive trauma energy weakens our autonomic nervous system, our immune system, our neurobiology, and our body's electromagnetic field.

Putting physical health aside for a moment, we can notice how traumas also impact our relationships. They pose emotional and physical challenges to all our unions with others. Unhealed repressed trauma can annihilate relationships.

As Peter Levine writes in *Waking the Tiger*, "Trauma is like a straightjacket that binds the mind and body in frozen fear. Paradoxi-cally, it is also a portal that can lead us to awakening and freedom." Trauma resolution cannot be understood cerebrally–it must be expe-rienced. So, as I attempt to explain how it works, please know that I am struggling to verbalize something that can only be experienced. Transforming trauma requires fusing (or touching at the edge) the energy frozen in the "trauma vortex" of our central nervous system with its polar opposite energy in the "healing (or resource) vortex." Fortunately, our miraculous systems continue to demonstrate that once we learn access to energetic healing we always have ample resource energy to counter-balance and renegotiate the trauma energy.

I have learned most about this sort of transformation by doing my own healing. I began to engage in body and energy-oriented therapies at about the same time. First I worked with Polarity Massage, then Rubenfeld Synergy, then Bio-Energetics and Core-Energetics; then The Wave Work®, Healing Imagery, Holotropic Breathwork, and Somatic Experiencing®. Many people have never heard of these heal-ing pathways, perhaps because they didn't need to search as conscien-tiously as I did. To the average reader these methods may sound like New Age modalities. They are not—many draw on ancient traditions.

When Dr. Stanislav Grof had to discontinue his promising research with LSD in the sixties because of its misuse, he was stumped. He had learned that by accessing nonordinary states of consciousness new dimensions of healing were available to us. Out of his desire to continue his research, he discovered ancient breathing and rhythm techniques, and crafted them into his Holotropic Breathwork process. The Wave Work® process was distilled from very refined and ancient yogic traditions. The surprising powers of Healing Imagery I studied with Dr. Gerald Epstein, were techniques of medicine used thousands of years ago in Egypt.

Most significant healing can only occur in what Stan Grof and Ken Wilbur refer to as "nonordinary" environments. When extraordinary things happened to us, we must do extraordinary things to heal ourselves—things like learning how to hear our bodies talk and guide us. This is where ritual comes in. It's all about nonordinary environments, be they private or shared.

Peter Levine writes:

> *If you are experiencing strange symptoms that no one seems able to explain, they could be arising from a traumatic reaction to a past event that you may not even remember. You are not alone. You are not crazy. There is a rational explanation for what is happening to you. You have not been irreversibly damaged, and it is possible to diminish or even eliminate your symptoms.*

Below are the five basic types of trauma I've come to know:

THE FIVE BASIC TYPES OF TRAUMA

1. Physical Trauma: accidents, surgery, illness, anesthesia, assaults.

2. Emotional Trauma: abandonment, terror (from bewildering rage behavior of another in developmental years, or horrifying exposures), humiliation, neglect, ridicule, encroachment (the feeling of having a caretaker in childhood, or siblings, highjack your life force).

3. Sexual Trauma: rape, molestation, unhealthy or premature exposure to sexual energy or acts, emotional (or covert) incest (becoming the energetic spousal equivalent to a seductive parent or guardian, without overt sex), and cultural ignorance that teaches that sexual pleasure (and diversity) is bad and shameful.

4. Endurance Trauma: a prolonged sense of feeling unsafe in one's world during childhood and/or later life. An example of this is being a child of an alcoholic or mentally ill parent. Often from day to day, the child does not know when the next crisis or traumatic episode will occur. They lie in wait as their autonomic nervous system gets fixed in fearful posture.

5. Developmental Trauma (DT): This always includes some or all of the above. The term reminds us that we were traumatized during our developmental years. DT directly relates to what shocked our self-regulatory systems and organic evolution (i.e. mothers who abused substances during pregnancy) from conception through our teen years. Many of us enter therapy today as a result of the barriers that DT causes in our adult lives, and the way it makes us act out in self-destructive patterns.

Torture, war, and other violent situations often twine together complex ropes of these five basic types of trauma. We may experience flashbacks, sudden panic, chronic sadness, and anxiety as a result of both old and new traumas. In many cases, we may feel shame. We may look to drugs to ease our pain. The good news is that progressive members of the healing community are learning more effective ways of healing all forms of trauma.

Moving Forward with Trauma Transformation

If we want to explore trauma transformation for ourselves or a loved one, what's most important is that we keep an open mind and heart. We may need to experience something our rational, linear mind has never considered. Our Curious Observer reminds us that we are larger than our thinking minds. Be willing to experiment if something feels right in your body and mind, and note any results.

In this form of healing and transformation, again, slow is fast. Trust yourself to do what makes sense to you without overwhelming yourself. Move only as fast as you are prepared to without being overwhelmed. Being overwhelmed sabotages all efforts to transform traumatic energies.

We are conditioned to resist directly examining the overwhelming experiences of our lives. Inherent cultural fear and lack of skills in this area hold us back. If we are going to create and participate in trauma healing rituals, a sense of hopefulness as a resource is helpful before we begin. Chapter Fourteen, "Transformation," of *Waking the Tiger* tells us this:

> *For a traumatized person, the journey toward a vital, sponta-neous life means more than alleviating symptoms—it means transformation.... Transformation is the process of changing something in relation to it's polar opposite.... Through trans-formation, the nervous system regains its capacity for self-regulation. Our emotions begin to lift us up rather than bring us down. They propel us into the exhilarating ability to soar and fly, giving us a more complete view of our place in nature. Our perceptions broaden to encompass receptivity and accep-tance of what is, without judgment.... Trust rather than anxi-ety, forms the field in which all experience occurs.*

As an SE practitioner who has worked with many severely trau-matized people, I know his words to be true. It is awesome to behold! This is a vivid example of turning our reality inside out. I speak here not just of shock trauma—physical, sexual, and such—but also of developmental trauma—all that growing-up stuff. Who would have ever thought we could take the most horrible events of life and, in a ritualized format, gracefully transmute them into aliveness, resilience, and creativity? It was a shocking revelation for me, one that I feel blessed to share.

In SE or any other Trauma Transformation Ritual, we are able to gradually reregulate the nervous system around traumatic episodes that are locked inside us. In the instant the regulation occurs, more calm and resource energy immediately emerges. We gradually learn from this ritual to find our resource energies, know them in the felt sense of our bodies, and then allow trauma memories to surface organically with whatever felt sense they are connected to. We then go back and forth between the two opposite physical experiences, gradually allowing one to touch the edge of the other. In doing so, we prove to ourselves what Levine suggested above, that "transformation is the process of changing something in relation to it's polar opposite." This process of healing is innate, a natural reorganization of a nervous system that was thrown out of whack. Trauma Transformation Rituals create an environment where such healing is possible.

Again, we find ourselves discussing opposite energies: explicitly expansive vs. explicitly contractive energies. Resource is expansive. When you feel contractive, you feel all dressed up with no place to go. The foot is on the accelerator and the brake at the same time. A lot of energy is going into the system but it too has nowhere to go, because we're contracted, and we burn out.

Ever felt sadness, depression, feelings of inadequacy, deadness? These are among the activation energies that create contraction. So are anxiety, hyperactivity, rage, and mania. This activation and contraction manifests differently in all of us. For some, it provides an addictive jolt of short-term energy, like dumping extra sugar in your coffee. For others, it takes the wind out of their sails or makes them do the foolish things usually caused by alcohol or drugs. Resource energy is, of course, the opposite of this and can be used to melt activation, creating transformation and more wholeness. Such an experience is then integrated, meaning it is ingested, digested, and metabolized. This transformative experience is not an emotional or intellectual journey; it's an instinctive one that then informs the emotional and the intellectual processes.

Below I will suggest a most simple Trauma Transformation Ritual that you can experiment with yourself. While a great deal of this internal reorganization can be done on one's own, it can be done more effectively and gracefully with a knowledgeable practitioner. This next ritual is a very safe one to start. It comes from Diane and Larry Heller's *Crash Course: A Self-Healing Guide to Auto Accident Trauma & Recovery.* They define trauma as "… any event that breaks the body's stimulus barrier, leading to overwhelming feelings of help-lessness." They offer this Boundary Rupture Ritual as a way to begin a relationship by discovering the body's felt senses where you may have ruptures related to past trauma. It is adapted from a bound-ary rupture exercise, originally designed by Darrel Sanchez, a trauma recovery specialist in Boulder, Colorado.

BOUNDARY RUPTURE RITUAL

Imagine that you are sitting or standing in a sphere. Gradually become aware of all 360 degrees around you. In doing this you are finding attunement with yourself. Try to sense the direction where you feel the safest and most protected so we can determine where your boundaries are most intact. This helps you become aware of what boundaries feel like energetically and to discover how you experience safety and protection in your body. You are now focusing your energy. Always start from where the boundaries feel most intact and build from strength. You may be astonished how exact you are in detecting the specific line of demarcation between what feels safe spatially and where the lack of safety begins. You may be able to literally draw a line in space once your attention is focused in this area. When you are working with a therapist, it is important to make sure that the area they are sitting in does not coincide with your area of boundary rupture. If they do sit in this area, you may have a sense of danger or activation rather than feeling helped by their presence. Or you may prefer them there (as a resource).

To continue the ritual, examine the next safest direction. Find resources to strengthen that area. Now you are amplifying the energy. How would your body want to add protection? Would it like a shield or the presence of a friendly protective ally? You are now directing the energy. As that direction gets stronger and you feel safer, go on to explore the next area until eventually you feel supported and safe from all directions. You may now remember different traumatic experiences you've encountered and thought were already resolved. This ritual reveals important information that only tapping into the boundary awareness seems to be able to provide.

When experimenting with the above ritual, if you find it a struggle to connect to the body's felt senses, it's time to remember self-compassion. Certain things come easier to some than others. If this is the case, try doing it again, only this time take a deep breath first, remind yourself there is no right or wrong outcome, drop into your Curious Observer, and notice even the slightest body sensations, allowing them time and space to develop. Welcome any images that may come. Many people do better the second time around. For those who can't get out of their heads on the first try or find themselves easily distracted, this too we must make loving room for. If you feel unsuccessful in the practice of this ritual, get a friend or practitioner to support your process. Sometimes just having a supportive person helping to hold the space can make a dramatic difference.

To explore Trauma Transformation Rituals in depth, I encourage people to work with a trusted practitioner who specializes in trauma resolution. It makes good sense to get in touch with all the resources available to you. This book includes several approaches to trauma resolution. It is not intended to be the be-all and end-all guide to trauma resolution, yet it goes to the core of trauma, demonstrates the healing basics, and advocates using Trauma Healing Rituals as a conduit to vibrant living.

Remember that we all access resources in our own manner and at our own pace. For more extensive exposure to the promise made here, and for many specific resources for trauma healing, check out these two websites: www.theinstitute.org/trauma.shtml and www.trauma-healing.com.

In exploring the roots that trauma healing and vibrant living share, it becomes evident that new, calmer, and more expansive energies become available to us. The balance of this chapter is devoted to helping the new energies made available through our Old Brain in trauma resolution to get in a new sync with our New Brain. This integration is done by considering frameworks of waves and principles through which we can direct these energies toward the vibrant living that this book is about.

Waves of Vibrant Living

As new energies become available to us, changing our thinking and behavior becomes easier and more graceful. I know this from experience and offer attitudes and principles I've discovered to help these energies move through us in a good way. I invite you to take what you want and leave the rest. These are only suggestions on how to develop a new sense of who you are and what it is you really want.

We've all had attitude changes at one time or another. In this new playground of vibrant living we want to take full, conscious responsibility for this ability to catch a new wave, to shift our heart, never forgetting that our aliveness depends on it.

As soon as we see the dynamism is gone in our present connection, if it can't be brought back pronto, then it may be time to move on. While being static may have been seen as a positive attribute, we know today it can be spiritual death. I've hung around a few relationships and organizations long after the juice was gone, out of some twisted kind of loyalty or fear of changing. Quite honestly, all those experiences taught me was how to fall back into what I now know as contraction. That is like the walking-dead experience of my childhood. Moving on when I finally saw the light was like a rebirth. A warm gentle wave of energy was able to move through me once again. How sweet! I never want to forget that I am responsible for keeping myself in either expansive or contractive relationships. Prayer, focused intention, and creative ritual can help us shift with the winds that call to us and allow new waves to move through us.

Here are some waves that I have found worth riding. They are useful for accessing the many communities that have sprung up on the Internet amidst a rapidly changing political, economic, and social structure—an accelerated dance of people connecting to accomplish certain goals and then moving on. This will trigger a chain of vibrant living that is so powerful, there's no telling where you'll end up. In fact, you won't know how good it gets till you get there.

Wave of Fluidity: First of all, fluidity is key. Don't get stuck, get *resourced*. Practice your ability to change roles, rules, plans, expectations, if the present ones are not panning out. Don't ram through obstacles. Go around them. Be able to enter into a new friendship or community without any expectations.

With this fluidity comes the ability to be considerate and yet respectfully frank with any new people you connect with, especially when things don't work out and you choose to part company. The more comfortable you are in ending a social situation, the more comfortable you can be in entering one. It is not fair to make demands that a group is not designed to meet or that a person is not trained to handle. We need to be able to negotiate and even initiate rapid changes in our chosen social group. If we are to stay on the cutting edge in terms of resources, we cannot afford to be rigid in our thinking. Try to avoid shallow generalizations and ask questions instead. We need to be able to be wrong or confused, to admit it, and to move on.

Wave of Abundance: Thanks to global news media, travel, and the worldwide Web, we can now see how infinite the playground of healing and other resources have become. They have always been this infinite, inwardly speaking. We have just been cut off from them as a culture. Ritual allows us to Google the universe and find inner resources we need when we need them. Shamans have known this for thousands of years and have always known abundance even in sparse, isolated terrains. Dandelion or clover can help cure a disease. In the right hands, a fungus can help light a fire. Sometimes the difference between abundance and suffering is know-how. It is important to have the attitude that you never know what you'll find or where you'll end up. Everything whatsoever is a mystery waiting to be solved. On this infinite playground, the experience of vibrant living can happen in all seven directions: east, south, west, north, up, down, and back to the center—all at once.

Not only can each person we meet connect us to others, but each group or organization can potentially be a wave to multiple resources as well. Develop the ability to make authentic conversation with strangers you meet whom you think might be good resources for you. However, try to go beyond small talk and use conversation as a linking tool to gain access to their knowledge, as well as to be friendly and caring—in other words, to become a resource for them. Earnest giving is always the best way to receive. One strategy to making ordinary conversation into an effective abundance tool is to remember to share with that person fairly early on what your current interests are, what kind of resources you have at your disposal, and what resources you're looking for from the universe. You'll be amazed at how fluidly you can make this happen without being inappropriate. This can save a lot of time. When developing connectivity, it is important to remember your first connection may not be the best one. If you are in scarcity mode, you will attach yourself to the first available port in the storm and not be able to enjoy all the subsequent resources provided by other communities and individuals.

Wave of Selectivity: In vibrant living we again borrow the phrase from 12-Step programs: "Take what you want and leave the rest." Many people and communities want us to agree to and commit to all the points on their agenda, to blend completely into their way of being, to be a loyal follower. We need to maintain our sovereignty as individuals and receive what we can from any given person or group without being pulled under and subsumed in a tangled web of conformity. Those who live vibrant lives are not followers but come to the table as humble but equal partners in the journey. We don't expect to agree on every point, but we are willing listeners. We evaluate our experience with a person or in a group by how much resource we can bring to the table minus the cost in resources it took to acquire it. We may have to sift through five tons of emotional slag to find two ounces of spiritual gold, but if it's authentic soul substance, it may be worth the trouble! If it's not, move on. Trust your body and let your feet do the voting. In our new wave of selectivity, *we* decide what is gold and what isn't, and *we* choose to move on or stay.

The Wave of Self-Reliance: To live vibrantly, we have to hold a strong bargaining position. That means being strong enough to go it alone. We all have a unique destiny. To realize it, we have to be able to move effectively in any direction we need to. We have to be reasonably able to take care of ourselves. Access the Five Wisdoms! These include being authentic, community-based healing, shared intentionality, shared belief, and grounding through resources. These are the keys to building all relationships and communities, and not getting thrown off center by arm-twisting recruiters and ideologues.

The Wave of Thinking Outside the Box: One wave we need to cultivate to really juice up our ability to get more out of our lives, relationships, and communities for healing and vibrant living is thinking outside the box. The energy needs to stay vibrant; it has to keep flowing. Our enthusiasm for the learning process can't get bottled up in a logjam of relationships or thinking. Just as individuals have occasional contractions of energy, so do relationships and groups. Occasional contraction is unavoidable, but combined with expansion we can feel whole. It's hard to expand inside a box, unless we are at an emotional place where the box provides the temporary sanctuary we need. In this case, it's just a matter of timing and self-trust. Animals and plants in captivity never grow quite as large as those in the wild, which have more room to grow. A flower pot is a good place to plant an acorn, but a bad place to grow it into a tree. If any of us were that acorn, we'd want the whole earth under our roots. The choice to stay or move on is yours. If you have a choice between being a warm body for someone's head count, being a dynamic and vibrant resource for your own evolution or for that of many people, choose the direction your feet tell you to move in. The possible exception to this is if you have already committed yourself. In that case it's a more complex self-negotiation and can be instructive about avoiding similar commitments in the future. This is a big part of vibrant living.

Vibrant Living Principles

The following are principles I've learned and live by:

Instant Verification: In vibrant living, the focus is on energy: energetic creativity, energetic healing, energetic exchange, etc., so we experience an immediate feeling of belonging or not belonging to a given situation or community. There will be an instantaneous resonance if the energy is right. If it's not obvious, we will feel that quickly as well. Only fear can jam our radar. A couple of deep breaths and perhaps verbal or nonverbal connection with one or two people should reregulate the system till a clear choice becomes obvious. Vibrant living means being confident enough to trust in our choices and invest in them energetically and emotionally when they feel right (even if appearances are misleading) or to walk away when they feel wrong. When your emotional stomach is growling for nourishment, it takes guts to say there are other fish in the sea—but there are. If there are three or four obvious areas of synchronicity with any one person or group, chances are you've hit on something worth saving and savoring. If it were me, I'd lower anchor for a while and enjoy the day.

Attraction: To stumble through the vast field of false promises, we need to be a little bit selfish, but ethically so. We need to shamanistically invoke the energy of the bumble bee and allow ourselves to be attracted to this person or group and trust the attraction provisionally, if not inherently. We follow our bliss. In other words, if it doesn't feel right, don't do it, don't join it, don't buy it; otherwise you end up in a dead end of ever-diminishing resources. Now I will contradict myself, particularly regarding groups and communities. By this point in the book, I hope readers can hold contradictions as part of the larger whole that is often in our best interest. My experience has also shown that the beauty of community is not always blissful (even at the beginning). An individual might experience pain at the start of joining the organization. The pain is not in the organization, but in the individual's resistance to it. Sometimes the individual shouldn't follow their bliss, but they should follow their heart and intuition and stick it out even if it feels uncomfortable. Trusting your intuition, your timing, and the possibility for meaningful connection will usually guide you.

Bumble bees are drawn to the right flowers by the colors of the petals, and this includes not only colors within the visible spectrum, but also those in the invisible ultraviolet spectrum as well. Likewise, the reasons for our gravitation towards one person or group may not be visible to us. Nonetheless, it's important that we trust that attraction. Like the bumble bee, we are cross-pollinating as we go on our attraction-driven travels. Having this wave will energize relationships, networking, activism, and *dynamic linking* (which we will explore in Chapter Fifteen). It's okay to be concerned for self; it is encouraged, as long as it's respectful of oneself and others.

Rejection: Just as there is a law of attraction, there is a law of rejection as well. When we apply for a job we open ourself up to rejection. Remember to be grown-up about this (see Chapter Seven's Grow-Up Ritual). The people with whom we are interacting are not our parents. We would certainly want the right to reject *them* if we felt less than a "good fit" with them. We can see it as a mutual rejection process: If they reject us, there is probably something about them that wouldn't make a "good fit" for us. We would never be an excellent complement to each other.

It is a fast dance indeed, driven by attraction and intention, but it is driven by purpose: to find out who we are and what we can be. We need to look beyond these few bumps in the road. Rejection is just nature's way of telling us someone is barking up the wrong tree, but that doesn't make us the dog.

An example comes to mind: My last book was turned down by most of the major publishers. I struggled with the fact that many of them really liked it, but turned it down anyway. Most of the publishers' responses were versions of: "The recovery market is oversaturated. It's dying." I had to accept that since they were knowledgeable of the profit-driven publishing business, they had a right to say no. But it didn't feel good. After this rejection, through a series of coincidences I was introduced to the nonprofit publishing world, and most notably North Atlantic Books, where my book found a very respectful home and excellent distribution. Then I was surrounded by a team of dedicated people that were more invested in getting new ideas out into the world than in profit projections. We never know where the dance is going to lead.

Pray for Connectivity: All the various interpersonal, electronic and communication tools in the world are not going to help us to live energetically if we are totally out of synch with the universe and are stuck in zero connectivity, zero creativity, and zero intuition. It is absolutely essential that we work on developing our inner dynamics at the same time as we are exploring our outer resources, or we will just go in circles. It is our innate intelligence that intuitively connects the invisible dots somewhere out in a world waiting to be discovered that makes vibrant living really work. Those dots will eventually make up the unfolding picture of our spiritual future. That kind of intuition cannot be learned from a book; however, it can be expanded upon greatly through the principles stressed throughout *this* book: creative ritual, focused intention, and shared belief. Have you ever called someone out of the blue and found that they had an important piece of news for you? That's a form of vibrant living. If you do a ritual each morning, or even a simple prayer, asking to be blessed with connectivity, it's a good bet that your connectivity will increase two-fold, as you are addressing the Old Brain directly, that source of our mysterious ability to draw what we desire into our lives. People offering you the answers you need are much more likely to call you out of the blue if you are asking the universe for help with connectivity. The same is true of using the Internet. There are millions of Web sites to be found on the Internet, available through any search engine, and that sea of data can be a maze of dead ends or a sea of exotic fish. Through developing intuition and that lucky feeling that spirit can give us, we can cut right through the ice and catch some very nice fish. Later, when we explore the dynamic linking of this vibrancy in our lives, we'll see how the two energies work hand-in-hand to bring about amazing progress in our lives.

Shared Intention: Any person, community, or resource group we encounter may have certain intentions and goals we share, and some we don't. As long as we are comfortable with this and don't consider these "cold" areas to be unethical, focus on the "hot" areas where you share the same vision as the others. They may teach you something about those other areas.

Know Your Baggage: When we scan the inner universe for resources, it is best to take with us as little baggage as possible, as it only inhibits our flight of imagination and blocks communication. Likewise, when we go out into the world to live vibrantly with other people and communities, we need to watch out for other people's baggage as we steer clear of our own. We understand the pace of this networking is swift, so we put our baggage in a safe storage place and expect others to do the same. If we get to a certain relationship or community and we keep tripping over unnecessary baggage, we need to make sure it's not our own, and then try to have it removed, or simply go our own way. Overall, it is hard for us to know what burdens are necessary or unnecessary for other people to carry. We haven't walked a mile in their moccasins. But if the baggage is more than we can handle, we should make a point of walking away without judgment or interference. Baggage is that which is not being communicated or is getting in the way of real communication.

Effective Compassionate Communication: According to Marshall B. Rosenberg's research in nonviolent communication, there are four steps to negotiating ones' needs that keep the lines of communication open.

STEP ONE: Observe what is happening in a given situation.

STEP TWO: Identify what one is feeling.

STEP THREE: Identify what one is needing.

STEP FOUR: Make a request for what one would like to see occur.

If this is not possible, there is probably more baggage floating around than at the baggage claim at O'Hare Airport. However, giving the four steps a shot may be worth the progress you get from practicing this Communication Ritual. After some practice, it has become the way I naturally communicate. It's an art that has never failed me. Rosenberg's findings are priceless gems.

Start Slow: Without naming it, vibrant living may already be present in your life, but only you can know how ready you are for vibrant living—to start it or to expand it. If you are new at it, start slow, go one step at a time, and pick up the pace naturally. Utilize friends and local grassroots organizations and find some of your waves there. If you know who you are and where you want to go, the train of high-speed global connectivity and intercommunity networking is already going full throttle, so jump on board. I am amazed at what's already available to us and have to modulate new engagements with self-care, always endeavoring to avoid falling into overwhelm. It's an interesting energetic edge to ride, and a new skill to build. We don't want so much aliveness and expansion that we start to fall apart. For me this modulation is a good daily practice of balance.

Although it may seem that this interlinking has come upon us very suddenly, it is the result of a trend towards greater interconnectivity. In the Protozoic era, significant events happened once every million years. Five hundred years ago, globally significant events started happening a few times a year, then once a month. Now they happen every few seconds. It's a warp-speed, superconductive world. Some choose to turn away from it all and find a slow simplicity in nature, but either way, remember that through ritual resourcing and tuning into the Old Brain we can break down in a minute what people used to take years to absorb. And ritual has been around for thousands of years.

Arriving at a New Future (Grounded in the Past)

In *Sleeper*, Woody Allen's character after realizing he has awakened two hundred years in the future says, "My analyst was a strict Freudian. If I'd lived all this time I'd be almost cured by now!" It's only been thirty years or so since that movie was released, but we have already arrived at Woody Allen's future. It is time to complete the journey of healing (utilizing ritual and other direct energetic tools) and move forward.

The old Newtonian/Cartesian paradigm of healing is grounded in materialist and mechanist models of reality, where body chemistry and energy patterns are fixed, except by interference from drugs, surgery, or some other therapy. It is difficult for this model to accommodate the idea that a shift in consciousness could trigger a shift in the material state of a person's body. When and if such shifts in consciousness do occur, they are expected to happen slowly as the person synthesizes a mental response to material changes in their body and world. The new quantum energy model of healing is based on energy, which is fluid, vibrant, illuminating, and can change like lightning. It also changes thought and material reality equally quickly, with a rhythm that's not bounded by time. Energy can work across distances as well as by direct contact, speeding up the healing process even more. Taking the quantum model, which many prominent scientists acknowledge they can't understand even when they work with it, and grounding that with the empirical research methods of the Newtonian worldview, we can combine the two different energies for a greater bandwidth of information and healing. This greater bandwidth is the holding together of two or more energies, without opposition, and noticing their innate potential to transform one another in a good way. This is what's gradually happening every day in the fusion of allopathic and holopathic medicine.

The above principles can be cultivated with practice. Move forward with ever increasing connectivity and a vision of acquiring a wide variety of high-quality resources and energies, information, communities, and personal contacts, and you have all the ingredients for vibrant living. Over time it will accelerate naturally as contacts multiply. Like everything else, there can be a shadow side to this kind of rapid expansion. I have watched myself and others periodically step back and find our grounding if the expansiveness becomes too much for us. It's all part of the dance if we respect ourselves first, listen to what our felt senses tell us we need, and then be respectful of others. There is a rhythm to expansion and contraction that must always be honored. The sooner we recognize how it works in us, the more graceful the transitions.

9

Specific Rituals for Tough Times

> If one advances confidently in the direction of his dreams, and endeavors to live the life he has imagined, he will meet with success unexpected in common hours.
>
> HENRY DAVID THOREAU

I've lived by these words for many years, and they have been a resource to me in some very tough times. While the wording is straight-forward, I've had to endure several raging storms to get back to their meaning. When I was eighteen years old and my bride-to-be had to have her leg amputated due to bone cancer, our dreams were annihilated. Later, when she was dying a hideous death, there was no time for dreams. When my own so-called terminal cancer hit resulting in two years of complete incapacitation, my dreams again were shattered. Then Gil, who literally carried me through those two years, was diagnosed with AIDS and I care-partnered him to his death several years later. Success unexpected in common hours, indeed! But there was. Sometimes without our even realizing it, in the midst of horrors, other worlds are opening. When I look back on the tragedies of my life, I see that I always emerged from them with new strength, imagining new dreams and trying to live them. These hardships (and others) have all taught me that we have an innate intelligence that wants us on an ascendant path, even if we don't realize it at the time. This chapter is intended to help us know this capacity and to have it with us, especially in those tough times.

Now we've practiced some ritual and felt what it can do—how it acts as a key to open doors to resources within and transforms everyday challenges into spiritual opportunities. Let us now apply those same principles to bigger challenges, which all of us must face sooner or later. We will see that the same principles that can pole-vault us over obstacles to finding a new car or getting to work on time can also power us through a major illness, divorce, or death of a loved one. It can even prepare us for our own death. All this can be accomplished by the techniques applied in a slower, deeper, more soul-searching way. It will require more out of us in the long run, and more application over time, but it will be there for us when we need it.

People say "Don't sweat the small stuff," and we have found with Everyday Rituals a way to do just that. We can now free everyday challenges without wearing ourselves out emotionally, knowing we are coming from a special place of hidden personal power. But it is how we encounter real adversity that will determine the outcome of our lives; and ritual as a resource can help us here too. Ritual can help us build up a greater reservoir of resources and connectedness; it can also help us access that reserve account when we are down and out.

One thing we can learn by reading of the lives of the great men and women of history is that, for the most part, they didn't get where they got by being lucky. More often than not, they faced repeated trauma and disappointment, sometimes in ways that would crush the average person, but they kept going. They adapted.

A person who packs it in the minute there is a major snafu is not going to last long in any business, spiritual quest, or important relationship. Even if you feel very connected to the universe now, you will eventually experience disaster. (The word "disaster" comes from a Latin word that means "separated from the stars," a state of disconnect from the universe.) Yes, disaster is a message from the universe telling us, "You're going about things the wrong way! You may want to redirect your efforts. But seldom, if ever, is disaster's message telling us, "Give up! It's no use!" That's how the frightened, abandoned inner child may hear the message of adversity, but through ritual we can tap into resources large enough to turn hardship into learning opportunities, and, eventually, future success as well. So we can quiet our inner child's crying by offering it love, light, and the possibility of happier circumstances.

We may want to teach our inner child about the sweet tears of connectivity, of loss, and of change. These tears can heal wrenching pain and celebrate the sweetness of being touched by deeper connection. If there are tears, there's often sweetness somewhere. That's where the resource energy is.

At least one part of ritual's secret power to overcome trouble—and the sinking feeling we get when the universe shoots a hole in our heart—is its ability to access information that is beyond the reach of rationale. It allows us to ask, "Why is this happening to me?" and get an answer, such as "Because the universe loves me," or "Because this is nature's way; we don't get to hold on, even when it hurts; life is about death and renewal." These lines of communication are truly great resources.

When disaster strikes, of course we do not feel cool, calm, and collected. We might find that our shadow-self comes to the foreground, bringing with it its collection of pet snakes. Nevertheless, at that moment, the universe is telling us something important we don't want to hear, and it's something that could make our lives not only better, but truly great if we could receive it. Through ritual we can better manage the shadow-self at those moments, and increase our ability to hear its message.

Every break-up of any long term intimate connection speaks volumes to us about our own choices, our childhood needs, self-deceptions, abuses, and insensitivities, and how to be more caring and compassion-ate to ourselves and others. Every trauma tells us how to live more wisely in the future so that we don't miss any important steps and don't lose our balance. Every cancerous tumor tells us how to better take care of our physical and emotional health. Every loss of a loved one tells us how to live every day with a greater sense of purpose, with each person with whom we choose to share our lives. It teaches us we need to examine our own mortality once in awhile and experience a taste of death even while alive. Ritual can help us do all these things.

If, through ritual, we can cope with the feelings associated with hardship, we will be able to better articulate our questions and fears, and even hear the answers more clearly.

No one can promise you such magnificent results every time; there are no guarantees in the disaster business. But once we understand the unlimited power of resource, we will see how ritual can become a key part of our long-term lifetime plan for happiness and success. It makes a lot of sense once we grasp that the IQ of the universe is quite high, and that we can let it do a lot of our "thinking" for us once we get out of our own way.

All of the "get-started" rituals offered in this chapter are each intended to initiate some familiarity with the One Taste of every-thing, everywhere. That place the Old Brain knows all about. If you do that with any success, we trust it will serve you in providing fur-ther light as we explore rituals in the upcoming themes of *Connectiv-ity*, *Vibrant Eros*, and *Dynamic Linking on an Infinite Playground*.

DIVORCE RITUAL

When I write about divorce ritual, it's not just for those who were married in a secular or religious ceremony, but also those who have shared a personal, loving commitment over time, whatever their ori-entation. I'm addressing all those really brave people who took the leap of faith to love and commit to one another. For many, a time comes when they decide the commitment no longer works for them.

Let's be honest: divorce is a major transition in life. Part death, part dismemberment, the experience of divorce is not taken lightly. It deserves the best of our abilities for grieving, self-healing, compassion, and learning. It deserves a special place of respect and a special set of rituals.

I've witnessed many clients, several close friends, and myself as well, go through relationship or marriage dissolution. The wrenching process usually isn't pretty to watch; neither is it comforting to see how often divorce is treated as a dirty little chapter that the parties should simply move through and forget. I recommend that everyone read Daphne Rose Kingma's book, *The Future of Love*. It places our relationship beginnings and endings in a present-day perspective, free of mythologies that no longer reflect who we have become in this contemporary age.

Having a ritual to acknowledge divorce helps us digest it. Divorce can be a key passage in a person's life, and it awakens a thirst for ritual closure. It can be another important initiation into who we are becoming. If we don't have this type of closure, the wounds can fester for years, leading to all sorts of negative emotional (and even physical) consequences. This is particularly troubling if children are in the picture.

Bernard Weiner, a consultant in ritual, offers the following options for dealing with this major life episode. (I have edited his thoughts to suit this book.)

1. A blessing way. If the splitting parties are divorcing rather amicably, there can be a ceremony, perhaps even officiated by their open-minded minister, counselor, friend, or rabbi, where each of them is ritually blessed as they leave this relationship and head out into their new life. Again, if things are relatively amicable, each partner might also write a blessing for their ex-spouse, wishing him or her well. I can imagine a large candle that is

blown out by both together; then each lights a separate candle as the blessing is spoken. Friends can deliver their comments. If there were children from this marriage, they should be present, observing how divorce doesn't have to be considered a mysterious, negative "end of the world," but an openly-acknowledged cause of distress and transition that can lead to positive developments for their parents—and, by extension, for them as well.

2. If the divorce is not a reasonably friendly one, and neither partner wants to be in the same room with the other, their friends and families might organize a separate divorce ceremony for each of them, where the ritual blessing might be given, and where their guests can speak to them from the heart, wishing them well and perhaps offering advice as they prepare to head off into their new lives. Perhaps each member of the witnessing audience can light a candle for the divorced man or woman, symbolizing the supporting network that will aid him or her in the new life. If there are children from this marriage, old enough to comprehend what is taking place, perhaps they should be present, as witnesses to the closure and the positive developments that may come from moving-on.

3. In any kind of divorce, especially extremely painful ones, each spouse needs to make as clean a break as possible. A ceremony might be devised where photos and other mementos of the relationship might be displayed on a ritual table. If the divorced person feels like keeping a photo for the sake of nostalgia, they could create a cleansing ritual to remove any negativity. If a lot of anger still exists, a ritual might be devised where photos (or mementos) are ceremonially burned (or crushed),

bringing symbolic closure and freedom from pain. (This
is not a ritual for young children.)

Rituals work best when they permit the participants and the witnesses to feel they've moved on to a new level of energy and emotion. Rituals devoid of this transformative element do not contain
the same amount of emotional and spiritual power. So, if you create
a Divorce Ritual make sure it contains the elements of ceremonial
transformation—just burning someone's photo does nothing except
relieve anger; it does not lead to the next step of healthy transformation unless the ritual ceremony includes steps taken in an ascendant
direction. I think you'll find that when you perform any ritual cer-
emonies at key passages in your life (and in the lives of those close to
you), everyone who participates is enriched—not only in the fun of
doing rituals together in a caring community, but with a deep connection to yourself. You can then move on with more strength, self-
assurance, and mindfulness.

I also suggest following and/or adapting a ritual in Marianne
Williamson's *Illuminata: Thoughts, Prayer, Rites of Passage*. Williamson advises that you ask your spiritual counselor or therapist to act as
officiator for your divorce ceremony, and she offers detailed prayers
of forgiveness and release. She suggests each spouse say to the other,
"I bless you and release you. Please forgive me; I forgive you. Go in
peace. You will remain in my heart."

I recently facilitated a Divorce Ritual with a couple who cared a
great deal for one another but could no longer live together. They
had gone through much over the years with alcoholism and code-
pendency overshadowing their lives. Once sober and in recovery for
some time, it became apparent that pain and *loss of self* were embed-
ded in their dynamics together. They both felt they would be better
off with a fresh start, needing new space to grow in.

Since they had both done ritual work in SE, they wanted to complete the divorce in a way that honored their history, along with feeling

whole in the separation. (As a psychotherapist, one of my saddest duties is to facilitate the separation of two good people who love each other.)

Life-Threatening Illness

There are few occasions that seem more disastrous than hearing those three words, "You have cancer." It is a life-changing moment.

In Richard Grossinger's quote in Chapter One, he speaks about our medical crises of how the active opposition between western (scientific) medicine and growing trends in energy medicine get in the way of optimal possibilities of recovery. In this section, we will begin to see the possibilities of convergence, a gradual transformation highlighted in a book by Ester M. Sternberg, M.D. titled *The Balance Within*. Sternberg, a well-respected physician and researcher, writes to other physicians saying:

> *Even the greatest skeptic must now admit that a wealth of evidence exists to prove in the most stringent scientific terms that functions of the mind do influence the health of the body and … affect our moods and emotions through molecules and nerve pathways. This level of proof of the myriad connections between the brain and the immune system was needed before the two cultures—the popular and the scientific—could begin to respect and talk to each other.*

This coming together is beginning to gradually happen as patients help educate our allopathic physicians in how we are caring for ourselves, and include them in the dialogue.

Unfortunately, when we are dealing with a life-threatening illness, we are in a poor position to be students or teachers. I see more and more how the entrenched arrogance of western scientific medicine is learning to respect other healing disciplines. Those of us who become seriously ill can't wait for a better world in this regard. We must empower ourselves and formulate our rituals for health to support the work of our physicians. To do this we'll need to employ some basics of ritual: intention, resource, and our Curious Observer.

Before totally accepting the horrific chemo protocol following my 1983 diagnosis of a fatal cancer, I went to see a holopathic spiritual healer from the Church of Religious Science. A tiny lady, she was a minister there, with an authorative voice: "Do not believe what they are saying, Michael, and do not feel doomed. You will survive this!"

Her words were so powerful, I believed her. It was the first good news I had in weeks. I honestly believe that this woman, a stranger to me, saved my life, and I later had the good fortune to call her and express my gratitude.

Getting Well Again by Carl Simonton, M.D. and Stephanie Matthews-Simonton, has many stories about how fatally diagnosed cancer patients worked to heal in community with visualization.

Below is a ritual for dealing with cancer and other life-threatening illnesses, including HIV/AIDS. It is much simpler than the one I used in '83, but I feel it will suffice as an adequate springboard for all that follows. I trust your own creativity and your Curious Observer, to adapt it best to your personal needs. If you need help, invite in a resourceful person that you have access to.

LIFE-THREATENING ILLNESS RITUAL

Write or type on a piece of letter-size paper a list of at least seventeen resources in your life, both inner ones and outer ones. They can be from your past, present, or future. They can be internal resources like, "I am a person who can be counted on by friends," or "I like my own value system." That's what I mean by internal. Or, they can be external like, "the day I graduated college" or "sleeping with my partner." As a grade school boy there was a time I would walk home from school for lunch.

My grandmother would warmly greet me and serve me tomato soup and a sandwich. I had her all to myself and she really loved and cared for me. I also had a teacher in high school that took a special interest in me when I was failing and made a true academic out of me. Pockets in time like these, many of them, continue to live in us, and they contain rich energy for the alchemy of transmuting our suffering and contributing to our good health. We call them resources and they contain the expansive energy that transforms contractive dis-ease.

Once you are satisfied with your resource list, turn it over or type a different document. This time I invite you to list at least seventeen things (intentions) you'd enjoy doing in the next five years if you are alive. They can be big things (within reason) or simple, pleasurable events or accomplishments. To make it easy, you can start each sentence with, "I want to …" When you have completed the list of seventeen (or as many as possible, you can always add more), circle the three that are most meaningful to you right now. Now take a moment and close your eyes and imagine that the three circled intentions have already mysteriously manifested. Let your imagination have fun with it. Totally imagine the manifestation in your being and what that would feel like. Invite your body to connect with that image and curiously notice the energy and feeling in your body. We call that "future resource." It can be very powerful in transmuting illness.

If you are physically able, stand up and gently rotate, shake and move your body. If you are not physically able to, do the best you can to simulate this, or just imagine yourself doing it. This begins your attunement process with yourself, your body's felt senses, and your Curious

Observer. You're bringing awareness and consciousness home—it's "your" time!

Begin to still your body in a sitting position with your shoeless feet on the floor. As you find a comfortable sitting position, begin allowing your body to feel supported by whatever you are sitting on. You don't need to work at sitting—you can just be supported, allowing yourself to just be, getting a sense that there is nothing to do and nowhere to go. Just sit, and notice from your Curious Observer. See if your body can find a relatively comfortable place for now.

Invite your body and your being to tap into the "future resource" discovered above. Allow that to permeate your being. Now invite in a protective ally, someone whom you know has been there for you at one time or many times. They can be living or dead. It is their energy we are calling into the experience, and it is that which lives in you. Let your body be with that energy along with the future resources. Notice your felt senses and experience. Give it all some time and space, allowing your mind to rest on the sidelines as you have a sensory experience.

When you know that you are experiencing a place of resource (expansiveness), invite into your being the following (do it in small chunks or as a whole, let your inner wisdom guide you): Your diagnosis, your physicians, your treatment regime, other complementary approaches you are including, and your fears. As you do this in your own particular (not perfect) way, notice the changes in your body sensations. Allow them time and space "to be." They deserve a place in your being. As you bring gentle awareness to these sensations and feelings, notice any subtle changes in them. What happens next? Do this for five to ten minutes, just tracking the sensations. See if the body has anything to illuminate in it's own mysterious way. Notice if there are any constrictions and notice where they are located. Gently register that awareness.

Now I invite you to shift your experience back to the sensations you had earlier of "future resource" and your protective ally. Notice how you can make the shift—gradually or swiftly. Notice the onset of the different sensations. Notice their nuances. Allow yourself to totally drop into this place of resource, curiously noticing what happens as you do. Don't force anything; simply give your being permission to bathe in resource. As you give this some time and space, you may once again notice expansiveness, even, perhaps, formlessness. At the time of your choosing, pick a tangible aspect of this expansiveness. It could be a color or light you are aware of. It could be a texture or "cloudy" formation. It could be an inner smile. Invite whatever feels tangible from your resource (if appropriate) to touch the edge of any contractions you have awakened from your earlier disease and treatment imagery.

By touching one form of energy to its opposite, you are creating and supporting the conditions for transformation. Just curiously notice what happens, giving time and space to whatever occurs. When the time feels right to you, move to the completion of this ritual.

Use your incredible imagination and ability for intention—gifts we share with the spirit that makes us and moves through us. Image yourself "moving through" your illness. Imagine yourself moving through all that it represents in your life now. Once you are on the other side, embrace the three "future resources" you've already circled and experienced within. Notice how that feels inside. Give yourself time. You are now directing your energy.

As you feel ready, bring ritual to a close, gradually reorienting yourself to your surroundings. Though your formal ritual is complete, your physiological and holistic self will continue the integration in its own unique style.

Two comments about important responsibilities regarding the above ritual. First, what I presented is a springboard that has worked for me. Your experience may be different. Please go with *your* experience if it feels like it's *moving toward aliveness*. If it is not, revisit my suggestions and play with them until they fit you better. Something inside you knows how to make them work.

Second, I want to acknowledge that all of us will die no matter what we do to heal ourselves. It would be insincere not to bring attention to this. With all the best rituals, holopathy, and allopathy integrated, all of us will leave this plane of existence. That mystery is beyond my grasp, but I can assure you that if you incorporate ritual as a resource your passing will be met with integrity and grace.

Take some comfort in the fact that you are a unique manifestation of the human spirit. Know that death could be yet another important initiation, then return to your brilliant future resources above and get on with living. Rumi (the great Sufi mystic and poet) once wrote, "Beyond ideas of right doing and wrong doing … there is a field—I'll meet you there."

Bereavement, Grief, and Death Rituals

Essential to an intuitive understanding of how ritual can help us in challenging and even disastrous circumstances is the understanding of grief and death and their profoundly healing roles in our lives.

This section is about the alchemy of transmuting grief into aliveness and creativity. Peg Elliot Mayo wrote about this beautifully in

Rituals for Living & Dying: "The terrible fire of grief is an energetic furnace, refining character, personality, intellect, and soul. It is a catalyst for creation. What is created may be dreadful—a distorted, unapproachable monument to despair—or a distillation of experience that is wholesome, useful, bright, and even wise."

A friend gave me a beautiful book titled *Ano Ano: The Seed* by Kristen Zambucka. It was an ancient tale about Polynesians and their struggles with existential crises. It illustrated to me that suffering had within it a transformational possibility.

Grief dwells in an inner reservoir. When we focus on a particular loss, connecting with those feelings, we gain a clearer perspective on other losses. If one allows it, there is always a sweetness and comfort in these reconnections. This is more accessible once we process the complex feelings, and a part of us comes alive again. It makes sense that grieving enlivens. If there had been no significant bonding in these relationships to begin with, we would not experience their loss as traumatic.

Furthermore, in the state of openness and vulnerability that is created through grieving, new learning and corrective experience come more easily. These can be times of significant change and transformation. Outer life experiences tend to be put in a perspective that reflects what is truly important in your life, and what is not.

Robert Gass, musician and vocalist who also conducts rituals on loss and opening the heart suggests, "One may always feel sadness … yet rather than being crippling, this sadness may one day become like a rich color in the palette of the soul." Grief is a healing feeling. If we allow ourselves to see it as a welcome friend, it will come naturally, and perhaps even leave us when we ask it to.

Healing grief is a very individual process. Each of us must be reassured that the sun will shine again while we are in the claws of grief. We must be comforted by an outer or inner resource, a sensation deep inside that healing will organically occur. We need to be with our unpleasant feelings and even allow ourselves to get lost in them as need be. We must also rise above our grief as we can. We must pull ourselves out of it periodically to socialize, even if we don't feel like it. We must dance with suffering, allowing it to lead sometimes in our private moments and in the nurturing presence of loved ones. We must make room for the feelings to move through us and be respected. Revisited memories are ghosts from the past that bring us profound and important connections with lost parts of our selves. With this reclaiming of our soul, we develop an expanded sense of aliveness. This process continues to quicken as we become more grounded in our wholeness.

TRANSFORMING GRIEF INTO CREATIVITY RITUAL

If you are already in deep grief when you read this, it may be hard to absorb what I'm writing, as the grief may have already enveloped your being. If that is so, I recommend that don't try to create this ritual right now, but rather register these words in your mind in the spirit of planting a seed that might grow later when the right amount of sunshine, soil, and watering (in other words, resources) becomes available. Give yourself time to wonder if this could possibly work for you. Then, when ready, create your new living ritual.

In this ritual we realize that we have a much greater capacity for rebuilding than we usually think possible. We will do so by holding opposite experiences in mind and body at the same time and letting each support the other.

Create the intention that this grief will not be a dreadful and distorted, unapproachable "monument to despair." Let it be an honor to the deceased and to the life you have shared, carrying over all that the deceased has given you into your future creative adventures.

The ritual begins with the intention to heal. Now gradually blend in outer and inner resources—energies that expand and elevate your sense of being. This does not preclude grief periodically grabbing you by the throat (even more often than you'd like) and throwing you down to the floor. The path to healing includes that. But when you've had enough of its bitter distillations running their natural course through your broken heart and mourning for the lost pieces of your life, re-engage your innate intelligence and create a new life ritual.

Go forward toward the true resource energies within you and throughout your life. Drop back into the Curious Observer within you, just noticing the paradox of it all, walking like a wounded fire fighter into the burning beauty and steaming pain, the blinding joy and heavy hurt of real grief and closure. Slowly, find your grounding here and your equanimity. You may be amazed what you will find on the other side of that insurmountable wall of pain.

When developing resources for your ritual, consider some of the following: Creative visualization, meditation, soothing music, support groups, creating a mantra for yourself (example: "a new life awaits me"), movement exercises that keep the body alive and vital, and, most importantly, bringing your energy down and away from your head. Intellectual thinking is no help when grieving. The head worries, but the body mysteriously inspires. Stay in the body as much as possible. Always work at feeling your feet on the floor, at least momentarily, to bring that energy down from the worry factory upstairs to a more creative place. All sound-making can be good: it creates a resonance in the body that also leads to equanimity and creativity. The more unusual the sound—the more it comes from you organically—the better for the creative energies. During my grieving periods, I found myself making weird sounds as soon as I was alone—in an elevator by myself, whenever I entered my home alone, whenever I ran or exercised. I just let those sounds come out of me, without wondering too much as to why. I still do, and they are very rejuvenating.

Weeping can be a profound resource, especially if you've lost a love. The weeping (watched and sometimes coached by the Curious Observer) can make room for creative juices and innate intelligence to more fully inhabit your being. Never force the weeping: let it be organic and grounded. Notice, you can sense gravity and support while letting your feelings fully express themselves. If it feels blocked, find a professional who knows how to support your process. In the mean time, find music that makes you weep at this particular time, and then find time alone to listen to it, with no distractions. Also find music to make you smile, that takes you out of that "lost" feeling and puts a bounce in your step again.

There are many resources you can draw from: You can sigh and take deep audible breaths. Conscious breathing is always good to amplify the restorative energies. If you are comfortable, consider accompanying the deep sense of breath with singing or chanting; go for it with gusto: singing and chanting are great as healing resources. Just remember to keep the worry head quiet, while allowing other parts of you to come forward.

I've given you a small range of resources to support your grief and new life rituals, but you can greatly expand on them. The important thing to remember is that you have resources to transform the contraction you may feel.

The Goodbye Ritual

I do not want to overlook the importance of saying goodbye. After waiting a few months or more after the loss, write or speak the words needed for completion. Saying goodbye and offering gratitude for all that was shared is a fundamental ingredient for any "New-Life Rituals" you've created. In this ritual, a degree of solemnity is suggested. Some other rituals may work well when performed with a light heart and a light touch, but *Goodbye Rituals* beg to be carried out with the greatest reverence and respect, and with tons of self-compassion, of course. Humor may come organically—just trust the Old Brain.

Death Ritual

Through ritual, many indigenous peoples have been able to honor death as an aspect of life to be fully understood and experienced. As natives of the land intuitively know, ritual that aids us in accepting our mortality will deepen our spiritual foundation as well. We become better friends with spirit. As my friend, Charles H. Lawrence, a Black Foot Indian, says, "I'm more interested in spirited people than in spirituality." Coming face to face with our mortality and of those we love (including pets) makes us *spirited people*.

I've come to see life as a light to be lived as brightly as possible until it burns out on the material plane of existence. When this happens to someone we care about, there is a dark spot in our existence and we can grieve in appropriate ways. Yet, my experience is also that all our deceased loved ones live inside and around us in a palpable ways. We just need to notice them.

One of the great dividends from my brushes with death is that my fear of it is gone. What a burden that was! How much more spirited I have become without that fear. Most of us have not yet come face to face with death, or perhaps that is happening now and is why you're reading this. If we haven't looked death in the face, or we are doing so at the moment, a big question can determine our future.

Can we transmute the "poison of fear" (as author Don Miguel Ruiz calls it) that we've inherited from past generations? I believe we can. We can live vibrantly and prepare for our light to dim here and shine elsewhere. It may be helpful to revisit how people who have lived in close contact with the earth have honored death as a life passage and heartfully and practically ministered to the bereaved.

In *Beyond Death: The Gates of Consciousness,* authors Stanislav and Christina Grof write:

> *The individual dying in ancient or pre-industrial culture is equipped with a religious or philosophical system that transcends death, and is likely to have had considerable experiential training and altered states of consciousness, including symbolic confrontations with death. The approach of death is faced in the nourishing context of the extended family, clan, or tribe, and with its support—sometimes even with specific and expert guidance through the successive stages of dying.*

The ritual below is for all of us facing death, the ones who know it could be just around the corner, and those who expect death's call in the future. In either case, the intention of the ritual is to use death to truly know what it means to be alive. We can use that aliveness to prepare for and create the most glorious death possible. We can create a feel-good tribute to who we have been, or to who we would have liked to be. We can do either and more. It's *our* death!

This ritual is crucially important to all of us, the living and the dying. Therefore, I will be direct and unsentimental.

There are two phases to this ritual, the external and the internal. Let's do the external first. It also has two parts. The first part of the outer ritual has to do with things left uncompleted in this life. We'll call this your "completion ritual." The second part of the outer ritual has to do with the physical "stuff" of your passing.

Here's how to do the first part. On a sheet of paper or computer document, write across the top of the page in dark letters or bold type: "If I die today, what unfinished business (emotional and practical) would I have regretfully left undone? This begins to create the framework for the ritual. Under that bold headline put three column headings. On the left put "People/Tasks" and in the center put "What Needs Doing" and on the far right the word "Completed?"

Once you've created the framework for the document, begin to notice what comes up for you in terms of creating a list for your completion ritual. Listen for the Curious Observer to comment as to what's relevant and what's not. This is not an egoistic do-good exercise; rather it is a soul-retrieval opportunity and a doorway to connectivity. You may want to put the document aside and let it be for a few minutes, hours, or days—your choice! When you return to it, come from your heart and your Curious Observer and begin to make your list of "People/Tasks" that are incomplete emotionally or physically. With each of those listings also fill in "What needs doing" for you to feel complete in that relationship or situation. Intend to fill-in the list in one sitting, knowing that you can always add to it later if you want to.

When this list is in some state of completion, place it in front of you in a comfortable way and recite a very private prayer. As you pray to the Creator of all that lives in our life force, ask for the courage and clarity to make completions as best you can and in your own appropriate time sequences. Also pray that you will know when to call on additional resources to complete your tasks. When you complete each one, put a heart symbol in the completed column, indicating a fuller, more whole-hearted space as a result of the completion. If for some reason (whatever you deem acceptable) you cannot complete one or more, do a small prayer ritual for each or all with the intention that they be completed and released in the spiritual and energetic realms. Here it is the intention that becomes paramount. You may also want to apply a good dose of self-compassion. Once you have done this, put a heart symbol in those columns until all of your incompletes have been addressed to the best of your ability (all things considered).

If you feel like you have not lived up to your potential (in all of life, or in a specific area, or in both; I know I once felt I had not given myself to life) and you may be dying in a few hours or days, do this: Place your favored hand on your chest so that you are prepared to have your flat hand move and circle your heart (clockwise) three times while very slowly repeating this phrase: "I love myself even though I realize, for a myriad of reasons, I did not live up to my potential. I love myself even though I realize, for a myriad of reasons, I did not live up to my potential. I love myself even though I realize, for a myriad of reasons, I did not live up to my potential." After repeating it three times in this fashion, an energy reversal is often achieved that will dissolve the regret. You can move on if you want to, knowing you did the best you could, all things considered.

When you've completed this first part of the outer ritual, take some time with the page you've been working with and bring a sense of reverence to it. Express gratitude that you have had the time and courage to create peace and a higher vibration of good energy while you are still alive to appreciate it. Also know that if and when you die you will have no regrets.

The second part of the outer ritual has to do with the physical "stuff" of your passing. How empowered do you want to be in regard to how you pass? How do you want your loved ones involved or not involved? What is important to you? If nothing is important to you, it's okay, just know that and be at peace with your choice. In this part of the outer death ritual, the key is bringing intention to areas of life we've been conditioned to ignore. This takes some concentration and focus. It may be helpful to invite in, as resource, a loved one, friend, social worker, or clergy person to assist you in moving the foggy clouds of cultural denial so you can have a death you feel as good as possible about. This planning often includes the kind of memorial or religious services you do or don't want and what you want done with your physical remains (body and possessions).

When you have formulated this second part of the outer death ritual to your satisfaction (notice the constant emphasis on "your"—it is important; others can draw energy from bereavement rituals—but your death is yours only), write it out and have one or two people close to you know of your choices. Once you have done this, let go into living, knowing you've done the best you could to prepare for the outer aspects of your death.

Now for the inner ritual. The inner ritual is all about forgiveness and remembering resource moments in your life. It's about love and light, preparing you for the smoothest transition possible. Nothing else is important, everything else is done. As we make our final passage from the physical, we want to attune, focus, amplify, and direct the most magnificent energies that we possess. These energies are love and forgiveness (which is an even higher vibration of love energy).

Pick your place for the ritual, or let the place pick you.
It occurred for me under the bright lights once while
being prepared for emergency open-heart surgery. With
a determination and will that is palpable, we want to go
deep into the heart of our being and allow a meaningful
moment to surface in awareness. Invite your body to
connect to that moment, noticing any inner sense of
connectivity. Then give yourself permission to have a
cavalcade of cascading images, slow or fast, of meaningful
moments. You may want to have special music in the
background, or hum or smile to help amplify the energy.
You may want to draw a picture. Anything that will hold
and amplify the energy is good. You choose!

As you bathe in the goodness of your own life, you want
to begin to direct this energy of love. I invite you to direct
this love into your second most powerful life-force (the
first being intention) of forgiveness. Use this energy, this
love, and this light within you and around you to forgive
yourself right now for everything! I am not suggesting a
piece-by-piece blow by blow forgiveness (we've all been
rotten scoundrels at times, intentionally or involuntarily,
consciously and unconsciously). Say "I forgive it all
right now, let it melt. You've been a good human; you've
completed this life. You deserve a loving pat on the
shoulder. You did it!"

Now, take another minute with this great energy and
forgive whoever hurt you the most in this life. As you
see their ignorant humaneness, just let your hurts melt in
the same way you forgave yourself. Wish that person (or
their spirit, if dead) a lightness of being, as they shed the
weight of your grudge. Let the forgiveness of that one
person create a wave of energy that forgives everyone who

you hold unpleasant feelings towards. It's all old news, no longer important. What matters now is how much love and light we can bring to the finish line. The more light we bring, the more graceful our passing.

Complete this ritual in whatever way feels right to you. The light is a good place to go to, whether we are living or dying.

Connectivity

Relationship Ritual as Medicine

Small is the number of them that see with their own eyes and feel with their own hearts.

ALBERT EINSTEIN

Ritual for Relationship

For many of us, the natural longing to fill that someone special slot in our consciousness with the right person has a profound impact on our lives. So it's safe to assume that many people will come to this chapter called *Relationship Ritual* seeking wisdom on how to make intimate relationships more accessible and fulfilling. But how can this be accomplished when each individual is so different? And not only are we different, as Einstein notes above, so few of us truly see with our own eyes and feel with our own hearts. In many ways our conditioning has taken us away from our inner compass. In ritual we find that compass and see that it still works. It is helpful to know that relationships are in themselves a healing force, not just for ourselves but for those we are in relationship with, and that once we find the right Relationship Rituals, they can be medicine to our souls, our hearts, minds, and bodies.

In this section on *connectivity*, we will explore rituals for creating more significant interactions and communications. This is central to how Relationship Rituals work as medicine for the soul and every other part of our being. This means developing focused rituals that expand our abilities to discover the life-giving relationship connections that we want and need.

A quick example of a Relationship Ritual that my partner and I created for a very close friend: He was fiftyish and had never managed to have a long-term significant relationship. He was not seeing with his own eyes or feeling with his own heart. He was sadly resigned to the cultural view that he was over the hill, out of shape, and unattractive. We invited our friend to join us in looking at greater possibilities for intimately connecting in his life. We bought him an inexpensive computer for Christmas and put an ad online. As nervous and doubtful as he was, he used us as a resource to craft an authentic personals profile. As crazy as it sounds, he met someone in less than nine months. I am delighted to report that several years later they are living together in loving union. This is just one example of the fun and gratification available through Relationship Rituals.

As I examine the possibilities of Relationship Rituals as medicine, I realize there's only one way to heal our selves and the planet. That is by replacing the fractured worldview of our culture that tells us how our relationships should be. And this cultural programming is so insidious that many of us are unaware how it drives our fears and obscures our instincts. In the world of *connectivity* we want to restore a worldview that is more holistic, multidimensional, and relational. The Old Brain knows better—as ritual will illuminate. Our self-centeredness is born out of the cultural parasite of fear that author Don Miguel Ruiz writes about in *The Mastery of Love*.

"I don't want to get hurt; I don't have what people want; too old; too fat; too skinny; not sexually perfect; don't want to get fenced in; don't want to hurt somebody; don't know how to do relationship; who'd want someone like me with emotional, physical, or communication challenges?" We want to transform this fear into expansive *giving*. This new worldview is based on the idea that giving love, rather than waiting for it, honors the web of life.

This is a big-picture perspective on why we need the medicine offered by relationship and *connectivity*. Let's bring it back to the here and now, to *you* and *me*. Without connection to the world, economic and social systems, sources of food, light, and warmth, we die.

Energy Medicine in Relationship Ritual

The first time I heard about energy medicine was before I learned to call it that. It was more than twenty-five years ago in a 12-Step program. People gave me incredible energy through their love and support, and they didn't even know me. There was a palpable spirit of giving and taking in this energy, and while nobody was calling it energy medicine, the program's slogan "to keep it you have to give it away," reminded us why energetic love often is the resource that makes one's sobriety possible.

That paradoxical expression feels fitting for this book, given the frequent references made to giving and receiving energy. Giving our energy away while taking care of ourselves helps us to become a resource for more expansive possibilities. We take the same energetic principle I used for staying sober in AA and apply it to health, vitality, and fulfillment.

Energy medicine contains the energies of love, light, and nurturance, with a healthy dose of a mysterious wisdom based on experiential knowledge. When we combine that with the intention to heal, we make real medicine. Such energy fields are created when two or more people share the same intention of being together for a particular purpose. When a client comes into my office, they are entering a predetermined energy field of intention and creation. It *is* a field of Relationship Ritual as medicine. My clients may not be aware of this energy field on an intellectual level, but they often respond to it on more subtle levels of energy. Real change and transformation occur more efficiently and consistently in these subtle energy fields, and are later integrated into intellectual functioning.

Experience has shown me that trying to create lasting transformation primarily through the intellect, or even through emotions, is far less effective than working with these subtle energy fields. The intellect, or cerebral upper brain, and the emotions, or the middle brain's limbic system, are expressions from these physical realities. However, the Old Brain, the one that supports the other two brains and our survival mechanisms is more connected to nature, the universe, and powerful invisible realities. It expresses itself energetically. We witness this by engaging with our Curious Observer as the Old Brain speaks to us through the body's felt senses and imagery. This all makes sense when we remember that we are energy first and foremost; and unseen realities like love and resource energy take priority over physical reality.

The important topic of relationship as healing is a challenging one. I've worked with my energy and the energy of others—sometimes unconsciously—for many years. In this chapter, I attempt to articulate for the first time what I know about intuitively. The offerings I originate at this point spring from the most private and trusted parts of myself and my experience, from great masters, and experiences I've had with the medicinal use of energy.

In Relationship Ritual, luminous energy often flows from embracing paradoxes. A paradoxical proposition or statement can be illogical, self-contradictory, or even absurd. Yet some relationship paradoxes we explore will prove to be logical upon investigation. When embraced from a multi-dimensional, rather than a binary (either/or) perspective, a *new* energy comes forth and offers many new possibilities for Relationship Ritual.

I encourage readers to practice the rituals in the order they are written, even if they decide not to do the actual ritual. Start from the beginning—the rituals build on one another. Put linear thinking aside, and join in the journey.

Here's the focus of the rituals and the medicine we will be exploring in this section:

- Connection with Self
- Connection with Others and Community
- Attracting a Life Partner
- Sustaining an Intimate Relationship

Connection with Self

In this ritual we form a conscious partnership with all parts of ourselves—shadows and angels included. We are conditioned to use binary thinking that hurts our relationships. In ritual we shift to Curious Observer and the Old Brain for guidance. We are acknowledging evolutionary processes and being informed by them.

Perhaps we can begin to see ourselves as complex, multidimensional beings, each possessing, and emanating from, a manifestation of the S.O.U.L. (Systemic Organization of Universal Love) explained in the book, *The Living Energy Universe,* by Russek and Schwartz mentioned earlier. Plotinus, the Greek philosopher, wrote a few thousand years ago: "There is one and the same soul in many bodies." It seems, according to Russek, Schwartz, and Plotinus that there is a larger soul of which we are energetic manifestations. I believe this oversoul's primary purpose is to progress toward healing and connection. Everything that gets in the way of that comes from intrusive thought systems that are not grounded in nature. These intrusions, often fear-based, are culturally promulgated and inherited. Often they are binary, dualistic, mechanistic, and hierarchical. To ascend toward greater healing and connection we embrace the subtle complexities of compassion, respect, and space-giving. When it comes to energetic relationships, space is love.

Knowing from experience that we can shift perceptions to a timeless dimension of the Old Brain helps us see that the future is plastic and flexible and that we will be present in the future. We are also architects of our future relationships. As co-creators with such a profound systemic organization, where are we missing the proactive cues? The most important question we can ask ourselves from this point on is: What does the future hold, and how can I influence it, especially with relationships?

This is why we start with the Connection with Self Ritual. Many of us have never made a true connection with self-realization. When we do this, we discover blossoming relations, first with ourselves, then others.

This section has been greatly informed by the writings of Don Miguel Ruiz, a modern Western trained physician and healer who was taught ancient shamanic practices and Toltec wisdoms, and whose near-death experience stunned him back to his ancestry.

Nicholas Cimorelli, from our book ritual circle, helped me focus on the highest good and express my intention to reach it clearly. I hope that our combined experience will help readers understand why deepening the connection with the self is the primary generator of relationship healing and sustenance.

CONNECTION WITH SELF RITUAL

Find a comfortable spot. This is your time, and it is sacred. Perhaps you may want to light a candle to sanctify the space. You may even want to prepare for the ritual in advance with a refreshing bath or shower as you imagine the future moments of connection with your self. If you do, dry off slowly with your softest, most luxurious-feeling towel, in a sensual way. You're going on a date with someone very special, someone you've known forever, who knows all about you. YOU! What a delightful date to prepare for!

Once you are ready to enter your sacred ritual space, start with noticing how comfortable your body is and if there is any way you can make it even more peaceful. If so, adjust to give your body what it desires. This is a ritual about love, and loving your body and its needs in the moment is the perfect way to start. Massage your heart with your left hand and then your right. Now touch your lips to the palm of your left hand in a kissing gesture, and place the hand on your heart again and say, "I love myself as I am. I bless myself!" Now try this with the right hand.

Some of these rituals may seem "over the top" or "outside the box" to you. They may even appear silly. Those are often the ones that work best. If this aspect of the ritual as playground journey is bothersome, remember to do these alone, and remember to be playful.

This is also a ritual about connectivity with our bodies and all present and lost parts of ourselves. We want to reconnect them all. To not do so would be to disrespect the reality that evolution exists and that we are manifestations of it. The best way to make an impact on it, and meaningfully to engage with it, is to bring love and understanding to it, and to ourselves—every teensy, weensy bit of us! So before beginning the ritual, take a ring, or pendant, and place it on an altar or sacred platform before you.

Just close your eyes and make contact with your Curious Observer. Let it begin to notice your mind being gently put to rest. Let it begin to notice your body, and how it has found a comfortable place. Notice any feelings associated with this. Perhaps put on an inner smile at the fact that you are giving yourself this time in a place specifically designed for your own comfort. This will amplify the energy of connection.

Just curiously notice the felt senses of the body, making lots of room for them. Notice any imagery that may present itself, knowing that whatever comes is there for a reason.

This fulfillment is very soulful, perhaps mysteriously so at first. Giving it time to shift and change will result in more space, expansiveness, and perhaps illumination.

Take a conscious breath and say hello to your inner connective experience. This is the real you, the birthright you own. It's an experience, not a thought. It's physical. Everything else that blocks this is baggage from old constructs. You can drop the baggage now! It isn't yours, never was, and never will be. It's simply a stacking of your experiences, and that of your culture, born out of quickly dissolving obsolete constructs. They no longer work! The constructs of dualism and one-upmanship don't work any more in terms of fulfillment. They are lies in your mind and consciousness. They tell you what you should do to insure that your deepest needs will NOT be fulfilled. With your right hand, slowly wipe your closed eyelids from left to right, wiping away all fear. Shake your hand out at arm's length. Now, with your left hand, slowly wipe the fear away from right to left. Make a vow to yourself to see clearly from now on, without fear.

In this part of the ritual, use your powerful, soulful imagination to make the lies and false constructs disappear into the cosmos where they can regenerate into something else. In mime gestures, pull the yarn of lies and false constructs out of your ears and throw them away, throw them far away where they will disappear into the cosmos. Engage your mind and your Curious Observer. Realistically note that even if you can't banish the lies completely and immediately, you can tame them and stop believing what they tell you.

You may also want to take a minute to recognize that almost everyone else carries a similar bag full of lies. They can't help it. Take a minute to imagine a world in which you no longer have to believe anyone else, unless you want to. Come back to your own Curious Observer and your own inner truth and make your own choices for a future that suits you, hopefully an expansive one with lots of connectivity to share. Let the inspiration come from within. You'll know it's right because it will gel with the experience of inner connectivity and you will no longer be burdened by the parasite of fear. Once we stop believing the pack of lies, they lose power over us, freeing us from a lot of unnecessary sorrow.

Notice the gift that comes next, when truth frees us from the lies. It's the gift of freedom. You now have the freedom to adore your own body and being. There is no better or worse body, no better or worse self. There is only the one that is you. When we completely accept our beingness, we will feel absolutely great about our bodies, regardless of shape or size, and we will feel happy.

Now take the ring or other memento from the sacred platform before you and hold it in your hand. Ask yourself, deep down in your heart, if you love yourself enough to connect all parts of you. This means accepting yourself with all your so-called flaws and quirks, "warts and all," and making a commitment to be there for yourself from this day on. It means to love and cherish yourself. If you can say yes to this, place the ring, or memento, on your body as a symbol of your inner connection.

This is the most important part of the ritual, in terms of amplifying and directing the energy. Coming from this place of inner connectivity, image yourself bringing this energy naturally and organically out into your world.

Notice the images your Curious Observer brings forth. Notice the parasite of fear disappear. As you bring non-judgmental love into your life, notice how your quotient of self-abuse becomes almost nonexistent because you are in self-love. As we allow that self-love to grow, even in our imaginations, we notice that we can treat others with the same love, the same honor, the same respect, and the same gratitude we give to our selves.

Notice if you can experience your soul honoring others in ways that are expansive to you. Just notice, give some time, smile in gratitude, and gently reorient yourself to the future in front of you. Notice how you may want to engage with it and impact it in different ways.

After doing this ritual once, some may find it valuable to go back to the fears and lies and actually write some of them down. This helps to demystify them. By slowly tearing up the paper they are written on, the autonomic nervous system will begin the process of liberation and internal reorganization of energies.

I hope that in performing the above Relationship Ritual, we recognize why *self-loving had to come first.* If not, the energy we are bringing to others may be contaminated with fear. We are alive only when our eyes can see life, which is love, not the fear of the old constructs. Experiencing love *coming out of you* is the only way to be happy. And this comes most naturally from cultivating unconditional love for our selves.

Please use the following rituals as a way to bring your medicine into the world and share it with special people. As some Native American friends of mine say, "It's big medicine!"

Connection with Others and Community

Our health, vitality, and well-being are always in relationship to everything else. All events are relational. I believe that every illness we have is connected to our relationships. As you proceed, let some of the pivotal illuminations from the last ritual pertaining to self-connection gently flow forward.

Faces and names flash before me when I think of connection with others and community as energetic resources. The one I think of first is Nicholas Cimorelli, whom I met more than fifteen years ago. We were both therapists in the exciting formative years of our private practices. I liked him immediately and discovered that his work intersected with my own. Trained in repressed trauma therapy, his clients provided insights into addiction recovery. I had the opposite situation: while trained in addiction recovery, my clients taught me about repressed trauma. Our collegial relationship has been extraordinarily enriching. As the years progressed, we were both mysteriously pulled toward the benefits of energy-based wisdoms in working with our clients. Nicholas is also the focalizer of the board of directors of the nonprofit institute that has supported and implemented our research over the years. He has become my energetic resource. It's been great to be able to share all this with him.

We met when we both volunteered to assist in the development of a state-funded mental health and addictions program at the Lesbian, Gay, Bisexual, and Transgender (LGBT) Community Center in New York City. The dynamic Dr. Barbara Warren, who was chief organizer of the project, has also become a long-time friend, and is presently sitting on our Institute's Board of Directors. In my work with Barbara and Nicholas, I learned a very powerful paradoxical lesson: that co-creating something that is both *selfless* and *selfish* at the same time can impact the future immeasurably. Most importantly, it can impact *my* future. Here again, as in the ritual dealing with connecting with self, love *coming out of me* is the only way to be happy.

Over the years we have shared in many professional communities and created a very personal one in which we became part of each other's *family of choice.* Being a member of a family of choice does not negate our *family of origin,* where we still honor our love and responsibilities. In my family of origin, I do most of the *resourcing,* and I do it out of a sense of honor and gratitude. So it's not hard to see why my family of choice is so very important to me.

After my near death experience in 1983, my system was cleared of the cultural parasites of fear. I should have been dead but I wasn't. There was no longer any place for fear to take hold. With ingrained fear gone, everything about my relationships changed. For one thing, I no longer felt like part of the mainstream. For another, I began planning my life in very short spans, knowing that death could come to my door at any minute. I know what that turn-your-life-upside-down moment feels like, and, since that time, I have been ready for it. I find myself new in every moment on an inventive playing field. I no longer relate to the word "insecurity," yet I can acknowledge my limitations.

I have since learned that you don't have to have a near-death experience in order to drop relationship fears. Look at your life from the end and work backward. It will lower your materialistic, ego-driven expectations and raise your spirit-driven expectations.

As you prepare to step out of the delusions of the fear-bound, dualistic paradigm, be on the lookout for other people and communities where you fit in better—but won't wreck your universe on your path to transformation!

Connection with Others and Community Ritual

One of the other things my near-death experience taught me was not to waste time with anything or anyone that is not meaningful. As we move into this ritual, let's recognize that we are all *terminally something.* Let's begin deciding how we want to use this energy we are filled with, this light and love it represents. Connectivity in relationship means feeling a bio-neurological, energetic sharing of energy fields; it means two people complementing and enriching one another. It is not about enduring someone who deadens your senses, or chatting mindlessly with someone whose wisdom you don't really seek. It is not about having the life sucked out of you by an energy vampire, or being one yourself. It is a natural free-flowing energetic give and take that starts with your offering of kindness and authenticity.

There isn't time to waste if we want to experience vitality and ful-fillment. Time for self-nurturance and self-care is not wasted time. It is premium resource time.

RITUAL MATERIALS: PAD AND PEN

Find a comfortable place for self-inquiry, a sacred space void of distractions. Take a moment to energetically dedicate your pen and note pad as tools for the journey. Also take a minute to invite in any other resource energies—like loved ones that are gone, or a particularly beautiful sunset experience—to help you glide into a more expansive place where there is no judgment and no agenda.

Take a pen and draw a line down the center of a blank piece of paper. Place a heading on the top of the left column that says, "People" and another heading, at the top of the right column, that says, "Communities." Flush left down each column, write the names of people and communities that you wish to evaluate in terms of the connectivity between yourself and them.

This "grounding" in our own authenticity will allow the following rituals relating to connection to help us "grow where we are planted." Since we cannot really grow from any place else, this is a very good place to start.

Read each of the following eighteen meaningful questions, and if the answer is yes, put a slash (/) mark to the immediate right of names of people and communities where yes is the true answer. Let your answers be instinctual. There are no rights or wrongs; no one else will see this.

Remember that we are merely creating a diagnostic picture of our areas of greatest connectivity—where it is and where it isn't. Don't over-analyze it or feel that you have to make drastic decisions based on what you see.

Do we share an alignment of our intentions around meaningful areas of life?

Does being in their presence uplift me *for the most part?*

Do I have a "felt sense" that I create a good energy field when I'm around them?

Do we ever amplify energy in a good way together?

Do I get a sense sometimes that we are being creative together?

Is there a sense that we share a soulful love for one another?

Can I often let my everyday defenses down in their company?

Can I be authentic and real with them?

Do I have the ability to clearly ask for what I want with them?

Can I *not* take it personally if they are unable/unwilling to give me what I want?

If asked for something, can I say no to them if that feels right for me?

Can I totally let them be as they are and still love them?

Can they totally let me be who I am and still love me?

Do I bring as much energy and spirit to the relationship as they do?

Do they bring as much energy and spirit to the relationship as I do?

Do my unique qualities and nature complement the relationship?

Do the other's unique qualities and nature complement the relationship?

Do I address any unspoken contracts that I sense in the relationship?

Take a minute now and notice the numbers of slash marks next to each name. Notice what your felt sense reaction is. This is not a time for judgment; it is a moment of reflection. The most important reflection, in terms of Relationship Ritual as medicine, is to learn where you are now and what kind of shifting you can bring to creating your future. Before ending this part of the ritual, perhaps take a moment to be grateful that you can examine your relationships without negating them, being fearful, or feeling like you have to do anything to fix them right now. Everything is as it should be; it could be no other way. Surrender to what is real and ground yourself in that. All good things come in time.

If there are no slash marks next to a particular person or community, it may be one you no longer want to invest

your energy in. You may want to honor the ones with
large numbers of slash marks and spend more time with
those. It's up to you.

If we can cultivate more of the above sensations of spiritual satisfaction in our relations with others and with communities, we will
be enriching the energetic medicine we bring and receive, in ever
expanding circles.

RITUAL FOR PERSONAL TRANSFORMATION

Find that special sacred place of your own making. Don't
be shy in including a special candle, cloth, memento,
photo of a loved one, or anything that can bring
additional resource energy to this important ritual.

After you make your body as comfortable as it wants to
be in your sacred space, it is good to eliminate possible
interruptions in advance. Gradually shift from nasal to
mouth breathing. As you breathe through your mouth,
visualize that your throat, mouth, and heart are staying
"open" just because you are consciously breathing through
your mouth. This helps amplify energy and supports the
felt senses to move and shift more freely through your
body. If your mouth gets dry, simply moisten your lips
with your tongue. This should relieve any distraction
caused by the dryness.

As you relax and notice what it's like to breathe through
the mouth, gradually tune into your Curious Observer,
slowly bringing awareness from your head down to your
body. Notice any felt sense that may enter into your body.
Notice any unpleasant ones, such as stiffness. Notice
any pleasant ones as well, such as a part of you that feels

calm or strong. Give yourself time to yawn and stretch, (nowhere to go, nothing to do) and allow these sensations all the space and time they would like. We trust the mysterious intelligence of the body and the Old Brain to move us in the direction of greater relational connectivity that brings us all the energy resources we want and need.

With your eyes now gently closed, still your breathing through your mouth, image the piece of paper in front of you from the earlier ritual—the one with the list of people communities that you marked with slashes. As you receive this image, invite your body to connect with it. Imagine that every time you touch the pen to any letter of any given name, the picture of the person appears before you. Notice any new awareness that develops as you connect your present felt senses with the image from the previous ritual. Whatever you notice, let it be, give it time and space.

Now invite into your memory the one person in your life who best makes you laugh or smile in a good way. Invite in whoever spontaneously comes to mind, or create an imaginary character. Now, stretching the boundless limits of your imagination a bit further, invite this person to embody you, to become a part of you for this ritual.

With this light hearted affection in mind, become a forgiving, unafraid, child-like, trusting person who sees the good in everyone and in every situation and is able to gather resources from almost anything.

Now, with that fullness of self, re-imagine that paper with the slash marks from the earlier exercise. This time let your imagination, empowered by all the new energies within you, see slash marks all over the paper.

See every relationship transformed in such a way that
you notice and appreciate these subtle openings of heart,
communication, and understanding that have already
occurred. You can feel them in a more resourced way. If
the doubting mind comes in, respectfully ask it to rest
a while as you bathe in and laugh with ALL the slash
marks everywhere.

Are there any additional names or communities that you
want to add to the list at this point? Notice the slash
marks all around them.

Take a minute now to notice that you have all the
friendship, all the important ingredients we identified, all
here, right now already!

Notice how your body is reacting—what new sensations
it is giving you. Contemplate those sensations as long
as it feels comfortable. When ready, gradually begin
breathing through your nose and softly open your eyes as
you transition out of the ritual.

In this chapter, we've had the opportunity to connect with ourselves, with others, and with our communities in ways that are more meaningful than we usually do. For those who are interested in either attracting a life partner or learning how to build and sustain a deeply enriching union with one, the next chapter is for you.

11

Attracting and Sustaining a Life Partnership

> The curious paradox is that when I accept myself just
> as I am, then I can change.
>
> CARL ROGERS

Attracting a Life Partner

Welcome to the world of paradox! It's a place of contradictions, oppositions, inconsistencies, ambiguities, and conflict. Have you ever considered that one reason for attracting a life partner is to ground and expand all the best energies and feelings we have? Imagine sharing love with someone whose presence makes you like being who you are, someone who supports your growing more into your uniqueness and fullest creative manifestation and expects nothing less from you. For many of us, this would require a complete shift in our thinking, our social behavior, and our self-image. Finding love often requires *turning our worlds inside out*. And that is the purpose of the next ritual.

This is not a how-to for finding a perfect partner. You can find those in magazines at the checkout lines in grocery stores. This chapter is about getting out of our own way and seeing through personal and cultural blind spots.

I met my present someone special almost fourteen years ago, when neither of us expected it. We had both *surrendered* to being single, at least until it really felt right. I had just endured a bad ending to a relationship which had taught me a great deal. Underneath that mess was the still-broken heart from losing Gil. I felt I was okay on my own for the time. Interestingly, at age forty-one, Elias had never had a long-term relationship. His standards were high, which is how he is with everything. Letting go and letting be played a role in his openness to a relationship with me.

Overcoming Binary Logjams

What I mean by a binary logjam is this: a situation where there seems to be only two possibilities, yes or no. When there only seem to be two alternatives, our possibilities will seem very limited. In the ritual that follows the discussion in this section, we will work on attracting a life partner by energetically grounding and expanding. We will make room for paradox in order to transform binary emotional logjams into free-flowing possibilities.

Following are a few of the cultural thought patterns that lock us out of our own lives. In each pair of statements, the statement marked "A" is boastful, with little nurturing or trust. The statement marked "B" is the voice of the hidden, orphaned child behind the mask of composure. Both views are true and are obstacles to finding a life partner because they are contradictory messages that take up all our energy. It is only when we resolve the fight between the two views that we can attract others.

It is recommended that the ritual preparation below be done in private and in sacred time. While it seems more like an exercise, don't let that fool you. The more authenticity, calmness, and good intention you bring to it, the more it will reveal mysterious powers and energies that will light your way on the relationship.

Here are the paradoxical pairs of statements to reflect upon in preparation for the heart of the Life Partner Ritual. Feel free to add a few of your own:

1. A. I know what I want! B. How am I supposed to know what or who is best for me?

2. A. I know how to be a good partner! B. Can someone tell me how to find a relationship that really works? I haven't got a clue.

3. A. I have an image of the perfect relationship. B. Can my fantasy ever become real?

4. A. There are lots of people like me looking for connection. B. There are so many lonely, isolated people. It's hopeless!

5. A. I need freedom to be exactly who I am, no matter what people think. B. I don't want anyone to know my shameful secrets.

6. A. I am not unattractive. I'm just always attracted to those who are unavailable. B. That unavailable person is the one without whom I can never feel alive and vital!

7. A. I feel stronger around a needy person. B. Why do I always end up with these weak, needy people?

8. A. Having an unhappy partnership is prison. B. Not having a partner is a life failure.

9. A. It is enough to be partnered with myself. B. I feel very lonely when following my own path.

10. A. A partner will appear when I am ready. B. When I don't have a partner I am mean, bitter, and self-destructive, and there's nothing I can do about it.

11. A. I see many possibilities unfolding even now. B. Everything seems blurry, like I need new glasses. I can't find my way out of the woods.

12. A. I must be open and receptive to new energy fields. B. Who wants to be hurt or embarrassed?

13. A. I want to surrender to whatever may come my way! B. I'm too busy with my life responsibilities to make time for a cozy romance.

14. A. I am in control of my emotions! B. Everyone is pushing my buttons!

15. A. I have let go of my wants and desires! B. Nice to meet you. Here is a list of my needs! Meet them! Now!

16. A. True and equal partnership is attainable! B. Oh, no it isn't!

I want to use these paradoxical statement pairs and any you care to add in a special Life Partner Ritual that will catapult us into the heart of paradox. At this place we hear a little voice that will guide us the rest of the way. **(Hint: the little voice is our innate intelligence revealed through the Curious Observer.)**

Life Partner Ritual

Preparation for ritual: Create a safe, quiet space for your ritual. Feel free to include candles, sensual music, and any objects that will serve as a resource for your ritual. Before actually doing the ritual, put on an outfit of clothing that you might wear to flirt with yourself. Find a wall mirror that can reflect back a good portion of you (a bathroom mirror at least, a full length wall dressing mirror at best). Have fun choosing your outfit. You will also need the above list of relational paradoxes along with any new ones you may have added. You will also want a place to lie down comfortably in dim light at the end of the ritual.

In the room with the mirror, bring in soft light and soothing music if possible, and any other artifacts or photos that can amplify the beneficial energy in the room. It is now your "Life Partner" ritual space. Now leave the room for a few minutes.

In preparation for reentering your sacred room, come back to your awkward/elegant self-seduction outfit. Remember you are seducing yourself. What would be fun and silly to wear or not wear to seduce yourself? Silly is important here; it helps crack open the blocks that otherwise preclude all possibilities for conscious life partnering, even with our selves. In the center of this openness, you will discover a voice. It will come from the felt senses in the energy fields that you have created, from imagery; it may come as words, or shape them later. Be patient and present to whatever comes from within and around you.

Your outfit is ready. Have the paradoxical statements handy to read in the ritual, and now you may enter the ritual space. Glance at that beauty in the mirror. If you have always felt physically unattractive, now is the time to notice, with a smile, that you are a unique manifestation of light in the universe, a universe in which there is not another hottie like you. Be willing to notice if your light always shines brightly, or if you rarely notice any shine at all. Now is a good time to look into your own eyes with humor, squint at your sexy body, gaze into your bright being, and notice yourself the way you suddenly notice something you really like. Dismiss any thoughts of self-disapproval with the words, "misperceptions of the dominant culture."

This part of the mirror ritual goes like this:

"My nose too big? Misperceptions of the dominant culture! I am beautiful!"

"Me too fat? Misperceptions of a 'Ken and Barbie' dominant culture! I too am beautiful."

"Too short? Me? Misperceptions of the dominant culture!"

"Eyebrows too heavy? Misperception of the dominant culture! My eyebrows are fine."

"Lips too large? Who are you kidding? That's just a misperception of the dominant culture."

"My eyes don't look funny. That is a misperception of the dominant culture which fails to see how exotic I really am!"

"My hair is a funny color! Misperception of the dominant culture. My hair is beautiful."

Make up your own statements as you need to.

Now apply this same technique as you see things about your personality you might be tempted to condemn or criticize. This is not to say that your personality can't be improved; however, it is important to accept your personality traits as they are without judgment before identifying those that are standing in your way that might be malleable to energetic change.

"I'm not too nervous, too loudmouth, too sensitive, too wild!"

"I'm not too quiet, too studious, too secretive, too wordy, too silly, too serious. I am FASCINATING!"

Now, take a minute to make sure the ritual area supports you as much as possible and that you are as comfortable there as you can be. Good! Please look into the mirror, holding the paradoxes, and begin reading the fifteen of them (plus any you add) very slowly. As you finish reading each one, take in the full meaning on both sides of the contradictions as you read it. Make room for it all without judgment or agenda. The medicine drizzles through the cracks in consciousness in the slow deliberate reading of each. Let your Curious Observer begin to notice the appearance of a unique corrective voice within you that longs to enlighten you and solve the puzzles of these binary logjams.

Read the whole list of paradoxes three times slowly (taking three deep breaths between each reading of the full list). As you do so, notice your senses, feelings, thoughts, and any positive, instructive inner voices that show up to rudder you around these rocky shoals. Register in a special place in consciousness anything you consider noteworthy.

When you have completed the list, read it three times, bow to yourself in the mirror as a way of saying thank you to your self for coming this far in the ritual. This will amplify all the energy that has been gestating. As gracefully as possible, find your way to the bed (the one with soft lighting) and lie on your back.

Lie there for a minute, noticing your state of being in this very moment without judgment or agenda. Now apply this breathing technique: Inhale and draw your creative, light energy down from your head and heart and into your buttocks, squeezing the energy tightly there. Hold it there briefly while rocking the spine slowly. If you feel the energy go up the back of your spine, tuck in your chin gently so the energy can move into your head. Roll your eyes up as if looking at the top of your head. This will help bring new energy to the top of your head. Do this breathing exercise three to six times at your choosing, managing your breath as feels right to you. When you feel you've done it and have sensed the energy movement in your body and your head, gently touch your tongue to the front upper roof of your mouth and notice if anything happens.

As you lie there breathing normally, gradually allow yourself to remember reading the paradoxes into the mirror and notice if you begin to hear an inner voice of guidance or knowing. If you don't notice it now, give it time to come to you. Don't force it. Much energy will be loosened up when you make room for the two sides of the paradoxes to coexist. As you open your body to energy, trust that a friendly, informed voice will come forth from within. It may not come as a voice but as something else that leads you, a directive force or meaningful occurrence. Invite your Curious Observer to notice what happens.

When you get the first glimpses of this voice, please follow it, if it is in alignment with respect for yourself and others. It is the wisdom in this voice that will mysteriously, step-by-step, lead you as an unseen guide toward the perfect relationship for you now. Let the voice keep lighting your next step on this frontier.

Openings

Now if we go back to the list of paradoxical statements used in the Life Partner Ritual, we will see something interesting. The contradictions between the statements can be transformed by energetically accepting that life is paradoxical and that we are larger than our perceived problems and contradictions. On our best days we can find a middle or third way. We need to find a *center* between extremes. Rather than take one virtue and overplay it until it becomes a flaw or weapon, let us learn to cultivate opposite virtues simultaneously.

This may be confusing for some at first, but if you look again at the Binary Logjam list and imagine you have the virtues of character to energetically and literally connect A and B, it all becomes clear.

1. I am decisive and think long term.
2. I am a loyal partner and know when to quit.
3. I am an idealist and am willing to work with the process.
4. I am optimistic and know when to be realistic.
5. I am expressive and know when to say "TMI!" (too much information).
6. I aim high and don't want the moon.
7. I like to *feel* strong and would rather *be* strong.
8. I reach out to others while learning to be self-sufficient.
9. I follow my own path and take time to share the journey of life with others.
10. I am focused on finding love and biding my time.
11. I think big and am aware of my limitations.
12. I am open-minded and self-preserving.
13. I am romantic and my feet are on the ground.
14. I am a feeling person and I won't be manipulated.
15. I am detached and in touch with my survival instincts.
16. I believe in equality and asymmetry.

Contemplate this list of opposite virtues, and consider them as resources for expansiveness and healing. Now imagine that a friend has come to you for guidance. Help them find a balance by encouraging them to seek and develop both their opposite virtues.

Sustaining an Intimate Relationship

In the Life Partner Ritual we explore new perspectives in energetic partnering. Energy has always been a component in relationships, yet now we are suggesting that relationships are all about energy. Let us use this understanding as a primary way of sorting out our relational world and seeing it through new lenses. We are looking for someone whose very energetic presence makes us really like being who we are. We want that someone to support our growth towards our uniqueness, and give us space to manifest and express ourselves creatively.

I remember being stirred by the words Scott Peck wrote in *The Road Less Traveled* more than twenty years ago: "I define love thus: The will to expand one's self for the purpose of nurturing one's own or another's spiritual growth…. We choose to love…. Love is the free exercise of choice … an action, an activity … that implies commitment and the exercise of wisdom."

In this section we move all the delicious words that many of us are so attracted to to another level (especially if we've done the Grow Up Ritual in Chapter Seven). Let's raise the level of expectation in an energetic relationship so that we not only sustain each other but also transform each other.

The Power of Two

The Power of Two concept is one I learned from The Body Electric School. In 1997 my partner and I attended the first five-day retreat they sponsored for gay male couples which explored sexuality as a doorway to the sacred. Held on the big island of Hawaii, it was a very liberating event. By exploring our erotic energy with each other that week in a sacred setting with fifteen other couples, many veils were dropped. We discovered an awesome power in the giving and receiving of sensual pleasure. During that time, the two of us also created a ring exchange ceremony for our union and stood barefoot on a rock ledge overlooking the Pacific Ocean during the ritual.

On the third day of the retreat, each couple was given an uncooked egg to take care of, a symbolic representation of the *third entity* in the relationship. Together we babied the egg for two days and took it everywhere. On the fifth day, we were asked to create a ritual to let go of the egg. We and another couple placed our eggs on a ledge that was being hit with ocean waves. We wrapped it in purple paper to protect it from the jostling and in honor of its sacred power. As we lit incense prior to releasing it, a wave swept over the egg and dyed it the most beautiful mosaic of white and brilliant purple.

The Power of Two has its origin in the awareness that we create a third *unseen* entity when we choose to bond with another. By bonding, I refer to what happens during the first three months to a year of being with a partner. At a certain point, we have shared many joys and struggles, and the unconscious of each person begins relating to this union differently than it would in more superficial relationships.

I discovered the existence of the *third entity* while investigating my own intimate relationships and those of my paired clients. It became easier to work with as I came to appreciate energy psychology, healing, and the principles of vibrant living. I now know that it takes three to create The Power of Two in the cosmos. In my union one entity is Michael and the uniqueness, love, light, and contradictions I bring to the union. The second entity is my partner and the uniqueness, love, light, and contradictions that he brings to the union. The third invisible entity we call the relationship, though it does not need a name. Once the third entity forms as an energy field, it represents the best of both of us and our contradictions. It is bigger than the both of us and paradoxically fragile at the same time.

When working with couples, sometimes I suggest they think of a plant as a metaphor for the third entity. It is a living, breathing organism that must be nurtured to survive and remain beautiful. If we do not care for the plant, it will no longer be able to bring us sustenance.

While a plant needs sun or light, air, and fertilizer to flourish, our human unions feed on communication and the exchange of sensual energies. Bringing the power of two into the cosmos is an experience, and it is felt in physical and primordial ways. My partner and I have no words for our experience, yet we *know* we are sharing a wider bandwidth of energy.

The following rituals are intended to dissolve outdated cultural constructs that deaden relationships. Ingredients we will need to bring to the ritual include willingness to be authentic and to learn something new.

In my own early relationships, I had labeled myself a *three-monther*. Once I was seeing someone and having sex for three months, the sex got stale, and I wanted to run for my life. I usually did. Sometimes I had a reason; sometimes I had to find one. I often wondered what was wrong with me. When I began this research in the mid '80s, I realized that it was at about the three-month period that I started to feel bonded to the other person and two things would begin to occur. They were a schism in my nervous system's ability to embrace both love or spiritual energies and sexual energies at the same time. The people I bonded with were fine, but my unconscious visceral projection of childhood traumas would take over, and I would project them onto anyone I had bonded with. I could no longer perform sexually and I didn't know why. Ultimately, they would get the message and leave.

The first illumination was that the bonding triggered something in my unconscious that went way back to my early ingrained sex/spirit split. I had internalized early on that God, love, and family were good, and that sex was dirty, bad, and sinful. While not everyone is a three-monther like me, many people I have counseled in long-term relationships struggle with sex lives that lack fulfillment after a bonding period evolves.

Like me, people in these relationships no longer feel comfortable asking for what they want for fear of being judged. On both sides of the dynamic, shame from shadowy corners obscures clarity. What emerges after the bonding are the physiological symptoms of early traumas that crushed our spirits.

The Polarity Stage

The other closely related bogeyman that enters is the unconscious ego power struggle, or the *polarity stage* of the union. This is the igniting in the unconscious, after bonding, of the early dynamics with our primary caregivers. For example, my mom abandoned me at age four. It does not take a genius to deduce that I probably have severe childhood abandonment issues. After bonding, I become very needy emotionally and physically. It just happens. This powerful drive from deep inside controls everything because of the fear of being *hurt again*.

Ironically, I have come to learn that nature is ahead of me on this one. My partners always had the opposite kind of issues: they were not afraid of abandonment but encroachment terrified them. Fear of encroachment happens when they've had one or more caretakers overly involved in their early lives. Often, this would be a secondary caregiver. In the end, they feel traumatized that they didn't have their own space, even if they were loved and cared for adequately.

Imagine the complicated dance that a partner and I would enter after bonding as our unconscious dictates take over. First, I'd drift away from sex and wouldn't know how to talk about it. Next, I would get touchy, clingy, and even loving—which would be confusing to my partner, who is already feeling smothered by his/her own need to *not* be taken over. It's a twisted mess, yet I've come to see it as a gift from the cosmos.

Before we can fully have the alchemy and unity we may desire with another, we must first dissolve the traumas from our primary relationships. That's why nature sees to it that we are mysteriously attracted to those with opposite energetic challenges. We were never taught that to have a rich, fulfilling, loving relationship where our erotic life can also flourish, we must first tend to those blockages.

The good news is *there is nothing wrong with us*. We are simply products of our cultural and personal evolutions. Once we bring the challenges out of the unconscious where they have ominous rule, we can work with another in intimacy and love and dissolve the barriers of the polarity stage of a relationship.

What is the polarity stage? After researching relationship dynamics for over fifteen years, I was serendipitously invited in 2001 to attend the first International Conference on Sex and Spirit hosted by the Findhorn Community in Scotland. It was there that I met researchers from the U.K., Nick Duffy and Helena Lovena. I was delighted that their research mirrored mine with one exception. What I had been calling the unconscious "power struggle" phase of a blossoming relationship, they named "the polarity stage."

As we move through the polarity stage, we begin to feel the *power of two* in the universe and it just keeps growing. This knowledge and language gave me a profound feeling of tremendous relief. It is as though I had just taken a great weight off my shoulders. This was my armor, of course, and the responsibility the child in me bore for trying to make my early relationships succeed. Now I understand that the very conflict I avoided was a necessary process in the development of an adult relationship.

I have created the Transmuting Polarization Ritual in honor of Nick and Helena's work, and of any of us who have stumbled through relationships.

Transmuting Polarization Ritual

This ritual is designed to enliven and sustain an intimate relationship while fostering its growth individually and as a union. It starts with preparing with the Transmuting Polarization Ritual and expands to the first three months of different Rituals for Couples. If practiced, it can also lead in time to an extraordinarily enriching erotic life.

This is a twelve-month ritual. After that time, you can choose to continue it in its present form, re-design it, or let it organically merge with everyday life.

The reasons for a twelve-month ritual cycle are manifold. For starters, the time commitment is essential to successfully completing the ritual. Each monthly one-hour performance of the ritual shakes loose and dissolves the frozen energy that has created barriers in the relationship. We would not want to do too much too fast, nor would it work very well. Therefore, there will be different yet palpable results from each of the twelve encounters. These results are immediately rewarding, and you will have a full month to notice the subtle and radical transformations in the union.

At the same time you will organically prepare for the next performance of the ritual by inviting your Curious Observer to inform the process. Usually one partner will notice more than the other, and sharing observations at the next ritual performance is encouraged. It is natural that one person might notice and be able to articulate more since we are working with many opposite energies, and what comes naturally to one may not to the other. There will probably be dramatic changes, yet the subtle ones often create just as many avenues for loving energy.

This ritual is being offered to you as a gateway resource, by which I mean an opening of all kinds of unrealized possibilities.

Your monthly rituals will focus and amplify the intention and process of transmutation. Anything that you offer up for healing—polarized emotions, psychology, ways of thinking, and energy fields—may then present themselves in new forms, and you and your partner will observe them together. In the process, the unique personal and cultural history of your relationship is likely to emerge. Remember that slow is fast. As we enter the one-year ritual, it's good to accept the fact that unconscious polarity dynamics tend to be entrenched for most couples. Any progress is good, and you will be amazed at how much fulfillment you can feel with even the smallest change. These deep and sometimes subtle feelings prime the pump for more shifts and openings to take place.

Start the ritual with the creating of sacred space, which will honor the importance of the ceremony from the beginning. Have a calendar for a full year handy that can be referred to over the next twelve months. Set aside on that calendar a convenient hour of sacred time for your sharing the ritual in each of the twelve months before you. Just make sure it is an hour unencumbered by other obligations. Some couples, after the first few months, may choose to do it bi-weekly (still holding the larger one year intention) because they enjoy it, can get more benefit from it, or just plain need it. Since this is your ritual, feel free to negotiate whatever feels right to both of you. There is no one right way. Most important is getting started and structuring a one-year plan that can be adaptable, yet will be respected. In setting up your calendar you are concurrently doing a Seed-Planting Ritual (Chapter Six) for a thriving union that will automatically get sensitive monthly attention, with shared intention and resource energy for fuller blossoming. The seed planting is organic as a couple aligns their intention to make this ritual important over the given time period, both amplifying and directing the energy.

One of you volunteer to be the "reader," the one who will be prepared to read at the ritual any grounding material to serve as a resource to the process. I invite the other to be the "convener" whose task it will be to watch the calendar to remind you both to prepare (if necessary) for the next upcoming ritual, and to set-up the space for the ritual. This means giving some forethought to the ambience, timing, lighting, and being sure that whatever else you need (such as talking object, reading material, etc.) is all in place when the ritual commences. The primary purpose for the talking object (be it a feather, a stick, a bead, or a stone) is to focus the energy on the one holding it while they are talking. In ancient traditions, when one held the talking stick, they spoke from the heart and from their experience and everyone else present actively listened, making the speakers' conditions their own. The talking object, which can be feather, stone, or memento, is passed from partner to partner as a tradition.

Once you have those designations, have fun choosing your talking object. A talking object, such as a talking stick or stone, has its history in wisdom circles through the ages. We call these gatherings "authenticity circles" because of the heartfelt manner in which we speak during these encounters. The one you choose now may stay with you through the year, or you can change it at anytime with respectful negotiation. It is important that you both have good feelings about the object, giving it the role of providing additional resource energy.

As an aid to you both in preparation for the first formal ritual, I encourage each partner to do (or redo) the Grow Up Ritual given in Chapter Three, however, this time having your relationship in mind. This particular ritual provides very good grist for the mill and will help generate the kind of energy we want at the first performance of the ritual. Perhaps after you each have experimented with it, you may want to make some notes as to what was illuminated and/or noteworthy to you in the process. Bring the notes to your first ritual.

What to bring to the first ritual and how to conduct it: It is the convener's role to bring the talking object, set up the meeting area so that it is comfortable (perhaps setting it up in advance with partner), and bring this or other

helpful texts for reference. The reader may want to be on
the look out for a poem or special passage to help set the
tone for the ritual, though both are invited to do so.

You also want to bring any notes from your performances
of the Grow Up Ritual to support your sharing about it.
In addition to that, I invite you both to write down on a
piece of paper in advance of meeting, three paradoxical
areas of personal sensitivity you have in the relationship.
For example: (1) Communication/Struggle with fluidity,
(2) Extended Family/I wish they didn't exist, and (3)
Fulfilling sex/Shadow fears.

They don't have to be perfect; they are intended
to be a starter kit for bringing heartfelt expression
about complexities into the light of compassion and
understanding. Don't share them with each other prior
to the ritual. Perhaps, by the time you both share your
sensitive paradoxes in the ritual space, there may be three
to five areas of challenged communication that you both
agree to honor and bring compassion to.

This ritual has three rituals to be performed one after another
with a one-month break. When you complete the three, you will be
empowered to design the next nine to complete the year of sacred
openings.

RITUAL FOR COUPLES: PART ONE/MONTH 1

Start the ritual on time with one minute of conscious
breathing and silence. Hold hands at the end of it
for a few seconds, or as long a time as you both feel
comfortable with. These activities allow for transition

from the "everyday" stuff to the coming together in mind, heart and spirit for this ritual. After a moment of silence with the talking object in hand, I invite the reader to slowly read the following prayer to begin focusing the energy:

> *May this ritual time together be for the highest good of each of us, our union, and our larger world.*

After the prayer, the reader passes the talking object to the convener, who will take ten minutes to share whatever they found noteworthy from doing the Grow-Up ritual, particularly as it relates to this relationship. As always, when holding the talking object, the one speaking will share from the experience of the "I" and from the heart with authenticity. Holding the object is always an invitation to share from personal experience, never about others, unless the primary focus is on the speaker's experience of engagement with another. The listener (the formal designation for the partner who is being totally present and "actively listening") will energetically create "a safe space" for the person speaking and listen actively with the intention of relating to what is being shared. In ritual, the person with the talking object always has full attention and is never interrupted, except for timing notification. The listener also is time-keeper and lets the speaker know when nine minutes have passed and that they have one more to complete their sharing for now. The ten-minute time period for sharing (like others to follow) is somewhat arbitrary, yet takes the reality of what's being done and the overall time into consideration. Feel free to adjust this to your liking once you get a feel for the process.

At the end of ten minutes, the speaker becomes quiet, and the listener in a ritualized and authentic expression says "Ho," as an acknowledgement that the sharing was received. The speaker then quietly passes the talking object to the partner, who becomes the next speaker and takes ten minutes to share his noteworthy experiences from the Grow-Up Ritual. This is not a time to comment on partners' earlier sharing; that can be done later. This is your time to speak authentically about your experiences with the ritual. The new listener now practices active listening, with the intention of relating to the sharing, and also creating a safe energy field. The new listener also keeps time and lets the speaker know when one minute is left.

As the speaker completes the ten minutes, the listener acknowledges the sharing with the expression "Ho," which in the future will always be used when someone shares something in the ritual space. We want to take the time to see that *everything shared will always be received and acknowledged.*

The talking object is now passed back to the listener who will take five minutes to share what it was like (from personal and felt sense experience) to share earlier and then to listen to their partner's sharing. The new listener will now keep time announcing when there is a minute left and expressing a "Ho" acknowledgment on completion. The talking stick is quietly passed back, and the same five-minute process is reversed.

After the acknowledgment with "Ho" concerning the above, take a ten-minute refreshment and bathroom break.

On return the reader gets the talking object and takes
up to ten minutes to share what he or she discovered as
three paradoxical areas of personal sensitivity. Follow the
same protocol as above (which will remain consistent).
After ten minutes the talking object is quietly passed and
the convener has ten minutes to share three paradoxical
areas of personal sensitivity. On completion of this, with
protocol in place, the object goes back to the reader
who takes five minutes to share what it was like sharing
their sensitivities and listening to their partners. On
completion, this is reversed (protocol still in place).

On completion, the reader reads the following prayer to
close the first formal ritual:

> *We give thanks for our ability and willingness to be*
> *together in this way, at this time, doing what we are*
> *doing. We respect that we are not here to fix anything or*
> *anyone. Our sole purpose is to give love, light, and space*
> *to what may have been in the dark. We trust that out of*
> *this compassionate space-giving to ourselves, each other*
> *and the union, that all will fall into place in a good way*
> *which we will observe without judgment or agenda. We*
> *give thanks!*

When the ritual is complete, remember it is always an option to
commune in whatever way you desire or you may want to try one of
the erotic rituals in this text. Whatever you do, a gentle, slow conscious transition back to the everyday world is recommended. We
don't want to jar our systems with outside stimuli too quickly. It can
interrupt the organic nature of inner shifts.

RITUAL FOR COUPLES: PART TWO/MONTH 2

It is suggested that part two be done a month after the above, in
line with the earlier planning for the year.

Preparation: Before gathering for ritual, each partner should take ten minutes of reflective time with a pen and paper. During that time, write down three things you like about your relationship and/or your partner. (Take whatever comes, there are no perfect answers, and you can always add to them later.) Now, leave some space and write three things in your relationship or your dynamics with your partner that, in your experience, could use some improvement or fine-tuning. It does not work well to finger-point here, but rather come from experience and perhaps say what makes you feel respected and cared about, and what does not. Stay in the first person. Rely mainly on "I" statements such as "I feel," "I want," "I need." Let your communication be grounded in respectfulness and compassion.

Start each performance of the ritual on time with one minute of conscious breathing and silence. Hold hands at the end of it for a few seconds or as long as you both feel comfortable with. These activities allow for transition from the "everyday" stuff and attunement to the coming together in mind, heart, and spirit for this ritual. After a moment of silence with the talking object in hand, the convener should invite the reader to slowly read the following prayer to begin focusing the energy:

May this ritual time together be for the highest good of each of us, our union, and our larger world.

This time, the reader will keep the talking object and take ten minutes to share three things they appreciate in the union and/or in their partner, reasons that help them keep choosing to stay in the relationship. When that sharing is complete, move on to the three things in your relationship or your dynamics with your partner that, in your experience, could use some improvement or fine-tuning.

As last time, the active listener will create a safe, energetic field for their partner and notify them when they have a minute left.

On completion, the convener says "Ho" to acknowledge receipt of sharing and is passed the talking object. Now it is the convener's time to take ten minutes to share three things they appreciate in the union and/or in their partner, reasons that help them to keep choosing to stay in the relationship. When that sharing is complete, move on to the three things in your relationship or your dynamics with your partner that, in your experience, could use some improvement or fine-tuning. The reader will actively listen and create a safe energetic field for their partner, notifying them when they have a minute left.

On completion, the reader says "Ho" to acknowledge receipt of sharing and is passed back the talking object. Now the reader takes five minutes to share reflections of what it was like to share three things that worked, three that could use improvement, and what it was like to hear their partner share their perspectives on the same points. The partner listens keenly, holds the space, and alerts reader when one minute is left.

On completion, the convener says "Ho" to acknowledge receipt of sharing and is passed back the talking object. Now the convener takes five minutes to share reflections of what it was like to share three things that worked and three that could use improvement, and what it was like to hear their partner share their perspectives on the same points. The partner listens keenly, holds the space, and alerts reader when one minute is left.

After acknowledging the above with the word "Ho," take a ten-minute refreshment and bathroom break.

On return from the break and resuming the ritual, I invite each of you to select one area of the relationship or dynamic that could use improvement. Personally, I'd select what appears to be the most difficult, as this makes whatever comes up next so much easier to resolve. Run them through the aforementioned "Four Steps of Compassionate Communication" below, first in your mind to yourself, then with your partner.

These steps for negotiating one's needs that keep the lines of communication clear, in other words, without baggage, are:

> STEP ONE: Observing what is happening in a given situation.
>
> STEP TWO: Identifying what one is feeling.
>
> STEP THREE: Identifying what one is needing.
>
> STEP FOUR: Making a request for what one would like to see occur.

Now the reader takes the talking object and shares his or her experience of expressing the desire for improvement using the above four steps: What I'm observing about the area I'd like to see improvement in for the union, what I feel about it, what I feel I need regarding it, and a request of what I would like to see occur.

On completion, the reader gets a "Ho," and the talking object gets passed to the convener, who repeats the exact same process using whatever area of desired improvement that he or she has chosen.

When the convener is finished, the reader gives a "Ho" and then proceeds to the closing prayer without comment. It is best not to discuss this sharing until it has time to move through and settle in your systems.

On completion, the reader reads the following prayer to close the second formal ritual:

> *We give thanks for our ability and willingness to be together in this way, at this time, doing exactly what we are doing. We respect that we are not here to fix any- thing or anyone. Our sole purpose is to give love, light, and space to what may have been in the dark. We trust that out of this compassionate space-giving to ourselves, each other, and the union, that all will fall into place in a good way, which we will observe without judgment or agenda. We give thanks!*

When the ritual is complete, be together in whatever way you desire. Perhaps you can try one of the erotic rituals in this text, or just hang out. Whatever you do, a gentle, slow, conscious transition back to the everyday world is recommended.

Ritual for Couples: Part Three/Month 3

It is recommended that part three be done about one month after the previous ritual, according to your prearranged calendar.

Preparation: Before gathering for the ritual each partner takes ten minutes of reflective time with a pen and paper. In that time, write down two things in your relationship that are nonsexual that make you feel awkward or embarrassed at times. Allow yourself to come up with examples of each. Leave some space. Now write one thing of a sexual or sensual nature that makes you feel awkward or embarrassed. Have some examples in mind. Prepare to elaborate. I encourage you to not be shy here and have the courage to go for what really affects you (rational or not). Try to avoid sharing what your partner already clearly knows, unless you deem it important to share again. This is a great time to get out what is not already in the air. This ritual gives us an opportunity that does not come everyday. Please use it for your highest good.

Start the ritual on time with one minute of conscious breathing and silence. Hold hands at the end of it for a few seconds or as long as you both feel comfortable with. These activities allow for transition from the 'everyday' stuff and for attunement to the coming together in mind, heart, and spirit for this ritual. After a moment of silence with the talking object in hand, I invite the reader to slowly read the following prayer to begin focusing the energy:

> *May this ritual time together be for the highest good of each of us, our union, and our larger world.*

The reader will then pass the talking object to the convener. As convener, you will take ten minutes to share two things in your relationship that are nonsexual that make you feel awkward or embarrassed at times. Also share examples of each. When you have completed that, move on to one thing of a sexual or sensual nature that makes you feel awkward or embarrassed. Give examples and elaborate. Don't be shy here; just speak your experience from the heart with authenticity.

As before, the active listener will create a safe energetic field for their partner and notify them when they have a minute left.

On completion the reader says "Ho" to acknowledge receipt of sharing and is passed the talking object. Now, as the reader, it is your turn to take ten minutes to share two things in your relationship that are nonsexual that make you feel awkward or embarrassed at times. Also share examples of each. When you have completed that, move on to one thing of a sexual or sensual nature that makes you feel awkward or embarrassed. Give examples and elaborate. Don't be shy here; just speak your experience from the heart with authenticity.

The reader will actively listen and create a safe energetic field for their partner and notify them when they have a minute left.

On completion the convener says "Ho" to acknowledge receipt of sharing and is passed back the talking object. Now the convener takes five minutes to share reflections of what it was like to share two awkward nonsexual and one sexual aspect of the relationship (with examples), and what it was like to hear their partner share their perspectives and examples on the same points. The partner listens keenly, holds the space and alerts the reader when one minute is left.

On completion, the reader says "Ho" to acknowledge receipt of sharing and is passed back the talking object. Now the reader takes five minutes to share reflections of what it was like to share two awkward nonsexual and one sexual aspect of the relationship (with examples), and what it was like to hear their partner share their perspectives and examples on the same points. The partner listens keenly, holds the space, and alerts the reader when one minute is left.

After acknowledgment with "Ho," take a ten-minute refreshment and bathroom break.

On return from the break, I invite each of you to select one area of the relationship where you would like to feel more supported or respected. We all feel under-appreciated at times. It is often part of the fundamental healing that our relationship is intended to complete. Having all been traumatized in our early primary relationships in one way or another, our unconscious links us with someone who can actually be part of the trauma healing. We do this by noticing what part of us most needs respect or tending to in the relationship, and how that relates to our early wounds or deprivations. This ritual can be a significant self-curative bridge from "falling in love" to mature love.

Again now, each partner chooses one area of the relationship where they would like to feel more supported or respected. It is important to ask for this, and the cleanest way to do that is to run your request through the "Four Steps of Compassionate Communication," in your mind before proceeding. You can also be light-hearted about this. There's humor in the absurdity of it all. Laughter makes for a light heart and that can heal anything.

Here are these steps again for negotiating one's needs. They keep the lines of communication clear.

> STEP ONE: Observing what is happening in a given situation.

> STEP TWO: Identifying what one is feeling.

Step Three: Identifying what one needs.

Step Four: Making a request for what one would like to see occur.

Now the convener takes the object and shares his or her experience of how she or he would like to feel more supported or respected in the union (and with regard to historic sensitivity) using these four steps: What I'm observing about the respect or support I'd like to receive in the union, what I feel about it, what I feel I need (specifically) regarding it, and a request of what I would like to see occur.

On completion, the convener gets a "Ho," and the talking object gets passed to the reader who repeats the exact same process using whatever area of support and respect that he or she has chosen.

When the reader is finished, the convener gives a "Ho." The reader then proceeds to the closing prayer without comment. It is best not to discuss this sharing until it has time to move through and settle in your systems.

On completion, the reader reads the following prayer to close the third formal ritual:

We give thanks for our ability and willingness to be together in this way, at this time, doing exactly what we are doing. We respect that we are not here to fix anything or anyone. Our sole purpose is to give love, light, and space to what may have been in the dark. We trust that out of this compassionate space-giving to ourselves, each other and the union, that all will fall into place in a good way which we will observe without judgment or agenda. We give thanks!

When this last phase of the ritual is complete, see what emerges and do what feels right in the moment. Whatever you do, a gentle, slow conscious transition back to the everyday world is recommended.

From this point on, I trust that as each month's ritual time comes up on the calendar, your conscious and unconscious minds and your Curious Observer will be prepared with *your focus points*, or ones that each of you selects from this book or another. Have fun negotiating them, knowing there's always time to do more rituals. I encourage building on Rosenberg's *Steps of Compassionate Communication* whenever possible. In time they will shape all your future intimate communications in a very good way.

I also invite you to see these long-term Power of Two relationship rituals as holistic and flexible rather than linear. However, it is your responsibility to each other and the third entity to keep it going. It must be sanctified as a monthly priority. Let your Curious Observer and the felt senses of your own bodies help you to evaluate the progress you are making with these rituals. Very simple, very sweet, and very powerful!

Vibrant Eros

12

Erotic Ritual

On with the dance!
Let joy be unconfined.

LORD BYRON

Eroticism is the powerful energy associated with Eros (sexual desire). It has been described as "the elixir of the Gods" and "God's best invention yet." And to those who listen to their Curious Observer and the Old Brain, Eros is the ultimate love medicine. The power of Eroticism is great, but it can also be dangerous to those who are not well-grounded. Personal limits must be respected at all times. In the next two chapters we will focus on using eroticism in energetic healing

According to Alain Danielou, author of numerous books on ancient myths and secrets of the universe, "Eroticism is the bond of attraction uniting two opposite and complementary poles." Yin and Yang represent the polarities between masculine and feminine energies, power and surrender, pleasure and pain, love and frustration, while eroticism offers an opportunity to bring fractured parts of our being together.

The power of Eros (or Love) is the ability to make us lose our sense of separateness. Love helps us be like the moth as it enters the flame, undistinguishable from the object of its fascination. Sufis have implied in their soaring poetry that the only way to approach the Godhead, the One, is not with fear and shame, but with ecstatic passion. My favorite poet, Rumi, wrote, "I am a fly in your honey, then closer, a moth caught in flame's allure, then empty sky stretched out in homage." What a wonderful way to approach the Divine! Yet many on the path of self-discovery or who are entering therapy are noticeably *separated* from God (a Higher Reality, or the Universe). This separation occurs out of a belief that we cannot be sexual and spiritual at the same time, when nothing could be further from the truth. This split between spirit and sex insures ongoing suffering. The sexual-spiritual split not only creates havoc with relationships, it undermines our relationship with the Divine, our ultimate healing resource.

It doesn't need to be this way. Georg Feurstein teaches in *Tantra: The Path to Ecstasy*, "… enjoy the sweet-tasting honey that is already on our tongue by enhancing our awareness."

It's important to discern what is called "sex" from "Eros." Sex is thought of as intercourse or some form of erotic stimulation, while Eros is a force field of energy that also includes spirit, connection, presence, and communication. Erotic connections offer a subtle and profound fulfillment beyond what I used to think of as just *having sex.*

Sex is a great driving force in the lives of many, while the pursuit of spirit, God, light, and goodness is a great driving force for others. Combining them opens up doors of perception to spirit and creativity. This union is known as Tantric. *Tantra,* a Sanskrit word, means an expansive system of all-encompassing reality that teaches the continuity between spirit and matter through our senses.

We are each unique manifestations of pure energy, yet in that uniqueness our perceptions of beauty and harmony can be quite different. Something *we* find beautiful and desire may be surprising to our friends, and even to our own civilized nature. Sexual energy predates civilization, and in creating organized communities to centralize power, civilizations have harnessed (and hampered) the power of Eros. Our mission is to expand the fullness of Eros to the profound healing resource that it is. Ritual can help gently break through the culturally imposed internal and social barriers. Like Plato before him, Ken Wilber describes Eros as a love energy opening an ascending path of a higher and wider sense of self. Lovers who truly love are taken out of themselves into a larger union with the beloved.

As you move into Erotic Ritual, be prepared as never before to dissolve the shame that may come up. Shame, a mechanism for restricting unethical social behavior, though initially influenced externally can become internalized and involuntary. In the case of sexuality, shame has been taught to us by parents or baby sitters before we were even old enough to talk. We encounter shame barriers that combat our erotic energy in the form of images and fears born of our civilized conditioning. This conditioning isn't right or wrong—it's simply a manifestation of our evolution. But we must determine whether this form of social conditioning is in our best interest, especially when making a conscious decision to access the best of who we are through Erotic Ritual. From Mario Jacoby's *Shame and the Origins of Self Esteem*:

> *In the biblical myth of Paradise, shame arises for the first time in connection with a growing consciousness. This dawning awareness concerns the separation of the self … from God, and it results in the loss of Paradise and original wholeness.*

Erotic Ritual is one of the most effective pathways back to the "wholeness and paradise" Jacoby refers to, and in the next pages I will offer *Erotic Rituals* for self-lovemaking and partnering with another.

The Sexual-Spiritual (or Love) Split Revisited

My interest in Erotic Ritual was ignited in the mid-'80s while leading a weekend retreat on *Spirituality in Recovery*. Serendipitously, one participant pressed for bringing the subject of sex into the weekend process, a challenge that launched my interest in the culturally-based sexual challenges that we all share. The field work and research that followed led me from the addictions work that had been my primary focus of the time, to underlying trauma, and sexual healing. As years passed, my knowledge was enhanced on how to use energy, ritual, and evolutionary awareness to resolve psychological issues and sexual/intimacy challenges.

The *sexual-spiritual (love) split*, is a deep psychic schism (within almost everyone) that *prohibits* loving relationships from forming and enduring, even though sexuality may be alive and growing, or vice versa (the sex dies after bonding occurs). The schism between sex and spirit, caused by generational, cultural, religious, and early programming, plants seeds deep in the unconscious that makes merging with another virtually impossible without the specific healing that Erotic Rituals offer.

Shifting Constructs: S.E.X.

To move into the world of Erotic Ritual, we must gently put our old constructs about sex aside. Many people equate sex with a means to procreation, but this is not the driving energy behind it. Most of us never developed a healthy conscious context for having erotic pleasure. We clumsily fall into sex, gradually shaping ideas about it from what we observed, and from our own experience. I have rarely met anyone who has an ongoing, rich, and fulfilling sexual life that did not have to go back to create new contexts for their erotic experiences. Each person has to create new ways of experiencing the meaning and purpose of all types of lovemaking, including with themselves.

Erotic Ritual also means "sacred and transcendent sex." Author, Jenny Wade, in her *Transcendent Sex: When Lovemaking Opens the Veil*, references that even in her title. She further states, "It is about the best kept secret in human history: that ordinary people, with no special training can find themselves in different spiritual realms when making love—an experience so profound that nothing will ever be the same." A sad observation for me in Jenny's research is that very few ever shared their transcendent experiences (even with lovers) until being questioned. Clearly our culture has limited ability to embrace the divine when it visits through the erotic. We are gradually learning that pleasure leads us toward the divine, therefore expanding the divinity in our lives.

To define sacred sexuality, it is important to rediscover and in some cases reinvent what sex means to us. Paramount for growth in this area is to break out of preconceived thinking. To help us step out of the cultural box, my partner and I turned the word into the acronym, **S.E.X.**, for *Soul Energy eXchange*. Couple that with an understanding of S.O.U.L., Systemic Organization of Universal Love, as defined in the book, *The Living Energy Universe*, by Gary Schwartz and Linda Russek, and you have Soulful Sex, the product of Erotic Ritual.

Erotic Ritual teaches us to live more from the level of the S.O.U.L., and can be freeing of fear, hatred, and anxiety. Deepak Chopra refers to the Curious Observer as a representation of the S.O.U.L. It is the knower. In Erotic Ritual we learn to take advantage of a connection between the personal soul and the universal soul to enrich our lives, without the "I" clamoring for attention.

This perspective is not limited to traditional concepts of sexuality as procreation, or even orgasm. S.E.X. is about sharing and exchanging energies that originate from our souls rather than just our heads or our genitals. It is about uniting our longing for wholeness with connection, yearnings that are naturally sacred and spiritual. It is about pleasuring and being pleasured in whatever consensual form that takes. As author Brandy Williams writes in *Ecstatic Ritual: Practical Sex Magic:*

Sex is the most engrossing human act. Intimate touch involves all the senses. At the moment of pleasure, of shivering contact with a partner or a stolen moment of self-love, all our normal duties, tasks, fears, failures, all things we do drop away. When our bodies feel healthy and our hearts clear, when we can give and accept pleasure freely and with sincerity, when we bring to intimate touch an awareness of the Divine, sex becomes sacred.

Erotic Ritual's Primary Energies

There are four primary forces in Erotic Ritual's Soul Energy eXchange (S.E.X.): love, pleasure, lingam, and yoni. Love is an energy transmitted from the heart. It can be felt through hands of a lover, or from a father or mother to a child. It is gender-neutral. Love means losing ourselves in the beloved. Pleasure takes many forms, but to define erotic pleasure, it is stimulation of the pleasure centers of the brain through visual and tactile stimulation. While some have a low threshold for erotic pleasure, others may find everything erotically pleasurable.

The kind of love we explore in Erotic Ritual is the love that moves us to listen and intuit what our lover wants, to care about their needs. It is best to have the constant energy of love as the foundation for everything in life. The energy of love can be triggered by the energy of pleasure, but it is at its greatest when love is present first.

The third and fourth energies, lingam and yoni, are Hindu Sanskrit terms for the erect penis and the vagina respectively. You can learn more about these energies by exploring Tantra, either in workshops, or in books such as *Tantra: The Art of Conscious Loving* by Charles and Caroline Muir. Understanding these terms can be supportive in breaking out of traditional, culture-bound thinking. Lingam energy can be thought of as masculine drive: the penis, the pursuer, initiation, aggression, and personal power. Lingam energy is often male-identified, yet this energy is found in all of us.

Yoni energy is feminine, receptive, creative, and artistic; the vagina or any part of the body that yields and opens to *receive* energy. Men also have yoni energy.

We have all experienced limiting conditioning in the expression of our lingam and/or yoni energies. We have all suffered some sort of trauma that blocks our love and pleasure energies as well. Unlocking trauma and toxic shame and thawing frozen erotic energies are the best paths to the sacred. Experimenting without judgment, using all four of these soulful energies is a direct route to the divine, to earth energy, to our ancient memories, and connection with the universe. As Robert Bly writes in *The Kabir Book*:

> *As the river gives into the ocean,*
> *what is inside me moves inside you …*

Perhaps more than in other rituals, we learn through Erotic Ritual that we are all expressions of a much larger source of communal energy. It melts barriers and we feel less alienated and alone.

Notice when you are having an erotic experience with someone (or yourself) that there is always a giving and a receiving of energy. Sometimes it's reciprocated, or sometimes one is consistently giving or receiving, and either is fine. Allow yourself to be really present in any prolonged erotic exchange, and you will find yourself in a *circle of energy*. (The yoni expression fully experiences the lingam expression, and vice versa.)

Sexual Concerns

The very personal sexual concerns people have shared with me have ranged from not feeling they are desirable, experiencing deadness in their pelvis, erectile challenges, orgasmic difficulties, or feeling limited with a partner they love. Sometimes it's an obsession over body parts—too big, too small, too tight, too wide. There are many similar burdens that a lot of people carry, sometimes silently. The principles of Erotic Ritual can be enormously helpful in renegotiating and resolving these hardships. With the right resources, including therapy in some cases (in addition to ritual practice) the barriers to erotic fulfillment will dissolve, creating possibilities for a blissful engagement with one's self and with another.

Relationships without Erotic Ritual

When the sex in a monogamous relationship is not fulfilling, a cornerstone of the union is weak and vulnerable. If fulfillment dwindles (or becomes barely existent) a foundation of the relationship is betrayed. Often because couples lack the communication skills required for sensitive dialogue, they go into denial, often lasting years. Addressing these problems with the assistance of Erotic Ritual can enhance those very skills.

Happily, I have been in a loving, growing, and sexually fulfilling relationship for many years now. It was one of my first experiences of what Peter Russell has been calling *"turning your reality inside out."* All the work has been worth it! Creating sacred time, opening up the heart, letting go of taboos, sharing shame-free sex, and being responsible and self-respecting have all been key. Loving sex heightens consciousness and pure love. In that vast, nurturing ocean there is no ego, nothing to defend, only a sense of just being and connection. Deepak Chopra wrote in *The Spontaneous Fulfillment of Desire:* "This ocean represents the non-local intelligence (beyond our physical being) and the wave represents our local intelligence. The two are intimately connected."

Communication in these sensitive areas can at first feel like hard work. With practice, after a while it becomes quite natural. When Elias and I explored having a life-partnership fourteen years ago, my primary request was that our sexual relations be the number one priority in our union. I had been in a number of long-term relationships where the sex-spirit split, along with undeveloped communication skills, caused sex and sensuality to wither, leaving a sense of deadness in a potentially thriving relationship. Having made a commitment, we began a life of conscious Erotic Ritual. Expansiveness and sexual gratification became a planned and sacrosanct part of our time together. If this seems to defy the spontaneity that I myself enjoy, let me suggest that respecting existing realities has a significant payoff. Without the earnest communication of our needs and desires, or without planning, we cannot build rich, enduring erotic lives.

Sexuality, Higher Consciousness, and Fantasy

Though the process can be awkward, it is essential to learn to communicate about our needs, desires, and fantasies. "Reclaiming adolescent awkwardness," is a phrase I use giving people permission to go to the uncomfortable places often necessary in healing the sexual-spiritual split; a requirement to form authentically intimate relationships.

In sexual counseling, many are curious about where their fantasies come from, often feeling shame for having them. I tell my clients good fantasies are like rainbows, mysterious and beautiful, sometimes fleeting, and they are to be respected.

There origins vary from abuses early in life to Freudian, or from recollections of pleasure from our past. Sometimes they mysteriously come from no conscious recollection whatsoever. Ritual can filter the shame out of our fantasies and allow us to fall more deeply in love with ourselves. Self-love is essential to grow in sacred sexuality and Erotic Ritual. Having fantasies doesn't mean we're bad or that something is wrong with us, as we don't have to act on them. *Only shame is Godless.* Removing the shame from our fantasies transforms them, and that contributes to keeping a long-term relationship sexually alive.

Many of us are afraid of letting our wild, primordial natures be exposed, thinking it could hurt someone, or ourselves, hence the importance of behaving responsibly. Margo Anand, author and pioneer of Erotic Ritual quotes a client named Jenny from her *The Art of Sexual Magic:* "If there's a strong, deep heart connection between two people, then love allows you to go totally wild, while at the same time remaining sensitive enough to stay playful without hurting each other." Anand further describes transforming shame, "Like a true alchemist, you learn how to turn the base metal of your own energy into the purest gold."

The Goat Story: History and Sensation

Several years ago when Elias and I were in Naples, Italy, we went to the Archeological Museum where we were fortunate enough to get a private guided tour of "the secret cabinet." Only recently opened to the public, this section of the museum houses erotic art that The Vatican has been furtively collecting for centuries but keeping under lock and key. The woman, who was very knowledgeable about erotic art, pointed out an ancient vase graphically decorated with an image of a satyr having sexual relations with a goat. In her non-plussed way, she clarified that at the time the vase was painted this act was considered perfectly natural. There were no judgments or laws inhibiting one's erotic pursuits. On further exploration I learned that the archetype of the goat is youthful, vigorous, powerful, and deeply connected to the earth. The goat lives in the moment, experiencing instinctively focused satisfying physical desire. Pan, the god of nature and sexuality, is depicted as part human, part goat. Unfortunately, due to horns and cloven hooves, images of the devil became associated with this god during the middle ages, a further expression of the growing sexual-spiritual split that still plagues western society.

Natural Resistance to Erotic Ritual

With all our knowledge we still encounter resistance to a loving fusion of our sexual and spiritual energies. The delicate nature of exploring repressed sexual history is likely to trigger that very resistance. When we appreciate the nature of our resistance to removing shame, our fantasies are an entryway to a joyous *circle of energy* where we can experience both full-body orgasm and full-hearted spirituality. Full-body orgasm refers to a pulsing burst of the four energies in S.E.X. that can take over every dimension of our physical and subtle energy being. When this happens, we can experience expansiveness and sometimes formlessness that is sublime and divine. It is a full-body encountering that is also uniquely restorative when we feel depleted and deeply relaxing when we are tense.

Since getting a sense of formlessness is not unusual to well-constructed Erotic Ritual (and many other rituals), it may be useful to have a visual representation of what that might look like. When I toured Alex Grey's Chapel of Sacred Mirrors in New York, I saw what my experience of energetic formlessness could look like. Once again, Alex was generous enough to allow me to reproduce his big magnificent painting in black and white on these little pages for you. I hope it gives you a glimpse of the primal universal energy experience, helping to make you more fearless.

Underneath our needs, desires, fears, and fantasies are powerful yet subtle feelings that yearn to be expressed. Giving them a voice helps us grow holistically and can help us dissolve shame. They can teach us about aggression and passivity, about our feminine and masculine energies, and about pleasuring and being pleasured.

True, spiritual lovemaking in Erotic Ritual is an interweaving of our higher and our shadow selves in a holistic fusing of their dualistic aspects.

A healthy appreciation of resistance represents a turning point in our sexual healing as we move toward Erotic Ritual. By connecting

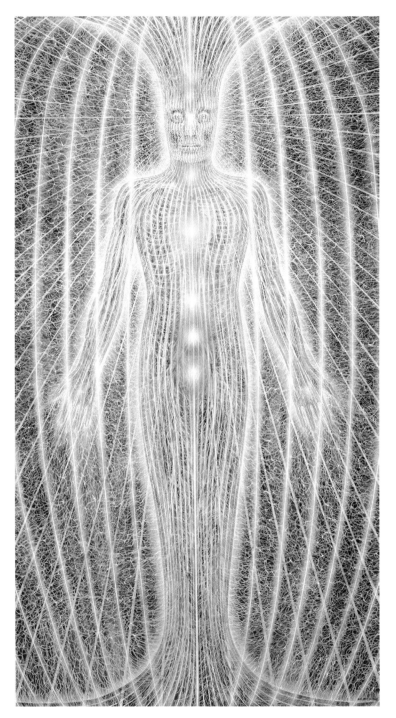

"Spiritual Energy System," painting by Alex Grey;
from *Sacred Mirrors: The Visionary Art of Alex Grey*

with your resistance, you have the opportunity to discern and untangle the diverse feelings and incidents that have formed themselves into a wall of shame. Whenever shame or energy blockage surfaces in a budding or long-term intimate relationship, the struggle to share it is part of the process of healthy development. As suggested by the author Max Scheler in his book, *Shame and Pride:* "It is from in and under the shame that our shimmering magic emerges."

Kinky?

Somehow, the word "kinky" has made its way into our sexual vocabulary. I love the word, as it means out of the norm. What is normal when we have so many primal animalistic energies running through us? It is important to explore what comes naturally to us. Often we may find ourselves gradually stretching some of the edges of these existing realities, but we can't presume to break down resistance barriers of others while experimenting with our own.

As the book branches out into the extraordinarily simple, beginner rituals, you can negotiate with any resistance. It will be beneficial to go through all of them.

Privacy vs. Secrecy

Whatever you choose to do with another or yourself you have a spiritual right to hold as private. You can share with others, if you want, but be careful not to lose the sanctity of your experience. Be discerning in your sharing. A secret is by nature imbued with shame and covertness. To the contrary, when you hold something private, it becomes part of your personal and spiritual identity, with no shame attached to it. There is a humble pride and gratitude that is all yours and that can make you strong.

13

Erotic Rituals for Everyone

Sex and beauty are inseparable, like life and consciousness. And the intelligence which goes with sex and beauty, and arises out of sex and beauty, is intuition.

D.H. LAWRENCE

Sex-Spirit Split Transformation Rituals

We begin the following three erotic rituals by bringing awareness to the body:

If you want to, you can use calming music in the background, something that you find soothing. I enjoy Brian Eno, Phillip Glass, Enya, Lorena McKennitt, Sheila Chandra, or Robbie Gass, but choose your own favorites, and trust your instincts.

Find a safe, comfortable space: your own ritual setting for a *Spiritual-Genital Integration Ritual.* Once settled, gradually bring your attention and Curious Observer to your sexual and sensual regions, whatever those are for you. First, do conscious, soft, and deep breathing focused in the solar plexus and the pelvic area. Now imagine breathing a warm golden light directly into your heart. As you notice you can do this, give the felt sense sensations time and space. If there are any interruptions from other thoughts or felt senses or images, give them some respectful time and space, then gently return to your heart and the warm golden light. Allow the heart to get as full of the warm golden light as it wants. It will know when it's right. Notice that. When this happens, imagine that you can take your breath all the way down from your nose to your lungs, through the golden light in your heart and down to the perineum, that lowermost part of the crotch between the vagina and the rectum or the scrotum and the rectum. At first, most people assume they can't breathe into their perineum, yet imagination can produce surprising results. See if you can notice some of that warm golden light naturally and organically finding its way into your whole pelvic region. Once you have practiced this ritual a few times with the intention of connecting your heart and your genitals, you can do it most anywhere to continue the healing. This ritual can be done while brushing your teeth, riding in a car, or for a few minutes before or after sleeping. While pleasant results are often immediate, with a little practice and patience, breathing of this sort will help lead to spiritual-genital integration. The breath connects spirit, or love, with energetically disconnected parts of our wholeness.

As a second ritual to further enhance the above, you can experiment with the Rotation Ritual. It can be combined with the conscious pelvic breathing.

Stand up straight, put your feet shoulder-length apart,
bend your knees, relax your jaw, and rotate your hips in a
circular motion, stretching out in all directions as far as is
comfortable while keeping your upper body gently erect.
Just the hips are moving. Imagine that you are standing
in the center of a mostly empty peanut butter jar and
you want to use your hip and pelvis, in a circular motion,
to clean the peanut butter off the sides of the jar. Keep
rotating, first in one direction and then the other. Lower
and raise yourself to clean the inside of that jar as best
you can. Attention to conscious breathing will be helpful.
Take a moment or two to giddily and randomly move
your pelvis, tuning into the energy and spontaneously
moving and following your inner current. Just go with
the flow for a few moments. You will begin, subtly at first,
feeling a renewed aliveness in this region that is sensual,
sexual, and centering—all at the same time. Notice the
energy waking up in that part of you, even just a little,
and image yourself smiling at this energy and watch
it amplify. When you've got the energy in a place that
feels right to you, focus it out to imagine it bringing
whatever you desire to you, just letting that happen.
Imagine and allow yourself to experience already having
what is desired. Be with it for a few minutes, and express
gratitude for the experience.

These rituals create different energy fields in and around you and
are excellent warm-ups for more pleasurable sexual experiences.

The following erotic meditation ritual is specifically designed for
transforming the split between our sexual and spiritual energies:

Light a candle to mark this experience as sacred. Find a
comfortable place to sit. Take a few minutes to have your
Curious Observer check in with your body. Be sure you are
as comfortable as you can be. Love yourself in this way. If
you are comfortable doing so, close your eyes so that your
felt senses are not obscured by visual distraction. If you
don't like closing your eyes, you might try gently squinting
them. Gradually bring your awareness down to your body;
notice your feet touching the floor; possibly feel the energy
between your feet and the floor. Notice the felt senses of
where your body is touching whatever you are sitting on.
Notice that you may be more aware of the contact between
your body and the seat in certain places. Noticing in this
way invites the felt senses (emanating from the Old Brain)
to begin to express themselves while at the same time
giving you a better sense of grounding.

Now that you are settled, you may want to start with a
simple prayer, like the one Daya taught me: "May this
ritual be for my highest good and for the good of all."

As you sit with the candle burning, your prayer said, your
felt sense awakened, image a time when you absolutely
knew you felt loved and cared for by someone (or a time
when you were loving and caring for another). Let the
image organically surface with as little editing as possible.
Take what comes. Once you have the image, circle the
absolute best moment(s) of it, excusing your mind from
giving the image distracting appendages. We want only the
finest part of the memory. Now invite your body to make
contact with that circled image, that resource. Gradually
notice and track the felt senses of your body. Give your self
time. Nothing else to do, nowhere to go. Just allow your

body to connect with the experience of true loving. In time you will most likely come to a place of expansiveness in your body, a sense of calm, well-being, and presence.

Knowing now that this experience belongs to you and lives within you, we are going to shift from it with the awareness that we can always come back to it or draw from its energy as a resource.

I want you to image the most private, secret (and juicy) sexual fantasy you have, the one you don't want others to know about. Or, if that isn't available to you, visualize that whatever you feel most sexually shameful about is happening to you. Once you have the image, circle the heart of it, the most poignant energy. Invite your body now to connect with the image. Bring gentle awareness to what happens now in the felt senses of the body, how they are different than before. Keep noticing the felt senses, and, whatever they are (don't try to make sense out of them, trust the body's innate intelligence for healing), give them time and space, always on the look-out to see if anything subtle or not-so-subtle happens next. Chances are that you will begin to find yourself in a contraction to at least some degree. Perhaps your breathing will become more shallow, or you'll experience tension, weight, or pain in your shoulders, neck, or elsewhere. It may be in the stomach, the heart, throat, or anywhere—just notice. If so, after giving the contraction(s) some time and space, notice if this contractive condition and energy might be emanating from any particular place in your body. See if it seems to start somewhere and then spreads to other areas. It may not, but if so, just register that awareness.

Gently shift back to the earlier image of feeling love in the felt senses of the body, and notice that you can do that. Take your time. Notice what happens. If you struggle at all, remember to drop back to your Curious Observer and release the mind from trying. Simply notice the image and experience of love being shared and how the felt senses of your body respond to that. When (and if) you again find yourself in an expansive state, continue to give it time and space. Notice if there are any colors associated with it, or textures or vibrations—anything that makes it even more palpable.

Now I'm going to ask you to take some of this energy, with its color, texture, or vibration, if you experience it that way (if not, just the calm energy alone) and pour it like sand into an imaginary pail, like a child would use at the beach. After you've filled the pail, imagine yourself covering the top with your hand to keep that lovely energy in the pail. Now shift back to the image of your secret, juicy sexual fantasy or shame. As you shift back, notice again the changes in the body sensations. Let them happen. Notice if you found where the contractions emanate from (the epicenter) and be aware of that. As the contractions become central to your being, I am going to ask you to imagine yourself picking up that sand pail full of expansive loving energy, with any colors it may have had from the loving image, and bringing it over to the image of contraction. Now I invite you to gently pour just a small amount of that energy over the contracted areas or the epicenter of the contraction. Pour it like a soft rain, and then just curiously notice if anything happens. If there are any changes in the felt senses of your experience, just give them time and space. As you do this, keep noticing if anything happens next. You may experience a third (or transformative) experience. Allow that to happen. Just keep noticing and giving space and time.

Now, if you want (and only if you want), I invite you to trust yourself and your body's intuition, and empty some more of the sand pail energy wherever it feels it needs to go, totally trusting your Curious Observer to guide the organic process. Just keep noticing what happens and trust that your body will guide you as to what to do, what not to do, and when to do it. Do this as long as you wish, adding energy from the pail as you are called to.

Before completing the ritual, I ask you to notice if anything was revealed to you in doing this experiment, if there were any illuminated images, new awarenesses, or felt senses in the body. Just take a moment to register them. When you are ready, gradually open your eyes and adjust to the light in the room.

You may want to write about this ritual or share it with a trusted friend or therapist. This can help platform your experience, while continuing to amplify the energy. Platforming is holding experiences in your energy field. As the body registers whatever you have platformed, it will gradually and organically move you toward similar and more expansive experiences.

Solo S.E.X. or Self-Lovemaking

Solo S.E.X. is my personal ritual. A place I go for escape from the everyday and a way to make love to myself. Some reading this may think that if you are in a partnership, you should not need to have solo S.E.X. This is another example of outdated information that contributes to feelings of shame and barriers to fulfilling lovemaking.

Making love with each other and with ourselves are two separate and distinct pleasures that can serve a union. To be in a partnership that honors and supports each other in both possibilities is a grand experience.

Self-lovemaking, particularly when we ritualize it, can be enormously informative in regards to what our Eros, ethos, and bodies want to teach us. For years my masturbation was not a declared ritual, and though it seemed to serve a valid purpose at the time, it was often like doing the wash.

In the early '80s I participated in a men's workshop on sexuality in which we watched a film of a man making love to himself in a prayerful way. It was quite beautiful and mind-altering. As I tried it myself, I reflected on the film when my mind and body log jammed. This is natural as we begin to bring love (spirit) and sex back together. I learned how to tenderly caress parts of myself, then switch to fantasy and back again.

If you are without an intimate partner, consider this: Contrary to what many believe, what is often considered casual sex can be enriching when experienced in the light of S.E.X. Here again we want to consider coming out of linear, dualistic thinking.

Many people tell me they are avoiding casual sex because they want a significant relationship. I honor and support that choice, yet I've learned a great deal from having serendipitous erotic encounters before I was in a more permanent relationship.

A Solo S.E.X. Ritual

Ritual Ingredients: Seven candles safely contained, a comfortable bath towel, a small, soft, hand or dish towel, and soothing music. These ingredients amplify the energy greatly, but are optional: I would not let the lack of them get in the way of proceeding.

First we set up for the ritual: Carve out sacred time (60–120 minutes, your choice) and space for yourself. Perhaps your home is best if no one else is there, or any place you feel safe and won't be interrupted. Turn off the phone ringer and any possibility of voice interruption. This is both a practical act and a symbolic one, involving your intention to remove yourself from the everyday world. Choose a location to conduct your Solo S.E.X. Ritual. On the bed, or on the floor, if carpeted, or if you have a mat of some kind and a pillow for your head. You may chose a chair, or anywhere you deem suitable, to make your ritual space for this occasion. Prepare the space so that it is ready for symbolically "holding" you and containing the energy when you begin the ritual. Wherever you are choosing for your self, make the area as clear and comfortable as possible. Place the seven candles around the area in a circle (if that works), or place them in a way that will create a pleasant setting.

If you have music, you may want to put it on softly now. Borrow three of the candles and bring them into the bathroom with you, place them strategically for a bath or shower, and light them. Once the candles are lit, the ritual has begun. If you have a bathtub, you may want to fill it with very warm, not hot, water. If you don't have a tub, a long warm shower will do. Before entering the bath or shower, if you have not already done so, slowly disrobe in a sensual way. Notice the felt senses of the body as you do this.

Have only the candlelight on (and any other natural light) when you enter the bath (or shower). The warm water is intended to greet and welcome you into the ritual, naturally beginning to relax the body's involuntary defenses (that it needs for the everyday world). If showering, allow it to be a slow conscious shower, feeling the sensation of the water spaying onto your skin. Notice the felt senses of your body responding to the sensations caused by the water. As you linger in the shower, listen to your body's calling as to how long to luxuriate there. If in the tub of warm water, notice the candles burning as you bring awareness to warm sensation of the water on your body. Notice if the warmth and the candles are assisting your body in relaxing. If so, give these awarenesses time and space. No rush. Nowhere to go, nothing to do. Just gently notice. Whatever you happen to notice, give it time and space with no judgment or agenda. See if you become aware of anything next in terms of body sensations, images, or feelings. Just give it all space and time. If resistance to relaxing is present, honor that, giving it space and time too. This opening part of the ritual is for finding attunement with yourself, as you temporarily put the outside world on hold for self-nourishment.

Trusting your instincts and the sharp intelligence of your body, slowly exit the bath or shower when that feels like the right thing to do. Take the bath towel and very slowly, slower than ever before, begin to dry your body in an unrushed way that awakens your sense of touch. Notice the subtle (or not so subtle) sensations as you lovingly dry the water from every part of your body. When drying your sacred erotic zones, you may want to go even slower, bringing additional attention to the felt sensations and doing it just the way it feels good. Take the time to notice and enjoy what good feels like. Before getting ready to complete whatever you need to do in the bathroom, you may want to take a moment and thank your body, however imperfect you might consider it to be, for getting you to this place in time and serving you in the ways that it does. It would be good to leave the bathroom naked with a sense of gratitude.

Move slowly and deliberately to the sacred space you prepared earlier for your continued self-loving ritual.

Safely bring the candles from the bathroom back to this
area as an additional resource and light all the candles.
Once the seven flames are burning to bring light and
support to your ritual, make yourself as comfortable as
possible in this space that you created for yourself.

Take a few minutes to just settle in and let your body
find its most comfortable situation. Remembering that
this is your time, and there's nothing to do and nowhere
to go, just gently check in with your body, noticing how
it has arranged itself. Just hang out in stillness for a few
minutes allowing your Curious Observer to notice what
this stillness is like. If you notice your mind coming in
to judge or create impatience, just gently put it aside,
returning to the felt sense experience of the moment.

Whenever you feel ready, check in with your body's
intelligence and desire and notice where it wants to be
touched. Fulfill that desire with your touch and then
notice how your body wants that touch to take place;
gentle and slow, deep, or fast. Whatever! Just notice the
calling and deliver the fulfillment.

After experimenting in this way for a while (you decide
how long), begin to bring attention to your erogenous
zones, again co-creating the experience and nature of the
touch with your body's desire. Notice, as you move along
at your own pace, the varied levels and states of arousal.
Slow the action down a bit to allow the sensations more
time and space. Curiously notice what happens as you
do this, then sensitively navigate your actions with the
natural flow of desire. If your mind comes in and wants to
direct the show a bit, experiment with that, knowing you
can always put it aside and ride the body's sensory call.

You can repeat the above as long as feels right for you, again you decide, it's your time. If you desire to shift to a higher state of arousal, perhaps in the direction of orgasm, notice how you want to do this. Give yourself all the permission in the world to give your body the arousal it wants in the way it wants it. You can use your mind and past experience to co-create this arousal with your body's felt sense, without overriding them. Go as slow as you can with this as you reach higher states of arousal. Notice that by slowing down just a bit and consciously breathing, you may be able to "plateau" the experience, hanging out there for periods of time and noticing whatever you notice. You may notice that lingering in higher states of arousal can be quite Godlike. Allow yourself to connect with and enjoy that Godlike state.

You can stay with the above as long as you are enjoying it, and, if you like, you can raise the level of arousal (using whatever means, fantasies, toys, etc.) moving toward orgasm if that's what your body wants. You do not have to climax. Stop when you like, and bathe in the glow of self love, and/or move toward an orgasmic state. If you go for orgasm, and you tend to manipulate yourself rapidly, you may want to experiment with pendulating between your regular style and a slower one. As you do this, keep noticing what your body is saying as it experiments with different sensations and try to work with it. If you reach a high state of arousal leading to orgasm, you may want to also experiment at this point. As you edge toward climax, see if you can slow down just a bit, and do some conscious breathing while touching your tongue to the top of your mouth (about a half inch behind your teeth). You might notice a tingling or electric feeling going through your body. This is a taste of the full-body orgasm that is separate from a climax. Whenever you are ready in this play station you've created, you may choose to move towards an orgasm. If so, go a bit slower than normal, breathe, and let your body instruct you. Stay as aware as possible so you can notice the benefits of the love making Solo S.E.X. Ritual.

If the time comes and you have an orgasm, be as much with the experience as you can. Allow your Curious Observer to join the climax, to coach it, and perhaps even prolong it. You deserve and your body may desire a very good release. On orgasm slow it all down again; see how much tolerance you have for the afterglow of being in such close contact with love and God. You may want to grab the small towel when ready and very gently let it embrace and absorb your juices, what some call your nectar from the Gods. Being still for just another few moments with towel in place, notice your sense of being. Also notice that if you are in a good place, feeling connected to yourself (and perhaps everything), notice if you want to pray for yourself or any loved ones or everyone. If you do, this place of being is a very powerful place to direct your prayer energies from. I've discovered that prayer always works best from a place of sensorial connectedness, pleasure, fulfillment, and gratitude.

Whenever you are ready, you may bring the ritual to a close by blowing out the candles. I encourage a slow and graceful reentry to the every-day. You are coming from a vulnerable place and you don't want to jar it with too much too fast. A gradual re-emergence will allow your experience to continue integrating long after you've closed the formal ritual. What you experienced lives in you and will forever inform future experiences, and you may find yourself connecting dots in your awareness for days afterward.

As you perform this ritual art again and perhaps repeat it periodically, you may often decide to creatively include mirrors and other elements to help amplify the energy. It's your play station, have fun with it!

More Self-Lovemaking

If at any time during these rituals you wish to increase the flow of the four primary energies, try focusing on them one at a time. Many people familiar with shamanic ritual invoke certain animals to share their energetic abilities during lovemaking. The attributes given to animals are fairly universal among primary societies. Ted Andrew's book, *Animal Powers,* is a reliable introduction to this vast energetic world.

We generally focus on the oversoul or spirit of the species and invite it to enter our consciousness temporarily. This takes practice, so begin by experimenting with this ritual alone. People suffering from sexual inhibitions and dysfunctions have reported breakthroughs where nothing else has worked.

Here are a few examples:

Love Energy: The dog brings us the energy of loyal and enduring love. The rabbit brings us the energy of frisky, gentle, but somewhat nervous love. The bear brings in energy of protective parental love. Choose one of these, or another animal you associate with loving, and then become that animal. Act out the movements of that animal as you play with yourself. Think of someone you love and radiate love to them as you caress yourself as that animal would. Fantasize that your loved one is lying in the forest and you saunter up as that animal to share love with them.

Pleasure Energy: The cat brings many of us a playful, carefree, and deeply relaxed sense of pleasure. The dolphin brings us a bouncy, happy, caring kind of playful pleasure. (Some invoke the spirit of Tigger from *Winnie the Pooh* for similar effect.) The monkey brings us silliness and the laugh-out-loud pleasures of the trickster. Choose one of these and enjoy guilt-free sexual play with yourself. Move as that animal moves, think as that animal thinks, and become one with your body. Again, think of the one you love. Imagine they are lying naked in a forest and you scamper up full of fun and pleasure to share with them.

Lingam (masculine) Energy: The billy goat brings boisterous male play energy into our sphere. The rooster brings cocky and confident male sexual energy to us. The fox brings smart, attractive, and stylish male energy into our world. The ox carries the enduring strength of male muscle into our realm. It helps us remain well grounded and offers itself in service to the female, i.e. to the land. The buck, aka "stag," the male deer with its large and many pointed antlers, is the king or chief of the male energy animals and brings us many of the qualities already mentioned. Regardless if you are now in a male body or a female body, as you play with yourself, choose one of these "male energy" animals and invite their energy to dwell with you and see what affect it has on your libido.

Yoni (feminine) Energy: The lamb brings receptive, peaceful female energy into our thoughts and our being. The doe brings graceful, unselfishly giving female energy into the ritual. The hen brings distinguished, home-making feminine energy into the mix. The horse brings beauty and strength into the energy field. The duck brings thoughtful reflective energy in, as does the loon. The wild boar brings a wild and independent female energy in. The otter is considered the clan mother of the "feminine energy" animals and is known for playfulness as well as strength and home-making and many other qualities. Whether you are currently occupying a male or female body, choose one of these animals and invoke that oversoul spirit to dwell with you and give you a boost of guilt-free feminine energy as you erotically enjoy yourself. Experiment with it, feel the loveliness and attractiveness of that animal (where appropriate) flow through you like a waterfall flowing down around your shoulders. Remember that animals in the wild don't have hang-ups about sex, and, except for the horny little mink, they don't overdo it either.

Have fun creating your lovemaking rituals. If you want to explore expanding this erotic energy with a partner, make sure to read the next chapter.

14

The Partnering Path

> The omnipotent process of sex, as it is woven into the
> whole texture of man's or woman's body, is the pattern
> of all of the process of our life.
>
> HAVELOCK ELLIS

Transformational S.E.X. for Couples

Transformational S.E.X. is the conscious sharing of the four energies (love, pleasure, lingam, and yoni). Such sharing amplifies the flow of many other healthy energies through both partners, especially creativity. These rituals break through resistance that has been built up as a protection against internal and external pressures.

Before moving into ritual space together, you may want to try the following ritual separately and then share the results with each other:

From a relaxed, felt senses position: Imagine yourself
and your partner, with open hearts, choosing to pleasure
each other and yourself. Imagine that all barriers to

intimacy and all "old news"—hurtful experiences you've had together—mysteriously vanish. You are honoring this new day and this new intention with which you are aligning yourselves spiritually. Notice that you have the intention to bring love, pleasure, lingam and/or yoni in whatever ways come most naturally to each of you. You find that in this new space you are easily able to share and negotiate with each other what feels good and what could be done to feel even better. Let this happen in Rumi's metaphorical "field" that is "beyond wrong thinking and right thinking." The rituals you embark on are not about thinking, they are about pleasure and divinity of a most personal and private nature. Imagine breathing and letting go into the bliss, whatever it may be, and knowing that you are going to God or the highest energy powers. Your partner is joining and supporting you in this awareness and experience. Notice how you and your bodies respond to this imagery without judgment. Use it as a place to grow from, a platform of the moment.

Before proceeding with the Erotic Ritual for Couples, the following are beneficial ways for couples to align their hearts and energies.

The suggestions can greatly fuel erotic ritual and sacred sex. Each time we go into the sacred erotic zone together, our intention should be to experience something that is surprising and fresh for us.

There are a few primary things I'd like to share with couples as they enter the world of erotic ritual: You are responsible for your own orgasm. Only you know how your body works and what it calls for in a given moment. While your partner may be an intuitive lover, you will find it beneficial to take responsibility for yourself.

Erotic ritual will be different for new couples and long-term couples. Transformational S.E.X. can be the impetus for necessary communication, renegotiation, forgiving, and healing. For new couples who possess a sense of adventure, erotic ritual should come relatively easy, though one person may want to take a leadership role. Often one partner is more naturally prepared for this than the other, and that can always be renegotiated down the road.

The following is a Forgiveness Ritual for longer-term couples, where there are often deep fears because of previous rejections or misunderstandings. If you both want to heal your sex-love schism (individually and as a union), try this:

FORGIVENESS RITUAL (LONG-TERM COUPLES)

Sit comfortably across from one another, perhaps on pillows on the floor. Put a candle between you to help focus and amplify the energy. This ritual involves saying the repetition of a few words of forgiveness by both of you at the same time. Before giving you the words, I want you to realize that you will be doing this for yourself and for each other at the same time. When it is complete, you will engage with each other, as prescribed (or as you adjust my suggestion to fit yourselves).

Put the palm of your favored hand on your own chest, preparing to circle your heart three times slowly as you prepare to say the following words to yourself:

Begin now to very slowly encircle your heart clockwise. This is best done with eyes closed (or squinting if you need to read). Go slow and notice the body's felt senses. As you do so, say together: "I forgive myself for any hurt I've caused myself and our union because of cultural ignorance, blind-spots, insensitivity, communication deficiencies, and possible transferences from past hurts." Say these words again while continuously circling the heart with your palm. "I forgive myself for any hurt

I've caused myself and our union because of cultural ignorance, blind-spots, insensitivity, communication deficiencies, and possible transferences from past hurts." Last time, still slowly encircling your hearts: "I forgive myself for any hurt I've caused myself and our union because of cultural ignorance, blind-spots, insensitivity, communication deficiencies, and possible transferences from past hurts."

Notice how you feel in your bodies and in your being, then share that with each other, whatever it may be. No judgment, no agenda. Now, softly gaze into each other's eyes for a moment and then say, one person at a time: "With this energy of self-forgiveness, however much I can manifest, I now extend its energy out to you and our union, forgiving you and both of us for any times of estrangement and pain either of us caused in our union. I recognize our challenges have been larger than we knew how to negotiate. I intend to improve these skills and honor your unique sensitivities, sensibilities, and needs."

Extinguish the candle to signal completion of the formal Forgiveness Ritual and embrace in whatever way feels right. Let the energy of the ritual organically grow in your union.

A ritual like the above *feeds* the invisible third entity in your union—the soul of the relationship. This entity can be compared to a plant. Authenticity brings it sunshine and our erotic rituals provide the water for it to flourish. In return, the plant gives us oxygen to fuel our union.

Both new and old couples can benefit from the following Seed Planting Ritual.

EROTIC RITUAL FOR COUPLES: PART ONE

This Giving and Receiving Ceremony requires ingredients and preparation: Candles safely contained, at least one (more if you like) in every room you will spend time in, including bathrooms. At least four small soft hand or dish towels, two nice bath towels. If any kind of lubricants, condoms, sex toys, or other paraphernalia have been part of your history, or you want to introduce them, have them out in advance. You should also have a special blanket to be used only in the performance of this ritual. Some good music like the Vangelis *1492* soundtrack, or whatever suits you (there is also a series of CDs called *Sex Lounge* that are quite good) can help amplify the energy. Part of the preparation is carving out the time. This will take negotiation. Most people do not do well at an erotic ritual of this sort after a long day's work. You want to be able to bring good energy to it. Personally, I tend to prefer a late Saturday afternoon, after a little nap. Then there is the afternoon coffee, the shower and cleansing ritual, and the space preparation. It can be very nice to have dinner in the energetic afterglow of the erotic ritual.

Aside from showering as a couple, exactly as in the Solo S.E.X. Ritual (please refer back), one or both of you may want to cleanse your private parts. If this is the case for one or both partners, you may want to make it a prelude or opening to the ritual.

Before cleansing and showering, set up your sacred space for the ritual that will follow your bathing. It can be the bed in a bedroom, a futon in front of a fireplace, or any place that works for the two of you; or you can have more than one place. The important thing is that the area is prepared in advance, with a sense of sacredness. You are preparing for something special and that energy is important. Be sure the ritual area has the necessary ingredients to keep the energy and flow as smooth as possible. Experiment and find out what works best for you and your partner.

Now follow the Solo S.E.X. Ritual until you have finished sensually drying yourself off after the shower. You may then want to put on some loose fitting comfortable clothes, a wrap or ceremonial gown. You may also choose to stay naked, whichever you both prefer. Be sure the phone ringers are off and no sound (like the answering machine) can enter the ritual space unless it is your chosen music or sounds from nature.

Light your candle in the ritual space, and, as you do, notice in yourself a feeling of gratitude that you have this time and space for whatever happens. See if you can bring the energy of appreciation into the ritual space, even if it's just for patting yourselves on the back for making it this far. Now sit opposite one another in the center of the ritual space. If using a bed, you will want to cover it with your special blanket.

As you sit across from one another, if you are clothed, begin to gently and sensually remove the clothing until you find yourselves as two naked beautiful humans sitting and facing one another. Hold hands, and notice each others breathing for a few minutes, seeing if you can synchronize one with the other. This is for attunement and amplification of energy. After doing that for a few minutes, with the intention of going slowly into the erotic unknown, drop back into your Curious Observer and see what it wants to do. If you can, ask your partner what comes to them, or, if it feels right, just gently move in that direction. Take about five to ten minutes for both of you to awkwardly/gracefully fulfill the desires coming from your Curious Observer.

Next, have the shorter of the two of you lay down in a comfortable way with lots of room around you. For the next twenty to thirty minutes, the partner lying down gets to have all the fun. They can explore the body's deep felt senses. Ask your partner to do for you anything that comes to you that would feel pleasurable. It could be as simple as a shoulder massage or the placing of a head on a chest. Or it could be more intense like a passionate kiss or a finger tantalizing an erogenous zone. The important ingredients here are the noticing of desire (even sometimes being surprised by it), the asking for what you want, and your partner doing their best to accommodate your desire. On a subtle and not so subtle energetic level, this in itself is nourishing, connective and fulfilling. In the designated time, just relax; enjoy the process, and, when the twenty to thirty minutes feel up for you, switch roles. When engaging in the ritual, both of you can also notice if there are any energetic responses or holdbacks in your body. Without judgment or agenda, do your best to share any constrictions (or joyous expansiveness) with your partner. Make room for them, honor them, shift as and if necessary (always listening to your body). We learn a great deal from these barriers (and joys) and they help us drop the unseen veils to greater intimacy and deeper lovemaking. Now, for twenty to thirty minutes, the taller partner will lie down, tuning into their felt senses and Curious Observer and asking for whatever desires come forth. Remember now, you're also in a play station.

Nothing has to be perfect and you can laugh and have fun too. You can also share barriers and/or joys that visit your visceral experience.

Once you've completed the Giving and Receiving Ceremony, begin to come out of the structured part of the ritual and tune into your bodies simultaneously. Don't forget to breath consciously periodically, it helps. Notice what desire comes up for you and see if your partner is willing. At this time you may want to move into higher states of arousal. Only, in doing so, try not to go back to what you always do (unless you want to), but see if your body leads you in any new directions, and ask for what you want. If your partner can possibly accommodate you, prolong and enjoy it as long as it works for both. If the arousal states move toward orgasm, you may want to experiment with slowing down, consciously breathing, and hanging out there for a while. In some Tantric teaching, it is thought that by touching the tip of your tongue to the top of your mouth and consciously breathing during sex, you may experience the body's erotic energy flowing in a full circle, and achieve a full body orgasm without climaxing—yet. At this point in the ritual, I invite you both to experiment at will, continuously tuning into yourself and respecting your partner. You can't go wrong.

Dance with Eros; take turns with who leads, each partner at times, Eros at others. Learn from Eros—it's there to teach us.

The last suggestion I will make is that if you ejaculate, treat the juices that may be on your bodies like they are nectars from the Gods, and if/when you clean up, use one of the small soft towels and do it with the appropriate reverence for completing the Eros ritual. These moments of just being are a good time to pray for yourself and for your loved one, quietly and privately or out load. Eros energy is passionate in many ways. It carries prayers really well. I suggest you transition out of the erotic ritual space slowly so that you do not jar the energy, and see how seamlessly you can both move to whate*ver you chose to do next.*

Notice if anything new comes up for you in this ritual. If so, share it with your partner so you can platform the experience.

EROTIC RITUAL FOR COUPLES: PART TWO

As part of another Transformational Sex Ceremony at a later time, give yourselves permission to "invite in" stimuli to increase the flow of erotic ritual's four primary energies into your body and consciousness. You can try focusing on them one at a time and welcome them in. Don't forget to laugh and smile. Each (or one) of you might consider choosing an erotic video or DVD that, for whatever reason, amps up your energies. You may need to go slow with this and be sensitive to your partner's sensitivities and sensibilities. Respectful communication and negotiation in advance is most helpful. Only include what you both are willing to explore, allowing for some risk-taking and expansion of comfort zones, if that feels okay. Visual erotic aids can be quite instructive and communicative. It is not necessarily important to play the fantasies out in the ritual, but de-shaming them and inviting their energy into the ritual helps drop veils and deepen intimacy, connectivity, and fulfillment.

As mentioned, another option is to have fun by invoking your favorite animal totem (of the moment, they often change) to better please your lover. It is exciting if both partners choose an animal and make a ritual dance, without costumes, dancing to the beat of their sexual inclinations, which include love, pleasure, masculine, and feminine energies. Ask your partner to guess which animal you are "channeling." The important thing is that you get beyond human barriers to the primary instincts associated with The Old Brain.

Here are some possibilities:

Love Energy: Choose the loyal dog, the gentle rabbit, or the protective bear. Act out the movements of that animal as you play with your lover. Then shape shift back into a human body, but with the mind of the animal, and use your hands to caress and transmit love to your lover. Feel the unconditional love of that animal flowing through you.

Pleasure Energy: Choose the relaxed cat, the playful dolphin, or the silly monkey. Move as that animal moves, think as that animal thinks, and become one with your body as you do. Give pleasure to your lover in a way you feel that your totem animal might. Then allow your lover to give you pleasure as if you were that same pleasure-minded creature.

Lingam (masculine) Energy: Choose the boisterous billy goat, the cocky rooster, the clever fox, the strong ox, the regal buck aka "stag." Regardless of whether you are now in a male body or a female body, choose one of these "male energy" animals and invite their energy to dwell with you and see what affect it has on your libido.

Yoni (feminine) Energy: Choose the receptive lamb, the unselfish doe, the distinguished hen, the beautiful horse, the thoughtful duck, the wild boar, the playful otter. Let it give you a boost of guilt-free feminine energy as you erotically engage and fascinate your partner. Experiment with it, feel the loveliness and attractiveness of that animal (where appropriate) flow through you like a waterfall flowing down around your shoulders. Use your eyes to express the feminine nature of the animal you have chosen to be, and let its innate sexuality enter you and take over, letting all human thoughts drift away.

Observe where the energy takes you. After you have reached a satisfying conclusion, gratefully send the animal away and become human once again.

Moving Forward with Innate Intelligence

In moving forward with erotic rituals, there are a few things to remember. Erotic Rituals are about surrendering to Spirit and Eros which is Soul Energy eXchange. This is a delightful process that allows all four distinct energies to illuminate, heal, and create a nexus for future creativity.

The offerings made in these chapters are baseline starter kits. They are intended to wake up erotic energy and ignite your creativity and curiosity.

It's good to evaluate our progress in erotic ritual. We need to ask ourselves: "What motives do I bring to sexuality? What do I want from the sexual aspect of my nature?"

We know our healing is progressing when our answers emphasize spiritual fulfillment and the desire for shared experiences of higher consciousness through Eros.

I close this section with a prayer I often share with my partner:

> *My prayer for us is that each erotic experience be vir-
> ginal, restorative, fun, and fulfilling ... and that the
> creativity it exudes be the full blossoming of who we are.*

Infinite Playground

15

Dynamic Linking on an Infinite Playground

> The interlinking of humanity that began with the emergence of language has now progressed to the point where information can be transmitted to anyone, anywhere, at the speed of light.
>
> Billions of messages are continually shuttling back and forth … linking the billions of minds of humanity together into a single system.
>
> Is this Gaia growing herself a nervous system?
>
> PETER RUSSELL

What Is Dynamic Linking?

Dynamic Linking is a new way of networking, relating to people and accessing inner and outer resources. It is a toolkit of communication skills, including accelerated on-line capabilities and other information systems combined with alternative resources and communities which are not generally mentioned in the mass media. Using ritual and focused intention, these resources can bring about an *information transformation*.

Act-UP (which created the first automated phone tree for volunteers), CulturalCreatives.org, "Greens," Peter Russell (peterussell.com), WisdomCircles.org, Marianne Williamson (renaissancealliance.org), MoveOn.org, TheHealingBridge.org, TheInstitute.org, the WTO protestors (various websites), Institute of Noetic Sciences (ions.org), livingjusticepress.com, and others have all been pioneers of this phenomenon.

Naomi Kline writes about how this Internet-action has created a whole new type of leaderless, nameless, but inherently powerful subculture. This resembles the slime mold organism Peter Russell writes about in *From Science to God*:

> *At the present time, evolution seems to have reached yet another twilight zone, the one between individual consciousness and global consciousness. Humanity currently displays characteristics of both levels; we are independent conscious units, who at times come together to function as an integrated whole for a common purpose. In this respect, society is reminiscent of a curious creature, the cellular slime mold, Dictyostelium discoideum, an "organism" which is somewhere between a collection of single-celled amoebas and a true multicellular organism. It is greater than the sum of its parts.*

Dynamic linking connects individuals with technology and the media differently than conventional methods. Our website (www.theinstitute.org) is only five years old and already has over 10,000 dynamic links on it. In this chapter, we will focus first on the revolution in linking communities and information resources. Then we will apply that concept to our inner resources, which take many shapes and forms. Lastly, we will access the healing community through ritual to keep us grounded with our egos in check.

Linking, a term made popular by the Internet, is the practice of connecting to a resource through a web link. Linking evokes images of links in a metal chain, a linear object. But in fact linking is not linear. Each website can link us to dozens of similar websites, which can link us to another dozen and so on.

Dynamic linking, on the other hand, is the ability to use all the mental and electronic tools available to accelerate this process and make it more fluid. By linking us to other similar communities that truly support our vision of the future, we are creating the communities Peter Russell writes about in *The Global Brain Awakens*.

I am dynamically linked to Peter Russell, who is on our Institute's Advisory Circle, and he is a Fellow with The Institute of Noetic Sciences, of which I am a long-time member. His book on the global brain inspired the creation of our community's website, and indeed his influence affected the writing of this book.

This section is not simply about the existence of linked networks but also about a new ritual that invites you to explore networks of *openings* for vibrant living. Dynamic linking is three-dimensional, an explosion of consciousness and community building that leads us to wider connectivity with the universe.

Many people live in quiet isolation, are unable to link beyond a community that no longer serves their needs, or they can't fit into any community. Some are frozen, trapped by loyalties to dead-end organizations and their own fear of the unknown.

I suggested to a client that community involvement might help her enjoy life. She had been in deep depression having ended another unworkable relationship. She responded by saying she doesn't like groups. Eventually, after gaining her trust, she committed (with trepidation) to a four-month community-based workshop focalized by an APH colleague of mine. For several years her participation continued in many community events and she eventually went on to become a focalizer. She pioneered the concept of bringing Wisdom Circles into corporations and energetic healing to federal government agencies. This woman who didn't like groups became a shining light and resource to countless people and organizations.

Some readers have reached a stage where they occasionally connect to communities. This has been adequate until now, but the future
requires more, as it offers more. As more people practice dynamic
linking, there are more communities to belong to. There are those
that we choose to link to over and over again, giving us a sense of
stability. While branching out in dynamic linking it's helpful to be
discerning over "righteous" organizations.

Righteous organizations come in many forms, such as religious,
self-help, environmental, political, and they want you to invest all
your energy in them. These groups act as Mommy and Daddy for
some, making it feel risky to seek other groups that may be better
for them.

A well-established, stable organization that encourages exploration
is an excellent starting place for a new adventure. Always remember
that if an organization feels more intrusive than grounding, you need
to move on.

Inner Dynamic Linking

Now that we have opened up the world of dynamic linking, we
can apply these ideas to our inner resources. At the foundation of
dynamic linking is the Five Wisdoms mentioned earlier: respect for
self, respect for others, and respect for other existing realities.

The Five Wisdoms can clear the gateway to inner dynamic linking
through ritual. Authenticity is the first of the five wisdoms. It means
going into the tender and complex areas of emotional vulnerability
within you or within a group. It is a necessary step before meaningful
ritual can occur.

Community is the second wisdom. It is the ability to bond and
create with other people. This is another gateway to the ritual of
dynamic linking. Through ritual we discover that there is a vast inner
community of non-physical allies waiting to help us. Some think of
them as angels, ghosts, ancestors, lost loves, animal powers, or rays of

light. Others visualize Jesus, Buddha, Krishna, or their fourth grade art teachers.

Intention is the third wisdom. It is the one necessary ingredient which defines ritual. Without intention, we are just going through the motions.

Belief is the fourth wisdom. A community that inspires belief can make the difference between success and failure in our efforts to transform ourselves.

The fifth wisdom is resource. It is wise to continually tap into our resources until it becomes natural. Remember, we have been conditioned to focus on our problems and what we *haven't* done. This is the direct opposite of resourcing, which comes from abundance rather than scarcity.

When combined or linked, these Five Wisdoms send a non-verbal message to the Old Brain, a powerhouse of concentrated human and universal energy. It does not generate thoughts as we conventionally think of them; it generates senses, intuitive hunches, and images. The Old Brain takes a different pathway towards our innate intelligence, which in turn links to our inner reality, which is God, soul, and Spirit.

These pathways correspond with the four parts of the self. The first is the path of the body, the second the path of the mind, the third the path of the heart, and the fourth the path of the spirit. All four paths are regulated by the Old Brain.

The Path of the Body

The Old Brain links us to the realm of animal instinct, the natural and uninhibited part of ourselves which is highly intuitive. The power enters in through the felt senses of the body. Through journeying deeply into the realm of the felt senses we can heal the sexual-spiritual split. Once these two aspects are rejoined, innate intelligence is more opened up.

We experience the "one taste," a highly sensual and satisfying linkup with the entire universe. The effects of this are staggering. It opens up a heightened physical awareness that can empower us to accomplish great things.

The Path of the Mind

The Old Brain itself hasn't much to say in everyday dialogue; rather, it connects consciousness to the cosmos. Einstein once commented that he was amazed the universe was *so* comprehensible, even though it wasn't *easily* comprehensible. It takes a certain kind of mind to perceive it. When we are confident intuitively, we develop a spirit that allows us to make fearless leaps of insight over gaps of missing information. When we combine intuition with fearless exploration and connectivity, we can see dramatic results in cognitive activity—what people call "genius." It can also open up a direct link to the universal mind, known as the source of all intelligence and love.

The connective super-mind is a direct reflection of total consciousness, a non-polarized cognitive entity that can communicate with the universe.

The Path of the Heart

From the Old Brain we can access the innate intelligence associated with emotional vibrancy, itself a great source of energy. As we sink into the darkness of this brain, we access a reservoir of love and compassion for all beings. It is interesting to note that all the great enlightened beings of history opened their hearts with compassion for the poor and weak. The path of the heart is one of the main gateways to total consciousness.

Once we open up the first gateway of the heart, love, and compassion, we encounter the next block—old traumas. Our compassion, guided by the Old Brain and the Curious Observer, can focus a great wave of loving energy on those traumatic wounds and heal them. When trauma is healed, there is an unlocking of cosmic energies such as joy, bliss, gratitude, happiness, well-being, and love. When we are open to this stage, we feel an emotional resilience that resonates with vibrancy. Beyond this, the detached Curious Observer records what we do, feel, think, and say in a neutral, objective manner, which can be very instructive.

The Path of Spirit

When we fully awaken the Old Brain, we find ourselves looking down into the well of mysteries—one which shamans often looked into. We gradually enter the spirit world, experiencing dreams and visions, and opening up to shamanic healing.

The higher self is a doorway to spirit that enlivens our spiritual nature. This journey of the soul leads us where there is no difference between the light in ourselves and the light that is everywhere. In this quantum reality we can be almost mistaken for God. Through ritual we open up the corridor that leads to pure spirit.

There is an infinite playground of resource energy in the center of our being, an energy that has been running things since the beginning of time. Through ritual, prayer, and focused intention, we can bring our deepest inner resources into play, in order to more fully and efficiently harvest all that we are.

A RITUAL FOR DYNAMIC LINKING

First, light a candle near your phone and/or computer and recite this prayer, "Protect me from any harmful energy. Protect my electronic helpers from bugs. Bless my special tools and make them doorways to that which is sacred." Then sit and meditate. Visualize a beautiful light around you. Allow yourself to feel "lucky" and blessed in all that you do. Breathe with an expansive air of confidence that what you touch will turn to gold for you in the long run. Count your breaths, twenty-one breaths, thinking of nothing else. Keep your mind blank, knowing that at the twenty-first breath, your hands will know what to do, even if "you" don't. Let an idea pop into your head from the Old Brain as to what you really need to learn about, and what's important in the big picture. Say: "It is my focused intention to find what I'm looking for, for the benefit of all beings. Let me not be distracted by anything that does not lead me to my intention. May my fingers be guided to that which I need to see and know. At the count of three, I will have the feel in my hands for what to click on and what to click off or what to do next."

If you have a computer, turn it on. Then, meditate with eyes closed, saying, "Today I will find my answers. I will find my people. I will find my way to health and consciousness." Then open your eyes and let your computer search become a part of the ritual. As you run your search engine, let your intuition tell you what words to search under, and which sites to click open. Notice which sites "light up" for you and which give you a feeling of impatience and restlessness. Trust your feelings. Use your inner resources to find your new outer ones.

This book has been designed to give you a glimpse of where inner and outer resources can take you if you follow them. Personal ritual and the exploration of inner energies can bring us into secret realms within the body, heart, mind, and spirit and lead us to a non-dualistic wholeness. At the same time, group and community ritual can lead us to the oneness of all life on this planet. Either way, a great awakening awaits us.

Epilogue

We have reached what philosopher Buckminster Fuller called our final evolutionary exam. Can we move beyond limiting modes of consciousness? Can we let go of our illusions and discover who we really are? Fuller said that "all humanity now has the option to become enduringly successful."

One-quarter of the population in the United States and Europe hungers for a deep change in their lives, according to the book, *The Cultural Creatives: How 50 Million People Are Changing the World,* by Paul H. Ray and Sherry Ruth Anderson. They want less stress, better health, and more spirituality. That represents approximately 50 million people in the U.S. and 90 million in the European Union.

It would be fraudulent to speak of ritual as an easy fix-all without any pain, awkwardness, or doubt. There is no perfection in this universe, except for what we sometimes experience as being part of oneness. The rituals in this book are not child's play, even though they are playful. Some are difficult and require self-dedication, a lot of focus and intention. Consider the possibility that once the energy inside you is increased in powerful, harmonious ways, you will be able to focus your energy towards others and toward the planet through rituals that are helpful, even miraculous.

Think about it: if *matter* is energy, as Einstein and those in the Quantum field assert, and *psychology* is energy, as so many therapists are asserting today, then there must be a place where physical images and mental images are one and the same. Through ritual we can open the doors of the subconscious mind and find this place. Once we find the source of healthy vibrant energy inside of us, we can heal. Perhaps, from that place, we can also heal the physical images around us, the diseases of the body, our healthcare systems, corporate paralysis, the ravages of pollution, the effects of global warming, all of it!

Miracles are nothing new; in fact, they aren't really miracles, but manifestations of a greater law of loving intention that has been present from the beginning of time and realized by many enlightened ones. Not all miracles are metaphysical. Some involve being at the right place at the right time, or saying the right words to a friend that changes their life. We can all increase our consciousness at any time. It's a lot like learning a new language, learning to read, or playing a new game. We just have to want it enough to break through a few simple barriers for miracles to occur. As Deepak Chopra writes: "Miracles are the shooting stars of everyday life. They bubble up from their hidden source, surround us with opportunities, and disappear."

WITH DEEP GRATITUDE TO
THE BOOK RITUAL CIRCLE,
AND ALL READERS,
FOR THIS OPPORTUNITY.

Glossary

Allopathic Medicine: Allopathy (which is most often considered "traditional" or "Western" medicine) breaks the body into parts—systems, cells, organs, limbs—identifies their particular functions and dysfunctions, and repairs each of them individually by use of chemicals, replacement parts, and cutting and mending processes. It is especially helpful for acute and sudden problems.

Alpha: The beginning.

Authentic Process Healing: Adapted from the work of Carl Rogers (the father of Humanistic Psychology). He states real healing can only take place in "the authentic sharing of personal experience." In honor of Carl Rogers, the phrase "Authentic Process Healing" now frames my research and practice and the name of our community.

Binary Logjam: This is an expression I coined to help explain a situation where there seems to be only two possibilities, yes, or no, and neither will do. Binary logjams come from personal and cultural thought patterns that lock us out of our own lives. They can also create blind spots that keep us from seeing what we want. We go unconscious. They are similar to bioenergetic blockages often caused by trauma to the body, emotions, or spirit. One gets an energetic logjam that can physically block them from the capacity for self advocacy. Making Room for Paradox and other rituals help us shift and transform binary emotional logjams into new, free-flowing possibilities.

Bioenergetics: The study of the transformation of energy in living organisms.

Bioenergetic Blockages: Constrictive blockages in the energy in living organisms that diminish living and cause disease (often caused by trauma). Also see Binary Logjams.

Coincidence: A notable concurrence of events having no apparent causal connection.

Collective Unconscious: The portion of the psyche whose unconscious contents is hereditary and belongs to all humankind.

Context: The total field of observation predicted by a point of view. Context includes any significant facts that qualify the meaning of a statement or event. For instance, the data in this book could be meaningless without putting it in the context of *Ritual as Resource.*

Contractive energy: This is the result of a constriction in our bodies and perceptions when in traumatic and threatening situations. When constriction fails to sufficiently focus the organism's energy to defend itself, the nervous system evokes other mechanisms such as freezing and dissociation to contain the hyper-arousal. This contractive energy lodged in our autonomic nervous systems is what we use resource energy to dissolve in the transformation of trauma.

Curious Observer: The invisible part of us that perceives our experiences (thinking, feeling, bodily felt-senses, and imaginings) without judgment or agenda. The Curious Observer perceives and knows all we see, do, feel, and think, by just noticing.

Discharge or Deactivation (regarding trauma's contractive energy): Organic regulation of the autonomic nervous system (ANS) through the reciprocal action of the sympathetic and parasympathetic branches of the ANS; the regulation of the opposite energies of activation and resource toward flow, resilience, and dynamic equilibrium.

Duality: The world of form, which is characterized by seeming separation of objects (reflected in the conceptual dichotomies such as "this/that," "here/there," "then/now," or "you/me'). This perception of limitation is produced by the senses because of the restriction implicit in a fixed point of view. Both time and space themselves are merely the measurable products of a higher implicit order.

Dynamic Linking: A new way of networking, relating to people and accessing inner and outer resources. It unleashes incredible energy inside the awakening consciousness. When you are dynamically linking, you *feel* it. There is a vibrant energy in the connection that is very different from that of just meeting people, swapping emails, or chatting on the phone. Using ritual and focused intention to further increase this connectivity, dynamic linking brings about an *informational transformation* that greatly expands and accelerates the individual's (or community's) growth and scope of experience.

EMDR: Eye Movement Desensitization and Reprocessing integrates elements of much effective psychotherapy. EMDR is an information processing therapy and uses an eight phase approach. During EMDR the client attends to past and present experiences in brief sequential doses while simultaneously focusing on an external stimulus. The client is then instructed to let new material become the focus of the next set of dual attention. This sequence of dual attention and personal association is repeated many times in the session. After EMDR processing, clients often report that the emotional distress related to the memory has been eliminated or greatly decreased, and that they have gained important cognitive insights.

Emotional Incest: Without overt sex, this is when a child becomes the energetic spousal equivalent to a seductive parent or guardian. This often has traumatic results.

Encroachment: Intrusion on personal boundaries.

Energy Medicine or Healing: Applying the knowledge and use of energy and energy fields as an effective remedy or cure for illness (dis-ease) in body, mind, or spirit.

Energy Field: An area of space characterized by a physical property that is normally invisible and intangible but under certain circumstances can interact with and even transform matter.

Eros: Sexual instinct encompassing longing and desire.

Expansive Energy: This is synonymous with resource energy. However, there are very expansive energetic states one can experience that feel like formlessness, oneness, or a wavelike sensation with all that exists. There also tend to be moments of awakening to a more transcendent consciousness.

Evolution: General term for the unfolding of behavior with the passage of time. Development or growth that produces higher and higher wholes; a movement from the lower to the higher.

Felt Sense: According to Eugene Gendlin, the man who coined the term in his book, *Focusing:* "A *felt sense* is not a mental experience but a physical one. *Physical*, as in a bodily awareness of a situation or person or event. An internal aura that encompasses everything you feel and know about a given subject at a given time—encompasses it and communicates it to you all at once, rather than detail by detail." Peter Levine adds: "The *felt sense* unifies a great deal of scattered data and gives it meaning."

Field: An area of space characterized by a physical property that is normally invisible and intangible but under certain circumstances can interact with matter. Classically, the action between two material objects separated in space is described in the language of fields. In *quantum field theory,* the interaction is viewed as an exchange of so-called messenger particles, which convey a particular force.

Focalizer: In our IAPH community, focalizer has come to mean a person who empowers himself and who is empowered by the community to bring focus to the matters at hand. A focalizer brings the community's energy to the highest level for the good of all.

Future Resource: A resource (described below) that is dreamed or imagined in the future, yet can still be accessed for pleasurable energies.

Gratitude: The sense of good will and appreciation for something received.

Holding the Space (also: *holding the energy*): This expresses a clear and strong intention by a person or persons to emanate a safe and understanding energy field in which healing can occur.

Holopathic Medicine: Holopathy (most often referred to as alternative or complementary medicine) views the person as an interconnected framework with many facets and angles, and aims to maintain integrity in that system by identifying barriers or weak spots in the integrity and supporting balance and energetic flow among all the parts of the self. Health is viewed as the integrity and the flow of energy through the web; healing is inseparable from the restoration of that integrity and flow. Holopathy is especially helpful for long-term problems or for problems based in habit, history, environment, and consciousness.

Liminal: Refers to the experience of a rare threshold, or the place between the worlds, the place between habits, the only place where true transformation can take place.

Lingam: The masculine drive energy, the penis, the pursuer, initiation, aggression, and personal power; the creation and *giving* of complex energies and glory. While lingam energy is often male-identified, in reality this energy is found in all human beings.

Matter: According to Ken Wilber and leading quantum physicists, matter is condensed consciousness. The unfolding and enfolding process creates successive localized manifestations that appear to our senses (and instruments?) as physical form.

Molecule: The smallest unit of a chemical compound which still posses the properties of the original substance.

Mythopoetic: Creation of myths.

Newtonian: Emphasizing the role of laws and predictable order in the universe and the role of experiment and observation in the discovery of truth.

Nonduality: Advanced scientific theory suggests that when individuals reach a certain attainable (and measurable) level of consciousness, they describe nonduality. When the limitation of a fixed location of perception is transcended, there's no longer an illusion either of separation, or of space and time as we generally know them. All things exist simultaneously in the unmanifest, enfolded, implicit universe, expressing itself as the manifest, unfolded, explicit perception of form.

Nonlinear: Diffuse or chaotic; not in accordance with probabilistic logical theory or mathematics; not solvable by differential equations.

This is the subject of the new science of chaos theory, which has given rise to an entirely new, non-Newtonian mathematics. Where linear systems are predictable, offering few surprises, nonlinear systems often offer more than we bargained for and tend to be self-organizing (with some chaos).

Numinous: Revealing or indicating the presence of spirit; awe-inspiring and evoking a sense of the sublime.

Omega: The end or the last word.

Paradigm: The dimensions of a context or field, as limited by parameters that inherently predict one's perception of reality. A paradigm is generally a definition of one's perceptions of reality according to its limitations.

Paradox: A counter-intuitive statement or proposition which could prove to be true.

Pendulating: To sway to and fro or oscillate between two opposite conditions or energies.

Platforming: Making a new *ground of being* somewhere inside yourself for expansive experiences. Platforming is about grounding resource and renewing a capacity for more of it.

Consider an imaginary "raised area" or "vortex" for accumulating more of these expansive experiences. A *platform* of holistic, sensorial experiences will naturally bring more of them to us.

Polarity Stage: This is a natural challenging period that manifests in long-term relationships after bonding occurs, igniting in our unconscious the early dynamics we had with our primary caregivers. It often appears like an ego power struggle, with blind spots common in communication. It is part of a healthy stage of human relationship development in our time. It is also nature's way of returning us to what needs to be healed before we can experience the ecstatic "power of two" alchemy in a union.

Power of Two: The Power of Two in the cosmos is a force that has its origin in the awareness that we create a third *unseen* entity when we choose to partner with another, particularly after bonding occurs.

It is an energetic force field. The melding together of energies at deeper emotional and spiritual levels makes a significant difference. This is a difference we have not been trained for, and yet we have access to a perfect, personal facilitator in the *third entity*—a representative of both individuals and the whole of the union.

Practice: The action, or an act, of practicing, and derived senses.

Resource: Any positive memory, person, place, action, or personal capacity that creates a soothing feeling in your body. We actively use these resources to help reduce nervous system overactivation and to stimulate a relaxation discharge response.

Reptilian brain: The brain that humans share with animals in the wild. It overseas such functions as reproduction, self-preservation, circulation of the blood, breathing, sleeping, and the contractions of muscles in response to external stimulation [like traumas and other overwhelming events]. This brain stem sits on top of the spinal column in the base of the skull. In this book I often refer to it as the Old Brain, yet it is referred to as the "reptilian brain" because all vertebrates from reptiles to mammals have one. This reptilian brain speaks to us through the *felt senses* of the body and imagery.

Resilience: Resuming a sense of wholeness after an energetic contraction.

Resonance: An interaction in which energy vibrations are noticed, shared, and amplified. This can exist as one person's experience or transmitted to one or many people. A great singer that mesmerizes has good resonance and also instinctively knows how to share and amplify that resonance with their audience. In subtler ways, we do the same in ritual.

Ritual: Usually refers to rite, an action sanctifying a certain process. For this book's purposes, we expand the meaning of the word "ritual" to include not only physical actions, but energetic, non-physical dimensions as well, such as intention, visualization, and realization. We use ritual for healing both our inner and outer existences. Ritual, partnered with scientific understanding of energy fields, gives birth to a new context in which to live a fuller and richer life.

Sacred: Devoted exclusively and set apart for worship and/or gratitude; holy and worthy of respect.

Sacred Sex: Creating a larger energetic field in which genital and all other pleasuring is made holy. A time in which masculine (lingam) and feminine (yoni) energies unite and cooperate, generating this larger *field* of awareness and wholeness.

Scientific: The method of inquiry into nature specifically designed to derive predictable laws for physical properties.

Sexual-Spiritual (love) Split: A deep psychic schism within almost everyone in our culture which *prohibits* loving relationships from forming and enduring, and which, at the same time, remain sexually alive and growing. The schism between sex and spirit is caused by generational, cultural, religious, and early programming that plants seeds deep in the unconscious that makes merging the two energies after bonding virtually impossible without the specific healing that *Erotic Rituals* offer.

S.E.X.: S.O.U.L. Energy e**X**change as it pertains to erotic ritual and lovemaking.

Shadow: As coined by Carl Jung, it is a complex compound of undeveloped feelings, ideas, desires, and the like—the animal instincts passed along through evolution. In this book it is expanded to include many instincts and feelings that were deemed unacceptable in developmental years (which could include aggression as well as tenderness).

Shaman: A medicine man (or woman); one acting as both energy healer (clergy) and doctor, who works with the supernatural.

Slow is fast: A paradoxical creed from energy medicine that helps us to connect with our Curious Observer. Taking in a breath of spirit ("spiritus" means breath in Latin), our body generally relaxes, allowing observations to emerge that are more clear and informed in more nuanced ways. This helps the transformation we seek, as we realize that only slowness can help restore and ground resilient organic systems.

Somatic Experiencing® (SE): A naturalistic approach to healing trauma. In the words of it's originator, Peter Levine: "It allows us to gradually bridge the chasm between 'heaven' and, 'hell' uniting the two polarities. Physiologically speaking, heaven is expansion and hell is contraction. With their gradual unification, trauma is gently healed."

Somatic Intelligence: The growing wisdom as we learn to "hear with new ears" and "envision with new eyes" from the felt senses of our bodies.

Spirituality: Being at one with the Universe, in tune with the infinite. Aware of spirit in all things, all events, and all circumstances, or the active longing for such.

S.O.U.L: **S**ystemic **O**rganization of **U**niversal **L**ove (from *The Living Energy Universe* by Linda Russek and Gary Schwartz). Other definitions of "soul" include: The eternal core of selfhood and being, the essence of one's full identity, and the God-like aspect of the self.

Synchronicity: Acausal connecting principle; a meaningful coincidence when an inner and outer event come together.

Tantra: A Sanskrit word meaning an expansive system of all-encompassing reality that teaches the continuity between spirit and matter through our felt senses.

The Old Brain: Often referred to as the Reptilian Brain, it is the brain that humans share with animals in the wild. It overseas such functions as reproduction, self-preservation, circulation of the blood, breathing, sleeping, and the contractions of muscles in response to external stimulation [like trauma and other overwhelming events]. This brain stem sits on top of the spinal column in the base of the skull. It is referred to as the "reptilian brain" because all vertebrates from reptiles to mammals have one. In the ritually awakened Old Brain there are no rigid barriers between the wisdom of our animal powers and those that are distinctly human. The Old Brain has no sense of linear time. Yesterday, today, and tomorrow do not exist. The past and the present are the same.

The Third Entity: In intimate relationship research a new awareness is becoming vitally important. It seems that we create a third *unseen* entity when we choose to partner with another, particularly after bonding occurs. It is an energetic force field. The melding together of energies at deeper emotional and spiritual levels makes a significant difference. This is a difference we have not been trained for, and yet we have access to a perfect, personal facilitator in the *third entity*—a representative of both individuals and the whole of the union. We take care of the invisible third entity and it takes care of us.

We can think of a plant as a metaphor for the third entity. It is a living, breathing organism that must be nurtured to survive and remain beautiful and life-giving to us. If we do not take the time to care for the plant, it will wither on the vine and no longer be able to bring us pleasure. While a plant needs sun or light, air, and perhaps fertilizer to flourish, our human unions feed on communication and the exchange of sensual and erotic energies.

Thought Field Therapy: Originated by Roger Callahan and evolved by practitioners John H. Diepold, Jr., Victoria Britt, and Sheila S. Bender in their book, *Evolving Thought Field Therapy*, it is, like Somatic Experiencing and EMDR, an Energy Psychology modality. This hybrid approach integrates many psychotherapy systems into its meridian-based (energy) foundation—drawing on applied kinesiology, the acupuncture meridian system, and muscle-testing, among others, to ameliorate symptoms.

Transcendent: Surprising, extraordinary, going beyond what is given or present in experience, hence beyond knowledge. Beyond the natural and rational, it is the unknowable character of ultimate reality and asserts the primacy of the spiritual, or energetic, as against the material.

Transformation: Generally, modification or change in the structure of something. In this book, regarding ritual, we use Peter

Levine's definition from *Waking the Tiger:* Transformation is when a fundamental shift occurs in our beings. It is the process of changing something in relation to its polar opposite.

Trauma Transformation (or Renegotiation): The overall process by which the traumatic response (constriction, hyper-vigilance, helplessness, and dissociation) transforms to natural vitality and aliveness.

Universe: According to David Hawkins in *Power vs. Force:* There may be seen to be an infinite number of dimensions to our universe. The familiar three-dimensional universe of conventional consensus is only one, and is merely an illusion created by our senses. The space between planetary bodies isn't empty, but filled with a sea of energy. One square inch of it could be said to be as great as that of the whole mass of the physical universe.

Vibrant: To pulsate or throb with vibrational energy or activity, as in *a vibrant personality.*

The Wave Work®: Originated by Dayashakti (Sandra Scherer) out of highly refined yogic traditions, this practice (best done with a partner or practitioner) is an opportunity to reach beyond the intellect to access a richer source of inner wisdom, our own innate intelligence. It is called Wave Work because we know from physics that all life is made up of particles of energy that move in waves. One movement leads into and influences the next until the waves come to rest.

Wholeness: Undivided, flowing movement, unbroken and all-encompassing but not complete and static.

Wider Bandwidth: In working with Energy Psychology, energy medicine, and ritual, one gradually becomes more open to, and conscious of, currents of vibrational energy. This often expands one's access to their innate intelligence and its teachings and directives. In regard to quickening and broadening our access to inner and outer resource, drawing on energy and computer terminology, developing a wider bandwidth is like changing your internet access from dial-up to broadband.

Wisdom Circle (sometimes referred to as "heart circles" or "authenticity circles")**:** A circle of people who honor that each of them contains that enduring spark of that wisdom at the heart of all creation. Gathering in such circles enables us to move more deeply into ourselves—into that core which continues to survive, hope, dream, and carry on. See wisdomcircle.org for guidelines.

Yin-Yang: The fusion of two cosmic forces, **Yin**, the feminine (receptive) and **Yang**, the masculine (active).

Yoni: Representation of the female sex organ in Hinduism and the feminine receptive energy.

I acknowledge Joyce Kovelman's *Once Upon A Soul* and David R. Hawkin's *Power vs. Force,* among others, for bringing current perspectives to many terms in this Glossary.

About the Author

Dr. Michael Picucci has had the opportunity to reinvent himself numerous times in the course of his lifetime and in doing so he has helped redefine what aging means in the early twenty-first century. He completed his doctoral education in the Psychology of Addictions Psychotherapy as he settled into his "silvering" years. This, and parallel learning opportunities, propelled him into the energetic healing of trauma and the relational and sexual challenges of our time. On numerous occasions he has been blessed with opportunities to

Photograph by Peter McGough

publicly express the evolution of his personal and professional discoveries, an experience which he met with immeasurable gratitude.

Dr. Picucci was also honored conjointly by the National Institutes on Health (NIH/NIDA) and the National Association of Professional Addiction Counselors (NAADAC) in 2000 with the Outstanding Leadership in Research Award. Subsequently, in 2001 the New York State's Addictions Counselor's Association honored him with their first-ever President's Award for his contributions. These acknowledgments were forthcoming after the publication of his last book which encompassed over ten years of research: *The Journey Toward Complete Recovery: Reclaiming Your Emotional, Spiritual & Sexual Wholeness*. His life is a profound demonstration of TRANS-FORMATION in upper case letters—from a shame-based perspective to a vitalistic one ameliorating suffering and supporting possibility.

His journey has been shared with his partner-in-life, Dr. Elias Guerrero, who, among other things, profoundly mirrors his love of the Catskill Mountains on weekends—an environment which supports most of Picucci's written works. In addition to his writings, Dr. Picucci maintains a vibrant private practice in downtown Manhattan. He also consults with organizations in the private, public, and health sectors, supporting alignment for strategic, organic transformation, and he facilitates retreats and workshops. He describes the authoring of this book as "a most sacred experience" through which he learned and shares an evolved understanding of the richness and possibilities available to all of us now.

Further Information & Resources

For Further information about additional resources, forthcoming books, CDs, DVD' workshops, presentations, and retreats on *Ritual as Resource* and "Authentic Process Healing" go to the Institute's website: www.theinstitute.org.

The Institute for Authentic Process Healing
A NOT FOR PROFIT CORPORATION
85 Fifth Avenue, Suite 905
New York, NY 10003
Email: info@theinstitute.org
Website: www.theinstitute.org

TO ORDER ADDITIONAL COPIES OF
Ritual as Resource
or CDs of spoken rituals

Please send _____book copies @ \$16.95 (US) each.
Please send_____ CDs copies @ \$16.00 (US) each.
Name_____
Address_____
City_____
State_____Zip_____
Country_____
Phone_____
E-mail_____

Book & CD totals (includes shipping in U.S.)
Books: \$16.95 each ×_____copies:_____
CDs: \$16.00 each × _____copies:_____

Make check payable to **The Institute** and mail to:
85 Fifth Avenue, Suite 905
New York, NY 10003

Credit card orders may be made online at:
www.michaelpicucci.net

To order the *Ritual as Resource* CD online, with all the rituals in this book clearly spoken, go to:
www.michaelpicucci.net